Dear
Armen:
Welcome home,
Thank you
for your
service.
—Jim
5-1-17

HEROES TO
THE END

HEROES TO THE END

AN ARMY CORRESPONDENT'S LAST DAYS IN VIETNAM

JIM SMITH

HEROES TO THE END
AN ARMY CORRESPONDENT'S LAST DAYS IN VIETNAM

iUniverse books may be ordered through booksellers or by contacting:

iUniverse
1663 Liberty Drive
Bloomington, IN 47403
www.iuniverse.com
1-800-Authors (1-800-288-4677)

ISBN: 978-1-4917-6812-9 (sc)
ISBN: 978-1-4917-6811-2 (e)

Library of Congress Control Number: 2015907764

Print information available on the last page.

iUniverse rev. date: 09/10/2015

ACKNOWLEDGMENTS

I'm dedicating this book to my wife, Lynn, and my son, Peter, who never lost faith in me. I'd like to thank my former Newsday colleague Jerry Zezima for his suggestion on the title and undying positivity and encouragement. I also thank Matt Franjola, my traveling buddy in Vietnam who carried the water and taught me the tricks of the war reporting trade. Thanks as well are due to the iUniverse staff and contract employees who did a careful and thorough editing job. Last of all, I thank all the servicemen who poured their hearts out to me and whose stories I tell here.

INTRODUCTION

This book is written through the eyes of the twenty-three-year-old that I was in Vietnam. I wrote it to validate my yearlong US Army tour from August 1971 to August 1972 and to pay tribute to the people I met and interviewed as a *Stars and Stripes* correspondent for seven months. My tour broke down into three phases: my five months as a clerk in Cam Ranh Bay on the central coast, three months spent primarily in the Saigon area during a quiet time in the war, and four exciting months spent mostly upcountry during the North Vietnamese Easter Offensive. By design, I placed the vignettes about phase one at the end of the book because I felt they were less compelling.

The latter stages of American involvement in Vietnam largely have been ignored by historians, authors, and moviemakers. There were "only" 759 American deaths in Vietnam in 1972. At President Richard Nixon's direction, a policy of Vietnamization saw combat responsibilities turned over to the South Vietnamese. American troop strength was cut from about two hundred thousand when I arrived to forty-nine thousand when I left. To keep American casualties down, US infantry units were pulled from the field one by one and sent home. Our role became to advise the South Vietnamese; support them with helicopters, tactical airstrikes, and B-52 bombings; and train them to fight on their own.

I was a specialist fourth class in the army but conducted myself as a civilian: long hair, safari suits, no rank insignia. I had worked four years as a sports reporter at *Newsday*, the Long Island newspaper, during college before I enlisted. My specialty in Vietnam was aftermath stories. I recorded accounts of combat survivors, walked with infantrymen on patrol, pulled guard duty in the jungle, flew in helicopters at treetop level as door gunners sprayed machine-gun fire, and interviewed civic action officers and Vietnamese officials about their hopes for the country's future.

As history shows, this North Vietnamese and Vietcong offensive was a prelude to the three-pronged April 1975 attacks, after we were long gone, that overwhelmed the South Vietnamese. They were aimed at Quang Tri and Hue in the north, Kontum in the Central Highlands, and the capital city of Saigon in the south. The difference was that in the spring of 1972, massive American air power helped the South Vietnamese beat back the attacks, regaining lost territory and provincial capitals. I and many of the remaining US troops felt we had helped stabilize the country and had duplicated the scenario in Korea where Vietnam would remain split in half in a perpetual stalemate. Some Americans at the time were upset they were unable to do more and volunteered for every last hairy mission available.

I stumbled across stories of Americans doing noble, unheralded things, right down to the end of our involvement. I told—and tell again, now—stories of heroism, compassion, and dumb luck. But this book is a broader look at what life was like in South Vietnam as US troops exited. Other vignettes involve Vietnamese refugees, American contractors, Bob Hope, a USO band, visiting NFL players, and South Korean troops. The book also looks at Rangers, military policemen, tank drivers, engineers, advisers at base camps, helicopter crew chiefs, civic action project coordinators, pilots of VIP aircraft, psychological operations specialists, maintenance men, and so forth.

I was in Tokyo meeting Stars and Stripes honchos April 4–11, 1972, during the beginning of the offensive and the most dangerous time for correspondents. I was never present during a firefight and—somewhat miraculously—never came under direct fire, except twice when enemy rockets exploded a couple of hundred feet away. Although I flew more than two hundred hours in helicopters, they were never struck by ground fire. I never saw any Americans wounded in action and only visited a hospital once. But I grew bolder as my tour wound down, going farther north, taking more chances, getting closer to the action and getting away with it.

I enjoyed my job so much that I refused a chance to come home three months early and actually put in for an extension of my tour; it was denied. I wound up having about seventy-five bylined articles in *Stars and Stripes*, the Defense Department's daily newspaper, and they form the basis of this book. But I've also included vignettes that were either censored or shortened, based on my original notes. The book took so long to write because I was a *Newsday* sports reporter from 1966 to 1999 (serving in the army from 1970 to 1973) and for the last fifteen years was an editor there, retiring December 31, 2014. I never seemed to have time to really focus on the book. I pitched proposals several times to publishers in the 1980s and '90s, but they weren't interested. Since I am now sixty-six, I decided to self-publish.

When Saigon fell in 1975, I had a traumatic episode in which I locked myself in my parents' bathroom and had blood spurting from my nose and mouth. I couldn't believe that all our blood, sweat, and tears in Vietnam had gone for nothing, that fifty-eight thousand had died. I didn't find out what survivor's guilt was until 1991; then I had a name for what I felt. In the past few years, I've become a member of Veterans for Peace and also a veterans' advocate and board chairman at United Veterans Beacon House, a Bay Shore, Long Island, nonprofit that runs transitional homes for homeless veterans. This book is a tribute to them and all those who put their asses on the line for us.

Jim Smith
May 2015
Williston Park, New York

CENSORSHIP

One of the first stories I submitted to *Stars and Stripes* was on theft, bad food, boredom, and inefficiency at the First Team Combat Training Center (CTC) in Bien Hoa, an air base north of Saigon. My boss Jim Lea killed the story and wrote me a long letter that basically told me I'd lose my job if I submitted another story that made the army look bad. The letter made me realize that I'd better choose subjects that I could write about with a clear journalistic conscience that also would be palatable to my bosses.

Here is a slightly edited version of the original January 29, 1972, story:

> Pity the poor in-country transfer, especially the soldier whose unit has stood down and who has been sent to the First Team Combat Training Center in Bien Hoa. The facilities are inadequate, the cadre are sometimes hostile, and theft is so common that a GI said, "I'm afraid to go anywhere because when I come back, all my stuff might be gone, and somebody else might be in my bed."
>
> The CTC is where every in-country transfer and newly arrived soldier assigned to the Third Brigade, First Cavalry Division, stops for at least one day. Noncombatants receive one day of training; combatants get three days' instruction. For most of the soldiers, the CTC is one big hassle.
>
> Speaking for the defense is Captain Brian F. Wells, commanding officer of the CTC. "A guy gets away with a

lot in the bush," he said. "There's no way we can transform them into stateside soldiers in three days, but we tell them, 'Get a haircut, take the beads off, get a cav. patch on.' … I don't think that's harassment. We're just trying to get them to obey the rules."

Speaking for the troops will be several enlisted men who have had a rough time at the CTC. Specialist Fourth Class Herman White Jr. is one. His former unit, the Twenty-Seventh Engineer Battalion in Phu Loi, stood down on January 17. He first was sent to Camp Alpha because there was no room at the CTC. The next day, he was shipped to the Ninetieth Replacement Center at Long Binh near Saigon. The following day, he came to the CTC. On January 25 he was still there, long after the men who had arrived with him and shipped out to new units.

"I finally got paid this morning," he said. "And I found out I'll be going to the 215th General Support Group. They found my finance records lying right in a filing cabinet. Nobody had touched them in a week. If I hadn't checked down there today, I might have been here another week."

White, who requested duty in Vietnam while stationed in Germany, is a bulldozer operator. He'd spent a year in Vietnam earlier in the war and enjoyed building roads. This tour, he said, he'd been used only to scrape the mud off jeeps. "I'm sorry I ever put in for here," White said. "But I ETS on 21 July. After that, I won't give a damn about this army."

In the seven days White had been at the CTC, he said he had stayed on his bunk reading, budging only for chow and the mandatory formations at 6:30, 12:30, and 6:00 p.m. every day. "I try to stay away from the lifers," he said. "One E-6 [staff sergeant] came in here last night, and my friend said, 'Hey, Sarge, I hear you're from Kentucky.' The guy says, 'No, I'm from Vietnam' and walks out. Then they wonder why there are fraggings."

Wells said he instructs all his cadre not to fraternize with "the trainees" and to "project the image of a noncommissioned officer." He said, "They're not unfriendly, but maybe some of them are tired. They had no breaks for Christmas or New Year's. We've gone about fifty straight days and trained something like 3,500 men. It's really rough. We realize that many of the men are good soldiers and have been bounced around a lot. We're sorry if they feel they're being harassed."

The CO said he knew about all the thievery going on but told each man when he arrived that if he had anything he wanted locked up, he would lock it up for him. "Most of them are too damn lazy to lock their valuables up," he said.

One victim was Specialist Fourth Class Calvin C. Nordlund, also of the Twenty-Seventh Engineer Battalion, who said he had a stereo cassette player stolen. "Everybody's had something stolen," he said. "Poncho liners, boonie hats, cameras, everything. They should have a guard in every barracks."

"Dig it," said Specialist Fourth Class Kenneth Bradley, who said he'd been at the CTC since January 13 but had not received orders since arriving from the 577th Engineer Battalion at Phan Rang. "I turned in a .22 automatic pistol and a bayonet. They wrapped it with tape and put it in a wall locker. When I asked a guy to see them the other day, they weren't there. Apparently, he'd just given the stuff to somebody else."

The men are restricted to the center after six in the evening unless they can get a pass to go to the PX or to make a phone call. But other cavalry troopers are allowed free access to the center. "People come through here," said Specialist Fourth Class Gregory Collier, formerly of the First/Twenty-Second Infantry, "and you don't know if they live here or not. They just walk in, pick something up, and they're gone. But we're fenced in here like animals in a cage."

As for the training, Nordlund said, "We know all this already. It's just a bunch of bull."

Roughly half of the men filtering through the CTC lately have been in-country transfers. But sometimes there are more. In a recent class of 288, only 113 were newly arrived from the world (as the United States was referred to). The men are briefed on the tactical situation at Bien Hoa and the mission of the First Cavalry Division. They receive classes in first aid, drug abuse, and human relations. They zero M16s at one of five firing ranges. They get a lecture on the care and maintenance of the M60 machine gun. Then there is a class on the Geneva Convention, code of conduct, and treatment of prisoners of war.

The infantry troopers get more intense training on the second and third days. They take classes in patrolling, base defense, setting of ambushes, and attacking of bunker complexes; then they rappel from a tower to simulate a drop by helicopter into a battlefield. There is instruction given on enemy weapons and a trip over the CTC's "Hanoi Village" combat reaction course. While all this is beneficial to "newfs," some of those who have been in the field a while resent having to go through it.

Most of the enlisted men and NCOs sleep in crowded, roach-infested, one-story barracks that hold about forty men in twenty double bunks. "The roaches are big, yeah," White said. "But they're all over Vietnam. This place is just too restrictive. Anybody can come in here, but we can't go out. I didn't have a patch on my fatigues one day, so one of the cadre made me fill sandbags all afternoon. At the time, I was flat broke. I couldn't even afford the money to have a patch sewn on. But they don't want to hear that. We filled out some papers telling what we thought of the place. I saw a sergeant take all the ones that had unfavorably comments on them and put them off to the side. He'll probably just throw them away."

He added, "The other day, I was outside the club with sandals and a T-shirt on. I asked a waitress to get me a soda. And this [NCO] starts hassling me, telling me to get away from the club. You'd think that with the cav. being such a big outfit, they'd treat you a little better. Maybe I'll be lucky enough to stay with my next unit until my tour is up without standing down. I sure hope so."

Wells said, "Our finance office is only equipped to handle forty men a day, and we're getting a hundred to a hundred fifty. Thus, we become a holding station until everybody is taken care of. This obviously will create a lot of problems. If I was coming through like they are and I'd been out in the bush sleeping in a mud puddle, I'd be happy to get a shower and clean sheets like we give them here. These guys don't appreciate anything."

"The food is horseshit," Bradley said. "The showers are cold; the toilets don't flush. The place stinks."

After I turned in the story, Lea sent me a letter that included these remarks:

Either rewrite this all the way or forget about it. The choice is yours on that but it can't go this way ... If this story did find its way to [*Stripes* honchos], there is a very great possibility that you would suddenly find yourself slinging hash in a field kitchen in the Delta ... There are papers which would—with a little polishing here and there—use this. I would not suggest you send it now to Newsday, though, unless they'll agree to a fake byline. If they used your byline, it would very quickly become known to ... whoever's bureau chief here and, again, you would—at best—find yourself slinging hash in the Delta. I say "at best" because the military would have many other options on your body.

After getting this note, I realized I couldn't conduct myself as if I was a *Newsday* reporter who happened to be in the army. I was an army reporter, and if I wanted my stories to run, I had to choose them wisely or run the risk of having a rifle thrust into my hands. I basically decided not to buck the system. For seven months, I used helicopters as taxis and was ferried to every city in South Vietnam. I specialized in secondhand accounts of heroism.

PART I

COMBAT HEROES

FREAKY KILLER

Specialist Fifth Class Paul Wells, twenty-one, from Montevello, California, was a door gunner for F Troop, Ninth Cavalry, a scout or reconnaissance company based in Bien Hoa that flew tiny OH-6 Cayuse light observation helicopters. When I talked to him in late January 1972, Wells said he had been in-country twenty-four straight months and never had been wounded, although his choppers twice had been shot down. He looked like Peter Fonda from *Easy Rider*. He was tall and thin with a sharp chin, mustache, neatly combed but long hair, and wire-rimmed glasses.

"Basically," Wells told me at a company party, "I'm not a violent person. Probably everybody in this company could kick my butt. But I do a job. And, like, when you blow a dude away, you can look down and say, 'Wow, I've accomplished this,' you know. I was pretty sheltered [as a child]. Back in the world I was conservative, shy, didn't have much confidence in myself in high school. I used to do my homework, watch TV, keep to myself. I figured I'd enlist in the army and maybe I'd grow up and find where my head's at."

An officer who had flown many times with Wells told me Wells was one of the best in the business. "He's the most relaxed gunner I've ever seen," said First Lieutenant Robert Kevan. "He'll say something like, 'Sir, ah, we're taking fire from four o'clock.' Just like that—cool and calm. He's unbelievable."

Wells's missions mostly involved visual reconnaissance with a gunship partner in an area forty miles east of Saigon. His bird floated over the treetops like a hummingbird. When he spotted an enemy bunker complex, he would tell his aircraft commander (AC) to make a series of passes over the target while he would stand on the right skid strapped in a harness

3

firing M60 machine gun bursts into it. He carried about a thousand rounds per mission.

"The gunner is the key man of our teams," Warrant Officer Joseph Moss said. "The mission rotates around him. He's the one that sees it, leads you into it, kills it, and then you take the credit—heh, heh. No, really, the gunner is important. He'll fly all day and then come back and pull maintenance on the aircraft."

After two six-month extensions of his Vietnam tour, Wells was scheduled to have been discharged on February 16, 1972. "You can't freak out up there," he said, "because if you do, the pilot's going to freak out. You've got to be cool."

A few days before I talked to Wells, he said his AC had taken a small-arms round in the buttocks during a mission.

"You need help?" Wells radioed.

"Yeah," the wounded man said.

Wells said he walked along the chopper's skids to the front of the aircraft, took control, and flew it to a clearing. As he was doing it, he told the pilot, "You realize I've never landed one of these before?"

Wells told me, "The danger doesn't bother me. I could've gotten killed the first day or the second day. Sure, I could dig going home in one piece—I don't want to make it sound like I don't give a damn. But if it happens, you know, like it happens. It's like getting up in the morning and taking a shower for me. It's just so natural. A couple of times I figured, 'Wow, they're doing an awful lot of shooting down there. We're going to have to get it together.' But I've never been hit, man. I don't know why. Somebody up there must dig the hell out of me."

THE HILLBILLY
CHICKEN MAN

Combat action was rare for American forces in Vietnam in January 1972. My first trip after being assigned to *Stars and Stripes* took me to Pleiku to cover US Army Secretary Robert F. Froehlke's visit and gather other stories. I stumbled onto a story about a Huey helicopter crew chief's brush with death two weeks earlier on January 6.

"We were on a Dustoff [rescue] mission about twenty miles northeast of Kontum, about fifteen clicks due east of Tan Canh," said Specialist Fifth Class Calvin "Hillbilly" Warren, twenty-four, of Brinkley, Arkansas. "We were to pick up these five wounded and four dead ARVNs [Army of the Republic of Vietnam troops]. We couldn't fire as we went in because the ARVNs were carrying the wounded to the LZ [landing zone] from all sides. We finally got down, made the pickup, took off, and then made a hard left bank and a hard right."

The Huey took a B-40 rocket in its tail rotor and small-arms fire in its engine. Warren was thrown out of the chopper, which crashed in three pieces. "We lost the engine before we hit the ground," he said. He fell unconscious in tall grass on a hillside. "When I woke up," he said, "the bird was about forty yards away, and here I was with my arm hanging over the main rotor blade. It had to be an act of God that it wasn't cut off." One of the wounded ARVNs wasn't so lucky. He was decapitated by the blade.

Warren's door gunner, Specialist Fourth Class Steven Hill, sprained his left ankle and took shrapnel in his right leg. But Warren escaped with only minor cuts and bruises, and neither of the other two crew members nor the other wounded ARVNs were hurt seriously. Moments after they went down, all eight were rescued by a Fourteenth Medevac Company chopper.

Warren was the most experienced crew chief in the Fifty-Second Aviation Battalion. With thirty-three months served in Vietnam on two tours, he was ready to go back into action two weeks after being shot down. "I dig cuttin' up Charlie's ass, but with the VNAF [Vietnam Air Force] taking over much of the combat assault missions," he said, "we're mostly doing supply runs right now. We fly to Fire Bases 5 and 6 with water, artillery shells. We do visual recon, medevacs. But we should have some action pretty soon. I was here in Tet of '69, and my feeling is Tet's going to be something big again this year." He was off by two months.

The thirty-two oak leaf clusters on his air medal showed that Warren had no reservations about going into combat. He said he'd flown more than a thousand missions and had been wounded twice during his first tour, when he'd worked mainly as a door gunner. "He's the best crew chief we have," said First Lieutenant Lee A. Merchen, his aircraft commander. "He's really dedicated. He'll work half the night if that's what it takes to get his bird running. He's happy-go-lucky. I'm impressed with him. He has more experience than most. There are not many of them around like him."

When I interviewed Warren, he said he'd been working on the main rotor blade of his helicopter for three days. "The blades have to have the same amount of pitch in 'em," he said, "to be tracked straight. It's like having a car's wheels out of line. We pull an inspection every day. It's like when you come in with a car—check the oil, all the gauges, lights, check for bullet holes, seapage, leaks, cracks, etc. My job's to keep the bird up. The gunner's job is to keep the guns clean and ready to fire, see that there's ammo and grenades, and help out the crew chief. We're like one big family. If I just let it go, it'll fall and kill us all ... We've had birds take fire, and they told us, 'Don't shoot back; the ARVNs are running it.'"

Warren said he had been a truck driver with the Eleventh Armored Cavalry in 1968–69. "They had a guy go home, and they asked me if I wanted to fly," he said. "I'd never flown anything before. It was OJT. One time on my last tour, I shot an M79 [grenade launcher] from a Loach, and the round exploded right outside, and shrapnel came back and hit me in the left leg ... Here, if we get a new gunner, he usually flies with me. I tell 'em from the start what to do. I'm on the left [in the backseat]; the gunner's on the right. The AC is in the front left [and his copilot in the front right]."

Warren said his first chopper on his current tour was a "Cadillac," the best-running bird in the company. When it crashed, it was the first time since May 26, 1971, that his company had lost an aircraft; it had about twenty Hueys. Warren said he helped maintenance men make intermediate inspections every twenty-five hours of flight time and periodic inspections every hundred hours.

Warren said he got his "Chicken Man" nickname due to hearsay because "other birds wouldn't do a Dustoff" and his chopper went in. He said on a normal day, his helicopter crew pulled twelve or thirteen rescue and supply missions. "We don't do much sleeping; I'll tell you that," he said. "I'd rather be out there where I can see Charlie and shoot at him rather than wait here for [incoming] rockets. We fight among ourselves sometimes, but when I went down, that bird came down and helped us. When the going gets tough, we're all for one and one for all."

I watched Warren work on his helicopter. "I'm going to try to get this one looking as good as the last one," he said as he polished its nose. "First, I'm going to put some black paint on, put on new drive shaft covers. I've got to put a decal on the front too—like the 'Hillbilly Chicken Man' or something. You can't take a bird up like this. It'll be a lot of work, but all the crew chiefs want to make their birds look the best. That's our job."

LOOKING FOR THE DUDES

Dawn was still almost an hour away at Bien Hoa as Warrant Officer Joseph Moss, in his early twenties, of Durango, Colorado, made a preflight inspection on his tiny OH-6 light observation helicopter (Loach) by flashlight in January 1972. It was chilly, and Moss was trying to shake off the cobwebs of a company party and poker game that had lasted until one thirty in the morning. "Damn," he said. "We'll have to get another bird. No sweat. This happens once in a while. We'll use 071." Moss had detected a minor mechanical glitch that had caused a caution light to glow on the instrument panel. "It was the oil chip light," he said. "It happens every once in a while. It means somewhere in the gearbox, gears are wearing out. You can't fly it like that."

The first orange rays of the sun were streaking the horizon as the soft-spoken, red-cheeked little pilot with sun-bleached blond hair got the substitute helicopter airborne. I was in the right-hand seat, having wanted to see what an F Troop visual reconnaissance mission was like. In the rear was a husky black private, Douglas Albright, the door gunner, from Denver, Colorado, equipped with a thousand M60 machine-gun rounds, six fragmentations grenades, six smoke grenades, ten white phosphorus grenades, and six concussion grenades, plus an M16 with twelve sixteen-round clips. Each man also had a .38-caliber pistol.

Cruising low, as a silky mist clung to the treetops, Moss pointed to the right. "See those rubber plantations down there?" he said. "The dudes hide in there. We have to send ground troops through periodically to flush them out. It's too expensive for us to do it by air because we have to pay for any trees we fire up—at least the US government does."

Moss landed at the airstrip at Xuan Loc, a provincial capital about forty miles east of Saigon, to take on fuel. Waiting there was an AH-1 Cobra helicopter gunship that would be the high bird on the hunter-killer mission. There were a half-dozen other choppers fueling up there and awaiting missions.

One of the best pilots in F Troop, Ninth Cavalry, Moss said he flew a mission a few weeks earlier when he had been called in to support American ground troops. "It was on January 3, about four in the afternoon," he said. "A Ranger company walked into a bunker complex. The mission was to cover the Rangers and the medevacs—loosen up the dinks so we could get the slicks [Hueys] in there and get 'em out. I had to go down to find where the VC were, identify the friendlies, see where they were taking fire from, see if I could suppress the fire, and let 'em move into a landing zone," he said.

"Then," he added, "we were gonna call for Blue Max [Cobras of F Battery, Seventy-Ninth Artillery]. We popped smoke and said, 'All of our people are within twenty-five meters of the smoke; everything else, you can blow away.' I called the medevacs in, but the first one took fire, flew away, and went down, and the second took fire and went down a click [kilometer] away. They decided to send me down to see where the fire was coming from. You get the feeling that you know you're going to take fire, that there's dudes down there. And about ten seconds after I got there [at tree level], the dudes opened up. One AK round came under my seat and through the console. Another one went through the air cooler and missed my gunner by six inches. It knocked some pieces of metal into the engine, and it blew. I took off for Fire Base Mace. But my RPMs were dropping, and I was losing power. I yelled to the gunner to throw out the ammo to lighten our load. I made a kind of run-in landing eight miles away, thirty to thirty-five miles east of Bien Hoa."

"I got out and looked," Moss said, "and we had only taken those two rounds." It was the first time Moss had been shot down, he said, in 250 missions. "I had a camera [Kodak Instamatic] that just happened to be sitting on the console between the seats, and one round did it a job. It makes a helluva good war souvenir, though. Not everybody has a bullet hole in their camera."

That incident was F Troop's last previous contact with the Communists, he said. Moss said one GI was killed and fourteen wounded during the confrontation, and three medical evacuation helicopters were shot down. "The dudes are out there," Moss said, "but they're just waiting for Tet [the lunar New Year in mid-February]. They avoid contact unless we corner them. We find a lot of evidence they're out there: bunkers, fighting positions, trails, tents … but we haven't seen a dude in weeks."

Moss said he had worked with twenty door gunners on his tour and said, "I depend on the gunner to make the mission a success. It takes time for me to handle the aircraft and for him to shoot and kill people."

Moss's radio crackled with news that his team had a mission. We trotted to the chopper and quickly were airborne. The area of operation was fifteen miles southeast of Xuan Loc. After several passes over the area, Albright spotted two short, shallow trenches and three log-reinforced bunkers, one of them brand new. They were ineffectively camouflaged with branches and leaves. I was too sick from the constant circling by this time to see anything or take notes. I closed my eyes, fighting off the impulse to vomit, and hung on.

The gunner, strapped in a shoulder harness, stood on the right-hand skid with his back braced against the chopper's outside wall. On Moss's order, he fired a few M60 machine-gun bursts at the complex as the chopper made dizzying passes thirty feet over the treetops. Albright dropped a grenade, and it exploded in the complex. When nothing stirred, Moss told him, "Get a Pete out."

Albright lobbed a white phosphorus (Willie Pete) canister that landed a yard from the bunker. A big cloud of white smoke marked the spot in the double-canopy jungle. The Loach flew off to the west. Now it was the Cobra's turn. In four dives, Captain Robert Timberlake unleashed his full load of ten- and seventeen-pound rockets and fired a few bursts of 7.62 mm minigun rounds. "That was a typical mission," said Moss as we flew back to Xuan Loc. "We went down, fired a short burst to try to get the little dudes to come out and fire at us, so the high bird could come in and fire them up. Our purpose is not to get killed. Came out real good. Destroyed the dudes' new hideaway. Too bad we didn't flush any out, though. You always want to do that,"

Albright said, "If you don't see any dudes, you don't know what they're doing. Our mission is to gather intelligence about what they're doing." Moss said, "We don't see 'em unless they want to be seen."

At some point after the mission was over, Moss and Timberlake had a simulated dogfight, taking turns in high and low positions a few hundred yards from each other and saying "Tacka-tacka-tacka" into their radios to simulate having fired rockets that "killed" the other. Great fun. I almost vomited again.

On the flight back to Bien Hoa, with my head reeling and appetite gone, Moss switched on the AFVN radio station, which was playing the Searchers' song "Needles and Pins." I chuckled because the song seemed appropriate. If there were any enemy soldiers in those bunkers, their bodies were perforated with hundreds of tiny, red, arrow-like nails from the Cobra's exploding rockets. I realized I had a morbid sense of humor.

SILVER DOLLAR

Jimmy Faulkner had death in his eyes. He wore a silver dollar on a leather necklace tight around his neck. The coin once deflected an AK-47 round in a firefight, so Faulkner never took it off. His nickname became "Silver Dollar." He was a specialist fourth class in H Company, Seventy-Fifth Infantry. Faulkner didn't have an ounce of fat on his lean, six-foot body and looked like a mercenary in camouflaged fatigues, black beret, spit-shined boots, and tapered trousers bloused neatly at his lower calves.

When I met him in March 1972, Faulkner said he had been in-country for sixteen months. The twenty-one-year-old from Carlsbad, California, said he had been on forty-five missions and was seeking approval for a second six-month extension to his tour. "There's still a war going on over here," he said, "even if the people back in the States don't believe it."

In late March 1972, H Company was the lone US Ranger outfit left in Vietnam, and it had seven six-man teams. The unit was based in Bien Hoa north of Saigon and operated in dense jungle east of the base, each man carrying 90 to 120 pounds of gear and armed to the teeth, for up to a week at a time. The Communists reportedly had put a bounty on the heads of the Rangers, but at the time, they had lost only two men in the previous thirteen months.

Faulkner said he was proud of the fact that he'd been along for the ride on the Son Tay rescue mission on November 21, 1970, when heavily armed US troops were helicoptered into North Vietnam to a prison camp supposedly holding Americans. Unfortunately, the POWs had been moved. The Americans had to be content with blowing a few North Vietnamese Army troops out of guard towers at an empty prison.

Faulkner said another highlight of his tour came in September 1971, when he and another Ranger took on a Communist mortar company. "We surprised them," he said. "We opened up on them, and they didn't know how many of us there were." The Vietcong had been trying to set up shop in the "rocket belt" east of Saigon. Faulkner said they fled, leaving behind their weapons and a few blood trails. Faulkner, the team leader, said he was awarded a Silver Star for his part in the engagement. He would not provide details and was not boastful. The brave ones never were.

On the previous Wednesday, March 22, 1972, Faulkner said, he and some Ranger teammates were involved in another skirmish twenty miles east of Bien Hoa. "We were surrounded by twenty-five or thirty of them," he said, "but the Cobras [helicopters] we called for arrived just in time, and they scattered. I had only one round left in my Thompson [submachine gun], and everybody was down to their last magazine. It was close, but there aren't any VC out there good enough to get us."

Faulkner added of the Rangers, "We're quieter than a line company. We can get right up on the VC before they know it. They're standing up to us more than before because they realize our numbers are getting less and our support's a little flaky. We've had contacts on the last four missions I've been on. Charlie is good. He's a good fighter. But he doesn't have the munitions or the know-how to match ours."

Most of the Rangers' kills came in ambushes. Faulkner said on his last mission his team killed four Communists and captured some AK-47 rifles and rocket launchers. "We're working one of the hottest areas around," he said. "We're going back out there tomorrow to see what we can find."

A friend of Faulkner, Sergeant John Sellens, twenty-one, another team leader from Manhattan, Kansas, who had been on seventy-three missions, said, "There's a war out there. When I was home on leave, a lot of people asked me what I was doing still in Vietnam. If they could go out with us, they'd see for themselves." Sellens said he had been in-country for sixteen months and, like Faulkner, had applied to extend his tour. The same was true of many other members of H Company.

"It's the best unit in Vietnam," said ammo supply man Thomas Jarocz, twenty-one, of Blair, Nebraska, who had been with the outfit for twenty months after two extensions. "I've done just about everything there is to do here. I don't care if they wake me up in the middle of the night. If they told me I was going to the field tomorrow, I'd be packing in a minute."

Sergeant Elvis W. Osborne Jr., twenty, of Forney, Texas, told me he'd reenlisted to stay with H Company. "I didn't want to leave with a drop after nine months," he said, "and I was going to reenlist anyway. So I figured it was as good a time as any. You can sit in the world and be a banker or something, but as far as pride and working together with people goes, this is it. You don't find any better people than you've got right here."

Sergeant First Class Robert Weaver, a Ranger instructor on his second tour, told me, "Everybody's over here to do a job. You've got some religious people in-country, but they consider [killing] a job they have to do. It's not that they're bloodthirsty. I don't know how to explain it. Maybe a couple enjoy going out and killing, but the majority are not out there just to be killers. They're just doing a job."

* * *

I visited H Company again in June 1972, after having spent a week in Bangkok on leave (June 4–11) with Faulkner a few weeks earlier. Silver Dollar's stereo was bouncing the electrical sounds of Alvin Lee's guitar off the graffiti-covered walls of his cluttered hooch. The song was "Goin' Home" by Ten Years After—from the Woodstock album. Faulkner, who said he had been to the festival in 1969, got up from a folding chair and popped the cassette tape out. "I'm sick of that one," he said. "I don't particularly want to go home. At least not this way."

Sellens strolled into the hooch, popped open a can of soda, and said, "You've got a dream, you know? You figure on the last mission, you'd really get a chance to do some people a job. We had a few scores to settle, but they wouldn't let us."

Sergeants Faulkner (he was promoted), Sellens, and John LeBrun were scheduled to ship out during the last week in June after having spent a total of seventy-four consecutive months in Vietnam among them. By their count, they had totaled 191 missions and been awarded twenty-two Bronze Stars and dozens of other medals. The three roommates said they were surprised when they got "drops" off their current extensions and were leaving the country without one last fling in the bush. In the previous four months, four of their buddies had been killed, and two had been wounded in three separate engagements. The men would not have the chance to avenge the deaths of their comrades.

When I found them, they were sunbathing, listening to music, and waiting for their orders. H Company was one of several units unaffected by the deactivation in early June of the Third Brigade, First Cavalry Division, because it was to remain as part of the two-thousand-man Task Force Gary Owen to help defend US men and installations in the Saigon area. Faulkner, Sellens, and LeBrun, however, were among twenty Rangers shipping out. About twenty were expected to remain.

"We all love this company," LeBrun said. "We wanted to stay here until the company went home. It feels funny just sitting around watching other people go to the field. We wanted to get out there again."

LeBrun, twenty-five, who was from Victoria, British Columbia, said he had been in Vietnam continuously since April 1969, except for four thirty-day leaves. "I believe in this war," he said. "I think it is just, and I'm glad I was here to help fight it. There are a lot of people going home in body bags but very few Rangers. This company did a lot of good work over here. Nobody can compare with our body count."

Sellens and LeBrun were being reassigned to Fort Carson, Colorado. Faulkner, sounding as if he was addicted to war, said he had reenlisted for five years and was headed to Panama to attend "all the schools I can and learn everything I can about fighting in the jungle. I'm going to stay down there a while. Then I'm coming back to Thailand or wherever I can to get back to the deal. I don't know. If there's some fighting in the remote regions of Panama, I'll stay there. I like to do war-type things. My dream is to be a mercenary for the British in South Africa or somewhere—if I don't get blown away first."

After seventy-nine missions, eighteen months in-country, and twelve Bronze Stars, Sellens said he had had enough of war. He said he planned to attend Kansas State University, get a physical education degree, and become a gym instructor and possibly a high school football coach. "What I did over here is my business," he said. "And if anybody asks the three of us about it, we can say it was cool and leave it at that because we don't want to tell war stories. But I don't think I want to carry a gun anymore."

The Fourteenth Military History Detachment of the First Cavalry Division made a book out of a contact Sellens and Faulkner were involved in on September 4, 1971, with three teammates. The group of five was lifted in by helicopter and chased an estimated Communist company (at least a hundred soldiers) out of a base camp in a surprise attack, killing dozens of them.

In early April 1972, on another mission, Sellens, Faulkner, and LeBrun were part of a ten-man Ranger group that was helicoptered over Loc Ninh seventy-five miles north of Saigon in the middle of the Easter Offensive. Their mission was to rescue three American advisers. But at the last minute, a decision was made that the landing zone was too hot. The mission was aborted. "They felt we would have lost the three advisers and all ten of us," LeBrun said. "We think we would have had thirteen people getting back on the two choppers."

Another regret the trio had was that there was no raid into North Vietnam to free US prisoners during the 1972 offensive, while the Communists' attention was focused on the South. "That would have been the ultimate mission," Sellens said. "I'm getting out soon, but if they ever ask for volunteers, that's one mission I'd like to come back here as a civilian for." Faulkner said, "If they got us on the ground, they wouldn't have to worry about getting us back. We'd find a way."

FOOTBALL HERO
TURNED RANGER

In his senior season at the US Military Academy in the fall of 1969, halfback Lynn Moore rushed for 983 yards, including an astonishing 208 on 40 carries in Army's 27–0 victory over Navy. Moore scored three touchdowns in that game, and another was called back because of a penalty. "If I could have gotten out of the army to play pro ball," Moore said, "I would have done it in a minute. But that would have been immaturity and inexperience speaking. Then, I didn't think anything was more important than signing autographs and speaking at banquets—being a celebrity. Now, I know there are more important things in life than football."

In late March 1972, Lieutenant Lynn Moore, twenty-four, was operations officer for H Company, Seventy-Fifth Infantry, the last US Ranger outfit left in Vietnam. Being a Ranger rearranged his priorities. While fellow Oklahoman Steve Owens of the Detroit Lions was leading the National Football Conference in rushing in 1971, Moore was leading reconnaissance patrols with the 101st Airborne Division west of Hue. When I met Moore in Bien Hoa, his responsibility was communicating with Ranger teams in the field, plotting their movements and phoning advice.

"Owens's rewards are money and fame," Moore said, "but when I can see guys coming back from the field alive after a mission I helped coordinate, it's just as big a reward for me. I don't know if I could make it in pro ball or whether I want to now. Most running backs are shot at thirty. I'll be twenty-seven when I finish my five years' active duty. Anyway, the game I'm playing right now is more important than any football game."

When I met him, Moore said he had been on ten missions with H Company's teams since he had been transferred to the Third Brigade, First Cavalry Division, in December 1971, after the 101st stood down. He said he did not have to go out in the bush but did so twice a month to check out his men and stay in touch with the situation in the field.

Moore said his last mission was a hot one. His team was surrounded by an estimated Communist platoon (about forty troops), and only the arrival of Cobra gunships and a rescue helicopter saved them. Moore said he emptied his last magazine at muzzle flashes in bushes as his chopper lifted off. "I was beginning to have second thoughts about going out," he said. "I'm going to keep going out, though."

He had made another important decision when he chose West Point over Oklahoma State, Arkansas, and Navy after starring on his Ponca City, Oklahoma, high school football team. A trip to West Point with an army assistant coach and a guided tour sold him. "I'd never been that far away from home before," he said. "The Navy people called me a few weeks later and said they were sorry for not calling sooner. But by then I had already made my decision."

Moore, six foot two, 195 pounds, played behind and alongside Charlie Jarvis during his first two seasons when the Black Knights of the Hudson finished 8–2 and 7–3 under new coach Tom Cahill and split two games against Navy. Highlights of his career included an eighty-three-yard run on the first play from scrimmage in a victory over Boston College, four touchdowns against Duke, and a ninety-five-yard kickoff return against Oregon. In his senior year, he was the workhorse of the offense and team captain when Army, with quarterback problems, went 4–5–1.

He was one of six honor graduates in a class of 247 from the Ranger School at Fort Benning, Georgia, in January 1971. He spent eight months as a platoon leader in an airborne unit at Fort Bragg, North Carolina, before coming to Vietnam in September 1971. Captain Peter Dencker, who graduated from West Point a year before Moore and was a defensive back on the football team, was Moore's H Company commanding officer. The executive officer, John Fenilli, a former end, also had been a teammate of Moore.

"I think we were prepared for this type of war environment by playing football," Dencker said. "The football team was very close and all volunteers, just like we are. And you work together in the bush, just like we used to do on the football field."

Moore said, "I like being a Ranger because of the esprit de corps. And so far, the army has enabled me to buy a nice car and supported my lifestyle. I'm happy with it. I've thought about maybe trying to make it in the pros or the Canadian League, but I don't know. There's a lot of excitement in being a Ranger too. I used to be scared before a football game, more scared than before a contact. In the locker room, you've got a lot of time to think about the game and get worried. In a firefight, it's just all of a sudden, and you're into it. There's no time to build up any great fear. It's just do or die."

TWO HEROES: GEDDES
MACLAREN AND JIM STEIN

The Vietnam War produced its share of unlikely heroes. One of them was Captain Geddes MacLaren, twenty-five, from Brunswick, Maryland. His job was making the so-called "goodies run" to firebases in western Pleiku and Kontum Provinces in the mountainous Central Highlands of South Vietnam. A couple of times a week, he'd fly in by chopper to a bunch of bases, bringing advisers their mail, magazines, C rations, and ammunition.

In April 1972, as the North Vietnamese Army overran several ARVN outposts along "Rocket Ridge" northwest of Kontum City, MacLaren flew in to Fire Base Yankee to extract two Americans. "What I didn't know," he said, "was that they had already been evacuated. When we got down, all that was left was a handful of [ARVN] Rangers and a lot of VC." MacLaren said the aircraft pilot realized what was going on and got them out of there in a hurry.

Another time, MacLaren said, his mission was to chopper in to the abandoned Fire Base 5 and remove the firing pins and breechblocks from artillery pieces so that the Communists could not use them. "We took several hits coming in," he said, "and I dove for cover on the LZ. I cut my nose. That's the worst I want to be wounded." MacLaren sprinted to the big guns, disarmed them, and scrambled back to the chopper. "The aircraft took a lot of fire going out," he said, "but we accomplished our mission."

On May 5–6, MacLaren said, he had the hairiest two days of his life. He was sent to replace another adviser at beleaguered Polei Kleng border Ranger camp fifteen miles west of Kontum and got another taste of combat. "We took three shells right near the chopper as we went in," he said. "They must have had a forward observer near the camp because later, every time an American stuck his head up, the shelling intensified."

MacLaren said he and First Lieutenant Paul McKenna, twenty-four, of New York City, called in twenty-three tactical airstrikes near the camp despite being under a barrage of shelling. "They systematically leveled the camp," he said. "They started in the middle with the command post. One direct hit collapsed the walls of five bunkers, blew a two-foot thick oak door off its hinges, and filled the room with smoke. I continued to call in airstrikes, and we dug our way out of the bunker and took up positions near the perimeter. Now, they started walking in rounds all over the compound. They shot down all our antennas, blew up all the buildings above ground, and destroyed most of our bunkers."

Then, MacLaren said, he did a crazy thing. He stood up in the open on a pile of sandbags, looked through his binoculars, and calmly directed airstrikes via his field telephone at onrushing Communist troops. "I guess it was sort of a crazy thing to do," he said, "but I couldn't see anything from inside the bunker I was in." The concussion from a mortar shell threw him to the ground, but he was unhurt. The battle continued throughout the next day. The advisers finally were extracted by chopper at 7:15 p.m. A few hours later, he said, the base was overrun, and the South Vietnamese defenders and their families were either killed or fled.

"The SOBs were jumping out of the bushes and firing AKs at us," MacLaren said. "We thought we had 'em for a while. We were calling in F-4s, A-1s, A-37s, Cobras, [AC-130] Spectre gunships, everything, but we couldn't knock them out."

* * *

Jim Stein, twenty-five, from Placerville, California, was on his second tour in Vietnam. On his first, from April 1969 to November 1970, he said he was shot down five times while flying Hueys for the 335th Aviation Company out of Bearcat and Dong Tam. Twice more, he brought back choppers that were badly damaged, one with thirty-two bullet holes in it, another with twenty.

"I volunteered for 'Nam," he told me. "I wanted to come back. I like to fly, to be in an aviation unit. I thought I could do better over here, really

21

doing something. I don't mind flying in combat situations. I'm trying to get all the combat time I can get. I want to be a career officer, and that really counts."

Just before he returned to Vietnam in March 1972, Stein said he took a light-observation-helicopter pilot course at Fort Rucker in Alabama. "It's a lot different [than flying Hueys]," he said, "but once you have the basic knowledge, it didn't take long to pick it up. The only course available was Loaches, so I said 'Okay, Loaches.' I wanted to fly them on my first tour but never got the chance … I requested flying Loaches and put in for this area. They said there's a lot of mountains, and I wanted to get mountain experience. I want to make aviation a career when I get out of the service and get as much experience as I can under all kinds of conditions."

Stein said he was shot down three times in a six-week span during the Communists' 1972 Easter Offensive but still made the daring rescue of MacLaren at Polei Kleng. (He received a Silver Star for it.)

"I do it because there are men on the ground that need help," he said. "I hope I never hear a pilot refuse to help somebody down there saying, 'It's too hot down there.' If somebody is in trouble, you go down and help. If you get shot down, you just go back and get another bird and finish the mission … All aircraft are vulnerable for ground fire, whether they're flying at six thousand feet and take .50 caliber or low and take AK. If a man wants a little more excitement, put him in a Loach—you'll get excitement. It makes you feel good when you come back with a bunch of intelligence or find a bunch of stuff that might prevent an attack on a city or whatever."

In April 1972, Stein said, small-arms fire knocked one of his birds out of the air. "We crashed near QL 14 [a road]," he said. "We were going through a pass on the way home. Two Loaches were flying together, and they opened up and got us. We had noticed that some ARVN jeeps were stopped, and we knew something was up. Just before we got the radio call [from ARVN troops], my wingman got hit and [Specialist Fourth Class Darryl Brandon] was wounded."

Stein added that the bullets "cut the drive link to the rotor head. We went down slowly with no further contact. I picked an area that had been heavily maintained. We crashed about ten meters from a road. A Loach is one of the best crashable aircraft. We hit and rolled over three times. The wingman [Warrant Officer Jack Rogers] disregarded his own safety and picked us up. We just happened to land in a safe area. We got some bruises, nothing major. It was the first time I'd been shot down where I couldn't put the aircraft down [softly]. We had a good roll."

On another mission, he said, Stein buzzed within twenty-five meters of an enemy bunker. His observer tossed a grenade into it and sprayed machine-gun fire around the area. The enemy returned fire, wounding the observer and crippling the chopper. But Stein and his partner again were rescued by a sister ship. "It was the last week of April," he said. "We were doing recon and screening for an ARVN element. We came upon the bunker, marked it [with a smoke grenade], and the guns [Cobra gunships] put rockets in there. We went back, marked it again, and there were still people inside. The guns came back, strafed the bunker with more rockets, but there were still people inside. We decided to engage them ourselves. We shot our .60, threw a frag inside from about twenty-five feet away, but the bunker was deep, and we still didn't knock it out. We took automatic fire that wounded the Oscar [observer Specialist Fourth Class Michael Holderman] and shot out the wires for the gauges. He kept engaging 'em and gave me time to fly the aircraft to a safe area, and my wingman [Warrant Officer Tony Fruge] picked me up. [Holderman] was medevaced."

In an early May mission, Stein said, he sniffed out some tire tracks, suspecting that tanks were hidden in what may have been camouflaged bunkers. He marked the area for airstrikes. After the bomb runs, Stein said, he dropped back to the deck to assess the damage and was greeted by .51-caliber fire from thirty feet away. His ship smashed into the ground, but a sister ship again rescued him.

Stein said he had rescued fourteen Americans in the first two months of the Easter Offensive. "Everybody is scared when they fly," he said. "But you don't think about it. If you do, it possesses you, and you can't do your job." He added about being hit that he knew he could be hit at six thousand feet or at treetop level. He said he was proud of his Silver Star but was just pleased he completed his mission. "It's the third-highest award the army gives," he said. "But I was more happy to see people's faces as you pull them out. It makes you feel the whole day's worth it, all worth it."

"Both Sides Showed
a Lot of Guts"

It was merely a sandbagged bald spot on top of a mountain outside Kontum City, but Fire Base Charlie was something NVA troops wanted and finally succeeded in taking on April 14, 1972. Charlie was one of a series of lonesome outposts on Rocket Ridge northwest of the provincial capital in the Central Highlands. Captain Phillip Handley, twenty-six, of Cordova, Alabama, had a ringside seat for the big fight.

Handley directed airstrikes from adjacent Fire Base Yankee, which itself was overrun a few days later. In Pleiku at the officers club at Camp Holloway, after his first shave, shower, and hot meal in ten days, Handley said, "The people on Charlie were far outnumbered. But they held on and held on. They never did break. They made the dinks take it bunker by bunker. They didn't get up and run. And the NVA, even though they lost about a thousand men, I guess, kept coming. Both sides showed a lot of guts."

"Wave after wave of tac. air pounded them," Handley said. "F-4s, Cobras, A-7s, A-37s … they hit them even after the ARVNs had evacuated." Handley said the NVA troops stayed at Charlie for a while but most fled after airstrikes leveled it and made the road adjacent to it impassable. I had to wonder why the NVA would sacrifice a thousand regular troops to take a base they could have circled around before attacking Kontum City.

"If what they wanted was an infiltration route," Handley said, "they've got it. But if they want the ridge northwest of Kontum, the big stuff is yet to come, and if they try to hit another one of those base camps, it'll take them a long time to recoup afterwards."

CAPTAIN GLEN S. IVEY

One day in Kontum, I was walking to the chopper pad at the MACV compound when I saw a familiar face striding briskly down the sidewalk.

"Hey, Smith, how's it goin'?"

"Captain Ivey, what are you doin' here?"

"Got myself transferred. I'm an adviser to an ARVN battalion."

"That's what you wanted?"

"Sure, man. This is where the action is. Tell all those guys in the rear at Bien Hoa hello for me, will you?"

"Sure will, Cap'n. Good luck."

Ivey, twenty-four, had been an information officer for the First Cavalry Division in a cushy, air-conditioned office fifteen miles north of Saigon and had steered me to several stories. He could have ridden out his tour without seeing combat but obviously had gotten fidgety.

A week later, I was at Fire Base 42, eight miles north of Pleiku, shortly after it had been hit by a company of North Vietnamese sappers. I was told about forty ARVN soldiers had been killed and eighty wounded. Thirty-six enemy dead lay in the wire. I was told that in the midst of the fierce predawn raid, which had been preceded by a barrage of mortars and rockets, there had been hand-to-hand fighting at several spots along the tiny camp's perimeter. An American adviser had stuck his head up out of a bunker to see what was going on. A VC had fired a B-40 rocket from point-blank range and blown the captain's head off.

His name was Glen S. Ivey.

* * *

At the firebase, I watched South Vietnamese soldiers slip a rope around the bullet-riddled body of a Communist soldier, hoist it from a blown-out bunker, and toss it into a heap of other bodies near the perimeter wire. The stench of death, mixed with the scent of smoldering trucks, burning bunker tops, and cooked-off ammo was suffocating.

The war had come to the doorstep of Pleiku. Official spokesmen said friendly losses in the surprise attack were a total of about a hundred killed or wounded.

It was the closest to Pleiku that Communist forces had struck since their countrywide offensive had begun on March 30. Fire Base 42 was one of three government garrisons along vital Highway 14, which connected Pleiku with Kontum, another provincial capital twenty-five miles north. The post normally was manned by elements of the Forty-Fifth Regiment of the Twenty-Third ARVN Division, but at the time of the attack, the lead element of a battalion of Second Airborne Brigade troops was inside after having completed a ten-mile sweep along the highway.

"It's a good thing the airborne was there," their American adviser Major Michael D. Haynes, thirty-four, of Columbus, Georgia, told me as we surveyed the damage the morning after the battle. "Otherwise, I don't know what would have happened. Look at our side [of the base] and the other side." (The enemy had not penetrated the perimeter wire on the side of the base defended by the airborne troops.)

Haynes edged his way along a caved-in bunker, slipped between two supply shacks that had been reduced to ashes, and looked at the camp from the middle. "The main attack came from the east. But look—look at how our men fought. The half of the camp defended by ARVN regulars was reduced to rubble. Most of the vehicles and artillery pieces were on that side."

Colonel Cran Tran Quoc Lich, commander of the airborne brigade, said, "We have better spirit, we're well trained, and we're more experienced. We've fought all over the country. But the infantry did well here too. Everybody did. If they hadn't, the NVA would own this place right now."

Lich said elements of the Seventh Battalion killed seventy-five Communists in fighting near Chu Pao, eight miles south of Kontum, during the first week of May and that the Ninth Airborne Battalion swept down the east side of the highway. The ARVN Forty-Fourth Regiment was choppered from An Khe to Chu Pao, where Communists had dug in mortar positions in caves and were preventing truck convoys from entering or leaving Kontum. But sources in Pleiku told me the infantrymen fled from the rock pile when they drew contact. Sources said the Forty-Fourth lost an entire company either killed or wounded.

"I'd be glad to have the mission to clear Chu Pao," Lich told me. "I asked General Dzu [Lieutenant General Ngo Dzu, II Corps commander] for that job a month ago. There's a regiment of NVA up there, and we need a lot of men to go in and clean them out. If somebody doesn't clear Chu Pao soon, we'll have a big problem when the enemy attacks Kontum. Our only resupply now is by air. When they attack, aircraft won't be able to get in."

Lich said he felt the attack on Fire Base 42 was an attempt to kill him. "They knew I was there," he said. "They knew if they killed me it would be very good for them."

The round-faced, crew-cut officer said his bunkers took several direct hits from the estimated two hundred rounds of assorted shells that hit the camp but that he was uninjured.

By noon, the firebase was returning to normal. The airborne troops had gone. The bodies of each side had been wrapped in cellophane bags and removed. US Cobra helicopters circled the area looking for a chance to pick off any retreating enemy soldiers. The remaining ARVNs cooked their rations and talked quietly.

All I could think about was Ivey.

DRAWING A LINE IN THE DIRT: JOHN PAUL VANN

When I visited Kontum City in the last week of April 1972, the mood was tense. North Vietnamese Army troops were advancing from the north and west. Many of the city's thirty thousand residents were packing to leave. Others vowed to stand and fight. John Paul Vann, the senior American adviser in II Corps, said allied forces did not plan on turning the provincial capital over to the Communists.

"I've been making predictions on the war for ten years," he said, "and I haven't been wrong yet. One of the biggest battles of the war is shaping up. And we have no intention of giving Kontum up. The plan is to fight and hold Kontum."

ARVN forces were overwhelmed earlier that week at Tan Canh and Dak To, and others had been evacuated from Rocket Ridge northwest of Kontum City. They were being regrouped and redeployed closer to Kontum to check the Communist advance. A firebase five miles north of the city was being manned by ARVN troops. They had been evacuated from Fire Base Delta after three Soviet-made tanks had appeared on a nearby hill. The troops did not have antitank weapons then, but they had them when I visited.

"And they know how to use them," a US adviser told me. "There's no way we're going to let these guys drive tanks into Kontum. Our men are anxious to get a shot at those Red tanks. Some of them have knocked out tanks up north [in Quang Tri Province], and they say they can do it down here too."

ARVN Colonel Ly Tong Ba, commander of the Twenty-Third ARVN Division, had his headquarters in Kontum City. "He's the most able field commander we have in II Corps," Vann said. "I believe Kontum will be held because friendly forces and civilians in the city are willing to pay the price to do it."

Vann said he believed 75 percent of the ARVN forces that were scattered when Tan Canh was overrun on April 24 had survived and were in the process of being redeployed. "The loss of Tan Canh and Dak To was anticipated," Vann said, "but he [Communist troops] will not take Kontum."

Crowds of refugees gathered in tent cities in school yards in Kontum. Some wounded staggered down the streets, supporting themselves with staffs and carrying a few items of clothing in wicker baskets. Asked what he would do if the NVA attacked the city, a bearded old man told me, "I don't know. I guess I will die … I can't walk any further."

As of May 2, I was told that 30 percent of the residents of Kontum City had been evacuated to Pleiku. "We're trying to get all the people who work for Americans in any capacity out first," a civilian adviser told me, "because they would be a prize target for any Vietcong who make it into the city."

Chinooks bearing up to seventy people at a time were making continuous dawn-to-dusk flights with people and equipment since April 29. Only women, children, and old men were being evacuated. Civilians were unable to flee south from Kontum to Pleiku along Highway 14 because the road was cut by the Communists. Sources told me that on May 2, ARVN Ranger and airborne troops evacuated Fire Base Lima, about four miles north of Kontum, in the face of heavy enemy pressure.

"There were beaucoup Communists all around that place," said a US officer who helped direct the evacuation. "It was only a matter of time before they were overrun."

LAST MEETING WITH VANN

My last face-to-face meeting with II Corps senior adviser John Paul Vann was on May 24, 1972, sixteen days before he died. Vann was the closest thing to a real hero that I met during my tour. He had been in and out of the country for most of the war and had historical perspective. He claimed in a news conference in Pleiku that the ongoing Communists' Easter Offensive was "a major tactical blunder." He added that "The enemy has fought a conventional war on a gamble that he would not be thrown back in the conventional manner. But it appears An Loc [sixty miles north of Saigon], Hue, and Kontum are going to hold."

Vann said the ARVN Twenty-Third Division, which was defending Kontum, "probably learned more about combat in the past three weeks than it learned in the past three years. I was very apprehensive about how the Twenty-Third would do when it first saw tanks. But once the Forty-Fourth Regiment killed some tanks, it got more confidence. Now, the threat of tanks doesn't panic the men."

Massive US B-52 strikes and tactical airstrikes helped the ARVNs blunt the NVA's drive into the Highlands. "I think Mr. Nixon decided to save South Vietnam," Vann said, "and I think South Vietnam a year from now is going to be a helluva lot stronger than it would have had the offensive not taken place. It's going to be much better prepared because they're going to have a helluva lot more experience in tactics and they're going to be much better led." But he added about current conditions, "This thing is a long way from being over."

Vann said twenty-three of the estimated forty Communist tanks in the area had been destroyed and that up to fifteen thousand enemy troops had been killed in the area since April 1. "Six months from now," Vann said,

"I don't think he will present the threat to Laos, Cambodia, and South Vietnam that he was able to mount before this offensive began. The rainy season is coming, and it will soon force the enemy to withdraw. When he does, I don't think he will be able to take any conventional armament—mortars, tanks, artillery pieces—with him. By next year, South Vietnam is going to be much better prepared to meet enemy attacks."

Vann said he was reasonably certain that Kontum would be held. But he said reports from agents indicated that the Communists were moving troops from the NVA's Third Division in coastal Binh Dinh Province to reinforce their troops around Kontum. "We hope the Third Division. beats itself to death on the door to Kontum," he said, "because we'll hit him with all the B-52s we can muster. I told people in Binh Dinh to wait until Kontum draws the Third Division away, and they'll be able to walk back into their old areas."

Vann said between May 14, when a tank-led assault on Kontum was repelled, and May 21, 1,150 Communists had died within two miles of the city, mostly from tactical airstrikes. He said ARVN losses during the period were 107 killed and about 300 wounded.

HOW VANN DIED

I was in the Bangkok Airport returning from a week's rest and relaxation on June 11, 1972 when I learned that John Paul Vann had been killed two days before that. It was ten thirty in the morning, and I was toting my baggage from a curbside cab when I saw his head shot on page 1 of *Stars and Stripes*. I knew he had to be dead. Why else would they run his photo?

"They got John Vann," I shouted. "Oh my God, no."

"He was asking for it—the hot dog," a voice behind me said. I whirled around, and the only reason I didn't punch the guy was because he was wearing the rank of a US Army captain.

"What the hell would you know about John Vann?" I asked, cutting it off there before I got into trouble.

It's really strange how people's minds work. A man is a hero until he gets it. Then he's a hot dog.

Death came to John Vann in a helicopter, and it figured that he died on what for him was a routine mission. He was flying from Pleiku to Kontum to spend the night at the front when his chopper crashed near Fire Base 42 along Highway 14.

I had more respect for Mr. Vann—for that is what I always called him—than for anybody else I met in Vietnam. Sometimes, though, I amused the veteran correspondents with the naïveté of the questions I asked. One time, I questioned him about the looting of the abandoned MACV advisers' compound at Kontum by ARVN soldiers.

"Young man," he said, "I don't know how many wars you've been through, but these are the hazards of war."

Another time, I had seen Americans dressed in black, unmarked fatigues and armed to the teeth choppered into Kontum. "Mr. Vann," I said, "would you comment on the American troops being dropped behind enemy lines in Kontum?"

"There are no Americans being dropped behind enemy lines," he said.

"But I saw them."

"There are no Americans being dropped behind enemy lines."

"There are some pretty weird-looking people up there."

"Well," Vann said, "there are some pretty weird-looking people right in this room."

CAPTAIN ROBERT
A. ROBERTSON

Captain Robertson was one of my best military sources in II Corps. He'd always make it sound like he didn't want to tell me anything, but he'd wind up dropping a little hint that would point me toward a story.

I first ran across Robertson when I did a story on an artillery unit based at Artillery Hill near Pleiku City. Robertson said he flew a forward air controller (FAC) mission the previous day in an O-1 Bird Dog light observation airplane to mark the artillery rounds that were fired in support of an ARVN operation. He popped smoke canisters over the targets and told the gunners where their rounds were falling. The only weapon he carried was a holstered .45-caliber pistol that he wore on his belt.

It seemed Robertson performed a variety of tasks, and I figured he was a CIA employee. I saw him all around the city—at floor shows at the club, driving around town in a jeep and sunning himself at the pool on Sundays. He was tall and thin with a red face and short, curly, brown hair.

I saw him once at Camp Holloway in Pleiku, and he told me the specifications of the new Bravo model Hueys that were being used to fire missiles at NVA tanks in the Highlands. One evening at dinner, he gave me correct casualty figures for both sides in an engagement at Dak Pek. "My source is the adviser to the ARVNs there," Robertson said. "He flew back here this afternoon." I thanked him.

I got little bits of information from Robertson here and there, but he didn't open up to me as much as he probably would have if I had not been an army enlisted man. But without guys like him, I never would have found out what really was going on. When he told me something, I could be sure it was true.

Robertson died in an accidental night helicopter crash in the Highlands on June 9, 1972, flying with John Paul Vann, the senior II Corps adviser, who also died in the crash.

SURVIVING A MISSILE HIT

It was a hot day at Lai Khe, and crewmen of VNAF helicopters were sleeping in the shade under their aircraft. I heard an American pilot say he was going up at one o'clock, so I asked if I could tag along. We flew at three thousand feet in a command and control (C&C) bird as the officer supervised the pickup and gunship cover of some elite South Vietnamese airborne troops during the battle to clear Highway 13 just south of An Loc, a provincial capital sixty miles north of Saigon.

I was too high to see much—so high that I couldn't see the troops scrambling aboard the choppers. But it was cool up there, and I just liked riding in choppers anyway. After nearly four hours aloft, interrupted by a stop for fuel, we landed back at Lai Khe. I asked the officer if I could talk to him for a story about the mission, but he wasn't listening. Some gunship crewmen had gathered, and one was gesturing wildly.

"What's up?" I said, with typical nonchalance.

"We had a bird shot down by a Strela [missile]," the man answered.

"What happened to the crew?"

"They lived."

"Where the hell are they?"

"One of 'em's in Third Field [Hospital] in Saigon. The other—Captain Mike Brown—last I heard was in the club."

"Thanks a lot."

I was off and walking briskly across the road to the US advisers' compound. On a day when I thought I had no story, I had stumbled onto one of the most exciting stories of my tour. And it was an exclusive because no other reporters were there. When I found Brown, he was eager to talk.

"Somebody yelled, 'Missile!' over the radio," he said. "I looked over my shoulder and saw the smoke trail. Then I felt a jolt. It happened so fast I couldn't do anything. The tail boom was blown off, and we started spiraling down to the right. I figured it was all over."

The scene was six miles south of An Loc in late June 1972, during the tail end of the Easter Offensive. Brown's AH-1 Cobra helicopter gunship was covering the extraction of about a thousand South Vietnamese troops from a hot landing zone near the town of Tan Khai. Brown had just broken out of a rocket run at a Communist position when his aircraft was hit in its exhaust stack by the heat-seeking SA-7 Strela missile. The twenty-eight-year-old from Sandpoint, Idaho, and his observer Captain Mark Gordon became the first US fliers to survive a crash after being hit by one of the Russian-made, shoulder-fired missiles. His helicopter landed in some trees. Gordon was evacuated to Third Field Hospital with possible back injuries. Brown was unmarked and sat drinking beer in the officers' club at Lai Khe when I met him.

"I thought my number was up," said the pilot, a Bluc Max member of F Battery, Seventy-Ninth Artillery Battalion. "I thought it was my turn to get it. I was flying up there every day and just asking for it. I said to myself on the way down that if I ever got out of this, I'd tell other people what I did."

Brown said after his chopper was hit, he immediately began autorotating the bird, meaning that he shut off all systems and allowed the air to spin the main rotor blade to break the fall as he spun with the nose of the aircraft at a forty-five-degree downward angle. Brown said he tried to jettison his rocket pods to lighten the load. No dice. When the tail section was blown off, the electrical circuits had been knocked out. He tried to fire his minigun and to expend the rest of his ten- and seventeen-pound rockets. No go.

"If we went down in a field," Brown said, "there was no chance for us."

It took about thirty seconds for the helicopter to hit the trees. "It seemed like a helluva lot longer than that," he said. "Neither of us was panicking, though. I'd thought a lot about what to do in this situation, and I did it."

About thirty feet above the treetops, Brown said, he raised the nose of the chopper so it would impact parallel to the ground. It hit and tangled in some trees. Gordon scrambled out of his canopy and to safety, but Brown's window was jammed. He pulled out a knife, smashed the Plexiglas on the left side, and lowered himself to the ground.

"We landed right in the middle of a bunker complex," Brown said. "We wanted to get out of there in a hurry and were afraid the bird would go up in flames because both of our birds that had been hit by missiles did. I'm really surprised ours didn't."

He added, "Three things saved us. One of the other birds yelled, 'Missile!' so I was ready for it. We landed in trees, which cushioned the shock. And before every flight, I always lock my shoulder harness. Not all Cobra people do. If I hadn't, I'd have been thrown through the windshield."

After they escaped the chopper, Brown and Gordon ran into a clearing and waved their arms. Two other Blue Max birds, based at Long Thanh, swooped down to treetop level. One crewman signaled with a thumbs-up to Brown that help was on the way. Ten minutes later, at about 2:40 in the afternoon, Brown said, a Huey landed and rescued the fliers, along with some weary ARVN airborne troops who had been involved in a bunker-to-bunker battle.

From the beginning of the Easter Offensive until the end of June, four other Blue Max birds were destroyed by enemy fire—two by missiles. All eight crewmen were killed. Brown said two of his buddies were downed by enemy fire two days before he was. They made a forced landing and were cut down by small-arms fire as they ran from their aircraft.

Captain Brown made a tape describing his actions in steering his disabled chopper through its dizzying turns. Copies were distributed to helicopter pilots throughout South Vietnam. After the incident, Brown said he had no desire to plunge right back into combat. "I think I could be of better use telling people about what I did," he said. Nobody could blame him for feeling that way.

KING OF TAC. AIR

In late April and early May 1972, Communist troops captured the district towns of Hoi An, Bong Son, and Tam Quan and took control of the northern third of the troublesome Binh Dinh Province, the most populous but least pacified province in South Vietnam. North Vietnamese Army (NVA) regulars sent ARVN troops and civilians fleeing by land and sea and gained domination over two hundred thousand people and fertile rice land.

In early June, elements of three regiments of the NVA's Third Division began a new push on Phu My, just south of the conquered territory and only thirty miles northwest of the strategic port city of Qui Nhon. If Phu My fell, it was conceivable that with a determined push in the Central Highlands, the Communists could cut South Vietnam in half. Without the cool, calculated direction of US airstrikes by Lieutenant Colonel Don Stovall during the siege of Phu My, June 2–5, that might have happened.

"I'm not going to stand here and say I was a hero or anything," Stovall said. "The people that flew the aircraft did all the damage." But the soft-spoken, articulate senior adviser to the Forty-First ARVN Regiment told me he directed 443 airstrikes that dumped over five million pounds of bombs and sent 996 sorties by American helicopter gunships against Communist positions in June. The heaviest fighting was June 2–5, when more than 1,500 Communists died within a mile of Phu My, according to an ARVN spokesman in Pleiku.

Lieutenant Colonel Bill Giese, commander of the Eagle Combat Aviation Battalion at An Son, told me, "Stovall singlehandedly controlled naval gunfire, where and when; ARVN artillery, where and when; gunships; air cavalry; [AC-130] Spectre; tac. air; B-52s ... everything. He

39

always knew precisely where the friendlies were, and he recommended to his [ARVN] counterpart where to employ his ground troops. He handled three radios at once, and there wasn't a single incident of friendlies being killed. It was the most outstanding job of fire support coordination I've ever witnessed."

On June 4, the NVA surrounded Landing Zone (LZ) Crystal, a dusty, sandbagged firebase just south of Phu My. The Communists had two .51-caliber antiaircraft artillery guns, two .57 mm recoilless rifles, a few mortars, and several thousand troops. "Even Stovall had to admit things were looking pretty bad," said Major Jim Ellis, who assisted Stovall. "But he just told everybody that we were going to stay here and win. He carried us through. If it hadn't been for him, we might not be here now."

Stovall did it all on less than five hours of sleep a night, friends said. He first directed helicopter gunships at enemy positions. Then he peeled off the Cobras to the west and brought in F-4s from the north and peeled them off to the south. At the same time, he had AC-130 Spectre gunships orbiting, their infrared sensors on, all night. Then Stovall brought in the awesome Arc Lights —B-52 strikes that shook every timber in his tiny compound.

Friends said incoming mortar rounds landed all around Stovall. Three made direct hits on his command shack. Five of the eleven members of his fire support team were wounded by shrapnel from rockets and artillery rounds. Stovall sustained a broken left arm as he jumped off an armored personnel carrier to take cover from artillery fire as he and ARVN troops headed out to retrieve the bodies of two F-4 crewmen whose plane had crashed four hundred meters outside LZ Crystal's perimeter wire.

Stovall suffered with the injury for four days before he was evacuated to Qui Nhon, where the bone was set and his arm was put in a cast. He returned to his post before the cast had hardened. Sources said a key factor in the defense of Phu My was information provided by a double deserter who revealed the NVA attack plans, allowing the ARVNs several hours to prepare for the initial Communist onslaught.

Bitter fighting later broke out in northern Binh Dinh, when ARVN troops fought to reclaim lost territory. Back in May, the senior US adviser in the Central Highlands, John Paul Vann, had predicted that the Third NVA Division would filter out of Binh Dinh to assist two NVA divisions that were driving on Kontum City. "I told the people in Binh Dinh to bide their time," Vann said, "and when the third beats itself to death against Kontum, they can walk back to their old areas."

It didn't quite work out that way, Stovall said, after a helicopter tour of northern Binh Dinh. "We ain't going to be able to walk back in there without a fight now," he said. "The enemy has prepared positions for a delaying action. We're in for a tough fight."

Twenty-Three Days
on the Ground

A US Air Force captain who lived for twenty-three days in the jungle north of Hanoi on fruit, nuts, berries, and water from a banana tree was rescued on June 2, 1972, and listed in good condition by a Seventh Air Force spokesman at a briefing I attended in Saigon the next day.

Captain Roger C. Locher, twenty-eight, from Sabetha, Kansas, lost fifteen pounds throughout the ordeal, during which he covered fifteen miles and avoided NVA troops after his F-4 Phantom was shot down by a MIG-21's heat-seeking missile on May 10. Locher was picked up by a Super Jolly Green Giant helicopter, escorted by F-4 and F-105 Thunderchief jet fighters. An A-1 Sandy airplane had spotted the downed airman, and HC-130 King command planes were used to refuel several Jolly Greens in the task force in flight, a spokesman said.

The aircraft braved heavy ground fire on their way to the downed airman's mountainside perch, spokesmen said. Rescue forces were driven off by MIGs on their first attempt to extract Locher on June 1. Locher was the weapons system operator in his F-4 and was flying his 407th combat mission when he was shot down. The pilot of the plane was listed as missing. The men had just shot down a MIG before they were shot down. Locher also was aboard aircraft that had shot down MIGs on February 21 and May 8.

Reached by the Associated Press at Udorn Royal Thai Air Force Base, Locher said that after his F-4 was hit, "We immediately went out of control, flopping from side to side. Then fire started coming out of the back of the cockpit. It seared my canopy with bubbles, and I couldn't see anymore. The airplane slowed down and went into a flat spin. I told the pilot, 'I think I'm going to have to get out. It's starting to burn pretty bad back here.' I yanked for what seemed to be an eternity on my primary ejection. The next thing I heard was a big blast. When I opened my eyes, I was in my parachute, and just about then I could see the airplane hit the ground right below."

"I looked around," he continued, "and was going into a kind of deep-dished valley. I aimed for a steep mountainside and came down through the trees ... I just sat down for a minute and listened."

The airman said finding water was easy. "One day, I went through somebody's garden," he said, "and stole some chives. They had some pretty good chives there." Another day, he said, "I eyed a banana tree all day. It didn't have any bananas on it, but I remembered I could get water out of it. Just before evening, I stuck a hole in it and got myself three pints of good banana water."

"I shaved a couple of times," Locher said. "There was nothing else to do. I used a surgical knife from my survival kit. I was getting to look pretty scrubby."

Locher had a few days' growth of beard and a big smile when the rescue chopper landed him at Udorn, and he was welcomed by the air force commander in Indochina, General John W. Vogt. "He gave me a bear hug," Locher said. "It's great to be back. It's a miracle. I was a long way up there. I didn't realize how far it is ... It was the first time I was shot down, and I hope it's the last."

He added, "I wanted to get to a particular spot. I had a goal. I made it partways, but I ran out of steam. I couldn't move too much the last few days, because I was so fatigued. I didn't have enough to eat. I ate assorted fruits from the trees and imagined they were steaks. I drank rain and stream water and imagined it was root beer. I was getting pretty hungry. But I never had any trouble sleeping, only when it rained."

Locher said several times NVA troops came within twenty feet of him in the dense jungle, but they never detected him. "I was pretty much camouflaged," he said. "The terrain was mountainous. Much of the time I laid down. A lot of things flashed through my mind. What I did wrong. It was a smattering of things I really can't explain."

He was unable to make radio contact with US aircraft until June 1, when he raised a pair of fighter-bombers, triggering his rescue. The Super Jolly Green Giant that rescued him was commanded by Captain Dale E. Stovall, of Toppenish, Washington. As the chopper swooped in to pluck Locher off the mountainside with a hoist, minigun fire sprayed by Sergeant Charles McQuid, of Evanston, Illinois, and Airman First Class Kenneth W. Cakebread, of San Jose, California, silenced Communist automatic weapons fire at the chopper.

Spokesmen said the HH-53 helicopter took fire from several enemy positions on its way out of North Vietnam. A1-Es, flying escort over the slow-moving chopper, destroyed a locomotive, several railroad cars, and a few trucks from which fire had been coming.

Locher was a graduate of Kansas State University with a degree in feed technology. He was single. The airman had extended his first one-year tour by twelve months and had served twenty straight months and flown sixty-eight missions over North Vietnam plus others over Laos and South Vietnam. A spokesman said he was to have been immediately reassigned out of the combat zone. "It looks like it probably will be that," Locher said. "Going down over the North pretty much wraps it up. If I would get it again, it would be the same as a death sentence."

SURVIVING IN
NO-MAN'S-LAND

The village of Mang Buk was in the middle of no-man's-land, forty miles north of Kontum City in the Central Highlands. US Air Force Sergeant Bill Lacer was stuck there for five days in late June 1972. Lacer, twenty-two, from Brandon, Florida, was a combat controller for aircraft operations. He and Sergeant Robert Chavez were sent to Mang Buk to work on some navigational equipment. Their chopper hardly had touched down when it came under intense small-arms and mortar fire. Chavez got back aboard, but the chopper had to lift off before Lacer could scramble back into it. He ran to the nearest Montagnard outpost.

Chavez bundled Lacer's gear inside a flak vest, and when the chopper made a low pass over the compound, he kicked it out the door. The chopper flew south to Pleiku. Lacer was the first American in Mang Buk in a long time and was treated as a VIP. He went on several patrols with the Montagnards, he said, because, "I didn't have anything better to do."

At each of the five friendly villages in the area that Lacer entered, the headman gave him a Montagnard bracelet. He also received three crossbows from the tribesmen. During the time he was at Mang Buk, there were continuous battles. "The compound catches steady incoming mortar rounds from all around the area," he said, "and snipers shoot at you when you move between bunkers. But those little guys [Montagnards] like to get out there and mop up. You should see the collection of weapons they've captured. The Communists are all over the place, but the little dudes get out and patrol and ambush—they really fight. One day, they located the

45

observation post that was directing the mortars, so they went out and cut the phone lines. Brought a big roll of that telephone wire back too."

Lacer, meanwhile, used an ARVN radio to contact Chavez at Pleiku. Bad weather prohibited a rescue attempt for four days, but on the fifth, a chopper went in and got Lacer. During his debriefing at Pleiku, the airfield came under a rocket attack. "I seem to draw that stuff like a magnet," Lacer said.

Chavez kidded Lacer, saying, "You were with me at Kontum, and we took incoming. You were with me at Song Be, and we got hit … When we get back to Tan Son Nhut [near Saigon, where they were based], you're going to be assigned to someone else's unit. We're bad for each other."

Lacer laughed and changed the subject. "Hey, Sarge," he said, "I hope somebody remembered that I was supposed to start my leave the day before yesterday."

A REPORTER KILLED
ON THE JOB

Newsweek's Alec Shimkin was tall and thin, and the dark-rimmed glasses he wore made him appear bookwormish. We often covered John Paul Vann's press conferences in Pleiku together, fed each other notes on occasion, and discussed the war over pizza and beer at the NCO club.

I hadn't seen Alec for some time when I read about what had happened to him near Quang Tri City in July 1972. He and UPI correspondent Chad Huntley were driving down a dirt road in a jeep to hook up with an ARVN airborne detachment near Highway 1. They saw a bunker system to the right of the road, Huntley later wrote, so they stopped and walked toward it. A grenade landed on the road behind Huntley.

"I yelled 'grenade!' and I ran across the road," Huntley wrote for UPI in a piece published by *Stars and Stripes*. "Alec, who was about 12 feet ahead of me, just stopped. I saw him thrust his arms high into the air and he yelled something in Vietnamese toward the bunker."

The first grenade bounced into a ditch, the former US Army Green Beret said. The second came down at his feet. He ran. Glancing back, Huntley said he saw a third grenade land at Shimkin's feet. "Alec just glanced at it," Huntley said. "Then he looked back at the man in the bunker ... and continued to plead with him in Vietnamese. About this time, the guy threw a fourth grenade at me, landing about a foot from me, so I jumped the fence in front of me, dived over a second fence and did a judo roll as I heard the explosion. When I looked back, I saw Shimkin crumbling. And I saw a fifth grenade being thrown at him."

It was presumed Shimkin had died; his body never was found. Huntley, putting his Special Forces training to use, rolled away from the two Communists who fired an AK-47 and then an M16 rifle at him. He said he was pinned down in a hollow by sniper fire for five hours. Then allied 105 mm howitzers walked in ten rounds on the bunkers near where Shimkin fell. Huntley said he spent the night in a cemetery and hitchhiked back down the highway to Hue two days later. "I found out later how we got so close to Quang Tri," he wrote. "Just a mixup in communications. Headquarters had moved and we were on the wrong road. No one's fault, really."

I made it my business never to get as close to the war as Huntley and Shimkin did. I preferred to sleep in the rear, fly around on choppers during the day to get my stories, and get back to a secure area by nightfall. It kept me alive.

PART II

DO-GOODERS

PART TWO

DO-GOODERS

TRYING TO LEAVE
WITH GOODWILL

As American troops were withdrawn from Vietnam, civic action programs in the villages surrounding their bases wound down. But US Army Captain John Wilcox, civic action officer of the Fifty-Second Aviation Battalion at Camp Holloway in Pleiku, wanted to get as much done as he could before leaving.

"Sure, we're not going to be here much longer," he told me in mid-January 1972. "But that doesn't mean we should stop working together. We want to do as much as we possibly can for as long as we are here."

Fighting against the clock, Wilcox had begun or planned to begin a series of projects to help Montagnards in several villages surrounding Holloway. The projects consisted of distributing clothes, building houses, and providing medical supplies. "The Montagnards—Vietnam's mountain people—are like Australia's aborigines," Wilcox said. "Some have highly developed villages and a very sophisticated society. But the people I deal with are living on land borrowed from a hamlet. They need everything imaginable."

In the village of Plei Ia Maih, he said, six to eight families of Montagnards lived in the same hut. Wilcox, with aid from volunteer enlisted men, planned to help the people build better houses, increase their livestock, and improve their farming methods. "B Troop bought a boar and a sow and told the village chief the pair of pigs should be used for reproduction only for at least several generations and not for eating as yet. They said to slaughter it on some great festive occasion in the future," Wilcox said.

At Tu Dam Orphanage, he said, members of D Troop gave presents and a party to children at Christmastime. In another project, the village of Plei Poim received eight hundred meters of electrical wire. "It was one of the more advanced hamlets," he said. "They had a generator and had scrounged together some light fixtures. They needed wire to get from the generator to a building which they will use for night meetings and classes."

Wilcox said he did not present the wire to the villagers but passed it to an ARVN officer to give to them. The money to buy it came from an assistance-in-kind fund. Wilcox said there were thirty-two such funds in-country at the time to help sponsor civic action projects. "We let the Montagnards think that the ARVNs are doing something for them," Wilcox said. "It makes the ARVNs feel good to see the people putting to use something that they gave them. I hope to act as a catalyst between the Vietnamese and the Montagnards here to try to decrease the resentment between them so that when we leave there won't be the constant bickering that you often find now."

Wilcox and his men visited a hospital in Kontum run by American civilian Pat Smith and brought excess medical supplies. He said his primary reason for the work he did was to ensure that after the Americans left, they would be remembered as friends.

STOKING VIETNAMESE
NATIONALISM

Vietnam historically had little national consciousness when I interviewed American and South Vietnamese officials on the subject in late January 1972. The family, not the state, was the most sacred institution. An old Vietnamese saying was "The government's authority stops at the village gate." But under the leadership of ARVN Colonel Lam Quang Phong, the South Vietnamese director general of youth, and his American adviser Major Aaron Williams, some steps were taken to cultivate a feeling of nationalism among children and young adults.

That nationalism was evident when about five hundred student volunteers worked in a densely packed area of downtown Saigon that had been ripped by a raging fire on January 24, 1972. The children, mostly members of the Youth of Goodwill, Police Boy Scouts, and Youth for Reconstruction, helped clear rubble, passed out food from their headquarters in a Buddhist temple, and helped build shelters to house the thousand people made homeless by the blaze. The fire destroyed more than two hundred dwellings and caused an estimated $250,000 in damage. But by February 1, 1972, most of the victims had at least some plywood walls and a tin roof over their heads, thanks to the volunteers.

Previously, especially in the aftermath of the Communist Tet Offensive of 1968, it generally was true that when an area was devastated by natural disaster or enemy attack, individual families reconstructed their own homes. A man worried about himself and his family first and his community second. That notion was starting to change by 1972.

"The people have come together and are close," Phong told me. "This is because of all that has happened to them. The young people realize that their future is right now and that when they help others, they are helping themselves. It's a stronger and a better young generation than we've ever had before. I'm very happy with them."

Phong's office, which was under the South Vietnamese Ministry of Education, had a staff of more than 1,500 men and women throughout the country coordinating and monitoring the activities of public and private youth groups. With a meager budget of about $10,000 a year, the organization sponsored sports contests and cultural events, held field trips, built youth centers, supervised civic action projects, and tried to foster the idea of group action.

Williams, the only American soldier assigned full-time in the field of Vietnamese youth activities, was Phong's link to the vast network of men and supplies that were available to the Vietnamese. At the time, there were twenty-three Vietnamese sports federations, forty-two private youth groups, and thirty-one foreign volunteer agencies operating in Vietnam. Williams visited many of them, offering advice and providing material and volunteers where they were needed. But Williams, who worked for the Civil Operations Rural Development Support (CORDS) joint US military-civilian agency, had no money to give.

"It's not like the old days," Phong said. "You are withdrawing, and you are a little stingy. Not him—he'd like to give me more. But we are pleased to receive anything we can from him because we know it comes from the heart."

Williams said he worked as a recreation supervisor for the New York City Parks Department in East Harlem before he was called back to active duty in 1961. He had served three tours in Germany and one previous tour in Vietnam in 1968, when he had been a district senior adviser in the Go Vap District north of Saigon. He said he loved working with children.

"I'm into kids because half the country is under sixteen," he said. "And records show that the youth over the years has been a tremendous source of manpower for the Vietcong movement. That's because there were no real programs for the kids. Now we're instituting some good programs at the hamlet level. We're holding soccer tournaments and other competitions. We're trying to get the kids away from their village and its aloofness. We want to get them into group activities and expose them to the ideas of other people in their country. Then they'll develop some national pride and won't look to the VC for help."

His office held a four-day bicycle race from Nha Trang to Saigon in which more than a hundred sixteen- to twenty-three-year-olds competed, Williams said, and were awarded team and individual prizes. Phong, a skin diver, soccer player, and general outdoorsman himself, spoke proudly of a trip to Kien Giang Island near the South Vietnamese border with Thailand. Five hundred youngsters made the trip in a two-thousand-ton vessel once used by the Vietnamese Navy as a hospital ship. Fifty of the children went under water with diving equipment while the rest received instruction.

"They wanted to stay another week," Phong said. "They were having such a good time. It used to be the children only knew about soccer, volleyball, and basketball. Now we're trying to introduce them to a wide range of sporting activities. We want to make them stronger, entertain them, and teach them to be—how do you say it?—good sports."

Williams estimated that 75 percent of all Vietnamese youth belonged to a sports club. The largest two were the Youth Volunteers with twenty thousand members and the Boy Scouts with fourteen thousand. "They're no different from any other kids," Williams said. "They're willing to learn, they seem to be very aware of the national situation—they know there's a war going on—and when there's a need for a civic action project, they really do the job. Sometimes, the kids will spend three or four days in a work camp on, say, road construction, working all day and getting together and singing or putting on shows by a campfire at night."

One handicap in youth activities, Williams said, was a lack of trained recreation supervisors and civic action specialists. "The military takes most of their qualified people," he said, "so we find ourselves in a situation where we're bringing people who have no background in the field and training them."

He added, "All over the country, there are civic action projects going on with no national coordination. Most people don't even know my office exists. But we want people to come to us if they run into a stone wall. I can contact the proper agency for help. I can get through the red tape quicker than somebody at the province level. I've got no money myself, but there are lots of people around who do."

Williams said he put fifty miles a day on his Scout station wagon driving around the Saigon area to meet with club and sports federation officials and also flew all over the country with Phong. "You know," he said, "if I wasn't in the army and I could stay over here indefinitely, what I'd like to do is get some of these surplus prefabricated buildings they have around here and build a sort of Boys Town somewhere near Saigon. I could get all these kids out of the bars and off the streets and have them go to school half a day and work at trades half a day. I've kicked the idea around with several of my Vietnamese friends. They seemed to like it. I hope they take the initiative on it after I'm gone."

With Phong spearheading the effort, it was felt there would be a lot more projects for Vietnamese youth. The fifty-six-year-old former Special Forces commander and province chief was an energetic man who liked children and wanted to see them happy. The colonel said he had been in the army since 1945 and was one medal short of having seven complete rows of awards on his chest. He had won thirteen Vietnamese Crosses of Gallantry. Phong said he had been interested in youth since 1945 when he saw what they did to help his regiment fight the French.

"We are building strong men and women physically now," he said, "but we don't indoctrinate them with the philosophy that suits us. We teach the children to be good citizens. We tell them to obey their parents and their teachers. We are believers—whether we are Catholic or Buddhist or whatever. The VC are not. We do not tamper with a child's beliefs. So we hope when they grow up they will love their country and won't be indoctrinated by the unbelievers. So many children want to come here and talk to me in my office. I tell my staff, by all means, to let them come in. I want them to come in and talk to me. I love the children. They are the future of my country."

CIVIC ACTION

Major Mitchell Leeds, of Philadelphia, saw his share of danger in Vietnam. When I interviewed him in Bien Hoa in February 1972, he said he had commanded a rifle company during his first tour and was a flier in his second. "I've done it all," he said. On his third tour, his job with the Third Brigade, First Cavalry Division, at the big base fifteen miles northeast of Saigon was perhaps the most important of his jobs in-country.

He was concerned not with killing Communists but with enhancing the image of the army among the Vietnamese people. Leeds said he wanted the people's last impression of American fighting men to be a good one. "If we leave here with the Vietnamese people hating us," Leeds said, "then we've blown everything. We want to leave here with the people liking us and us liking them."

To accomplish that task, Leeds's office assisted in civic action projects, conducted psychological operations, and investigated accidents involving the Vietnamese and Americans in the Bien Hoa area. Instead of getting smaller, his staff was increased in early 1972 to fifteen full-time troops and many volunteers.

Two brigades of the First Cavalry Division went home to Fort Hood in April 1971, leaving only the Third Brigade to defend Americans and their installations within a forty-mile radius of Saigon. "We thought we might be going home too," Leeds said, "but when we found out we were staying, I was put in charge of S-5 [civilian-military operations] because I saw a need for imagination and a chance to really help these people. I handpicked my staff, and we were able to start making progress."

With a civic action fund of $250 a month Captain Chesley Durgin, of Lee, New Hampshire, was able to do things like buy irrigation pipes for a local mental hospital and hold Christmas parties for 1,613 children at five orphanages. Durgin, twenty-four, had been deputy defense coordinator with the First Armored Cavalry Division at An Khe in the Central Highlands before joining Leeds's staff in November 1971.

"I just wanted to do something to help people not as fortunate as myself," Durgin said. "At An Khe I got a bad impression of the Vietnamese people because I was trapped on the firebase and all I saw were the maids and the prostitutes and the pimps. Here, I've been able to see the real people working for themselves and creating a better environment."

Durgin had helped by scrounging garden and farming equipment for local villagers and by taking excess fruit, food, and bread from the brigade's mess hall to them. "The mess sergeants are only too happy to help out," he said. "I hit them for things a couple of times a week. The stuff would only be going to waste otherwise. I take the mess sergeants out with me to see the kids, so they know the food is going to the right place."

Brigade doctors and dentists made frequent trips to areas around Bien Hoa, treating people for illnesses, pulling teeth, passing out toothbrushes and toothpaste and instructions on how to use them. Volunteer enlisted men taught English to local officials, assisted in house-building, ditch-digging, and road-construction projects. "Whenever there's something to be done," Durgin said, "we get all the men we need for it."

Specialist Fifth Class Charles Lutz, a volunteer English teacher who had a BA in English from La Salle (Pennsylvania) University, said, "I just enjoy doing it. I like to see how other people think. I know a lot of Vietnamese want very much to learn English to help them deal with Americans, and I can help them do it. And besides, there's no way out of this base. If I didn't do this, I'd never know what was out there."

Captain Thomas Mastaglio, twenty-four, a former field artillery officer, headed the brigade's psychological operations branch. Mastaglio said the mission of psyops was to "demoralize the enemy by broadcasting messages to him and dropping leaflets to him, capitalizing on his losses in battle, lack of food, ammo, poor leadership—anything that could cause dissension in his ranks."

Mastaglio flew in a "speaker bird" Huey helicopter several times a week in the surrounding area, playing Vietnamese language tapes over his four 250-watt loudspeakers to Communist guerillas presumably in the jungle below. "I'd like to tell you that we're getting twenty prisoners a week and that the dudes are running in fear back to the Cambodian border," he said, "but the VC are just biding their time right now."

The one prisoner the psyops team took in November did provide some important intelligence, however. "The guy was shot in both legs," Mastaglio said, "and he just gave up to us. He said that when our speaker bird had flown over his unit, it had broadcast the names of his unit's commanders, which we'd gathered from our intelligence sources. He said it struck fear into their hearts and they moved their battalion headquarters but left him there because he would have slowed them down."

Mastaglio's team passed out candy and health kits, showed movies and cartoons to adults and children in villages, and offered rewards to anyone providing information leading to the capture of a Communist or a weapon. He also coordinated with a team of air force planes that dropped leaflets on regular runs from Tan Son Nhut Air Base on suspected Communist troop locations, offering fair treatment to those who surrendered.

The third component of Leeds's office was the reaction assistance team, in which the thirty-six-year-old major was heavily involved. "Our function is to prevent civil confrontation," Leeds said. "The minute we hear about an accident—and very often it is just moments after it happened—we run for our jeep. We've got an interpreter and a driver standing by at all times. We make payments to the family and help them fill out claims forms. But the main thing is to get there before there can be any misunderstanding."

Leeds added, "We investigate all accidents within seventy-two hours and try to process all claims within thirty days. We're courteous with the people. We do all we can to keep up the image of the US government, We've gotten around a lot in the past few months. The people know us now. They know they'll get a fair deal."

He said GIs went out of their way to help a Vietnamese accident victim even if the accident was *his* fault. "We had a guy drive his vehicle down the wrong side of the street and hit one of our trucks recently," he said. "His fault, right? But if he dies, it's still our fault in the people's eyes. So we took him from a Vietnamese hospital, where he was lying bleeding on the floor, and had him treated [for minor cuts and bruises] at one of ours."

"We had him fill out a claims form," Leeds said, "gave him a beer, and gave him a little money anyway. And he gave half the money back to us because he said it was too much. Now that's the ultimate right there. That's what we're striving for."

Leeds's office also conducted classes on Vietnamese customs and traditions for First Cavalry Division troops. "We tell the men not to call the people 'gooks' or 'dinks,'" Leeds said. "We want them to treat the people with respect so they will then be respected."

He said the emphasis in all his office's projects was on joint action. "Three years ago," Leeds said, "we'd just walk into a town and say we're going to build a road and that's that. Now, the people have to want it, and they have to work for it. We're not going to hand it to them."

Leeds's men wore their equivalent rank in Vietnamese on their shirts to be more easily identifiable to villagers. "The people know what team we're on when we visit them," he said. "They know we're there to help them. And there's just nowhere to stop. There's so much we can do for them. No—change that—there's just so many ways we can help the Vietnamese people to help themselves."

VIETNAMIZATION
WAS WORKING

When Colonel Elvin O. Wyatt arrived in Nha Trang in April 1971 as chief of the US Air Force Advisory Team (AFAT) 7, he held his first commander's call in a theater. He had more than 150 men working for him. By mid-February 1972, when I interviewed him, he had thirty-six. "I could probably fit them all into this office," Wyatt said on February 15.

By May 1, Wyatt, forty-five, with twenty-two years in the service, was scheduled to have left Vietnam. He said he would be exiting with a feeling of accomplishment. "If there's any place that Vietnamization is working, it's here. If the question is, 'Can they do it without us?' the answer is yes."

The mission of AFAT 7 was to assist the VNAF in operating its Air Training Center (ATC) at Nha Trang Air Base two hundred miles northeast of Saigon on the coast. "Our presence here has expedited the development of the school by two years," Wyatt said. "That justifies having been here, and the fact that the school turns out the quality of people it does justifies our leaving. These people are as professional as anybody. We are not needed anymore."

The ATC had a faculty of more than a hundred, most of whom had been trained in the United States. Wyatt's staff taught English to the Vietnamese supervisors. The center graduated more than 7,500 students in 1971 from its various schools: flying, air-ground operations assistance, general military training, general services, technical command and staff, English language and communications, and electronics. Many former students returned as teachers.

"These people don't want to go to the United States at all," Wyatt said, "just like you didn't want to come to Vietnam. They have great pride in their country and in being Vietnamese. But the fact is that they have to use American equipment and they have to read American manuals. So first we have to teach them the language before they get specific technical instruction."

One of the most successful of the center's schools, Wyatt said, was the Officers' Aircraft Maintenance School. In a little less than a year, 180 Vietnamese graduates completed a thirty-two-week course that Wyatt said was identical to that given to US airmen at Chanute (Illinois) Air Base. "The success of this program is typical of what we've done," Wyatt said. "In essence, we send a Vietnamese to America to learn how to fix a telephone, for example. Then we teach him to teach fixing telephones. Then we bring him back here and have him teach his people how to fix telephones. The technique works."

Wyatt added, "I've been all over the world and seen nearly every country on the face of the earth. This is the most interesting assignment I've ever had. When you've lived with the Vietnamese and listened to them talk about their wishes for their country, it's great. They anticipate their economy will bloom, as it did in Japan and Korea. They're talking in terms of it happening within five years. With what I've seen of their ability to learn technical skills, I don't doubt it at all."

Sergeant Duncan Parker, an instructor, said that his students' ability to learn English was "amazing." He added, "In a matter of weeks, their vocabulary blooms, and they're able to talk to you about a variety of things."

Instruction at the English school was given five days a week, six hours a day, for from three weeks to five months, depending on the amount of English an airman needed to accomplish his job. "If a man is going to be a cook, he doesn't need English," Wyatt said, "but if he's going to be a pilot or an electrician, for example, he does. Based on the success of our students when they go to more-intensive language training courses in the states, I think we have the best English-language school in Vietnam."

More than four hundred VNAF officers, cadets, and enlisted men were enrolled in the school at the time I visited and most were slated for trips to the United States for additional training. The VNAF had come a long way from its beginning in 1955, when it had ninety-four pilots. By 1972, it had more than forty-five thousand men, and its growth traced to the involvement of American advisers.

GOD SQUAD MEMBER

Here's one of the most unusual stories I had published. US Air Force Captain Robert Shadduck, whom I visited in early February 1972, had applied for an early-out discharge from the air force—to become a Jesuit priest.

"I prayed on it a lot," the twenty-seven-year-old said at Cam Ranh Bay Air Base. "I've had a lot of other offers to teach in a secular environment ... But my whole life has been a sort of preparation for this step. I feel I want to live a more perfect Christian life by living the vows. It doesn't mean I'm called to a higher level of holiness than anybody else. But I'll be better serving Christ by serving others."

Shadduck arrived at CRB, 190 miles northeast of Saigon, in April 1971 and was named disaster preparedness officer. His job was formulating contingency plans for base defense in the event of an attack, but mostly he worked as an unordained chaplain. April 2, 1972, was Shadduck's date for returning to the states, but since his four-year service commitment was up on September 14, he applied for and was granted an early out from the air force.

He had been accepted for training in the Jesuit order in June 1968 and planned two years of study as a novitiate, during which he would take the vows of poverty, chastity, and obedience and learn the rules of St. Ignatius Loyola, founder of the Jesuits (Society of Jesus). Then there would be two years of juniorate in which he would finish work on his master's degree in biology, probably at Loyola University in Los Angeles, from where he had graduated in 1967 with a BS in physiological biochemistry. Next would come scholasticate, three more years during which he would teach as a layman. Then three more years of religious study. Finally, Shadduck hoped to be ordained a priest and work primarily as a teacher.

"It's an elite group," he said. "The Jesuits are well respected as writers, educators, and teachers. The order was very hard for me to get into. You wouldn't believe all the questions they asked me and the tests I had to take. But it's the type of spirituality I want. I like the spirit of individuality Jesuits have. They're not overly outspoken, but they're generally experts in their field."

Shadduck had been an altar boy since sixth grade, been educated by Marianist brothers at Chaminade Prep in Canoga Park, California, and had spent three years studying to be a Marianist after graduating in 1965. Instead, he chose college and was exposed to Jesuit teachings at Loyola. From 1963 to 1968, he said, he had been the master of ceremonies for Bishop John Ward, auxiliary bishop of the diocese of Los Angeles, a post equivalent to being a general's aid.

"I've always been deeply involved with the Mass," Shadduck said. "I enjoyed working on the altar. I've always gravitated toward being a priest. My family was very religious, and my parents encouraged me to go to Mass and love the Lord."

Shadduck said he could accept the Catholic Church's refusal to allow priests to marry. "I don't think it would be good if priests could marry," he said. "A priest still has real desires and the capacity to love. But he must replace the love of a woman with his love for God."

Asked about the decline in priestly vocations in the early '70s, he said, "There have been lulls in the history of the church before. I feel it's just taking a deep breath before making another surge."

Shadduck said he enjoyed his work as a chaplain in Vietnam, had made trips with donations to a local orphanage, and had given instruction to GIs who wound up converting to Roman Catholicism. "I feel I can help the church," he said, "make it real to people—especially the students I hope to teach. The Jesuits seem to be holding their own as far as vocations are concerned. But you know, today you don't want to become a priest because you want to be a priest. You become a priest because it is God's will for you. I believe this is what God wants me to do."

AFRO WORKSHOP

US Air Force Technical Sergeant John Norris and about seventy other black airmen launched the Afro Cultural Workshop at Cam Ranh Bay Air Base in late February 1972 with Norris as its president. It was the first black organization of any consequence there since the facility opened in 1965. "With the base phasing down," said Norris, "a lot of people are getting complacent. They don't seem to care about anything. I remind them that if the base closes tomorrow, they'll still be black, and they'll still have responsibilities. We want the men going home to be better people as a result of their experience in Vietnam."

Norris, in his late thirties when I met him, said the aims of the workshop were to promote the study of black history, encourage interracial harmony, bridge the gap between enlisted men and noncommissioned officers, and help fight the drug problem by giving anyone who wanted to rap a place to do it twenty-four hours a day.

He told me 150 airmen had confessed to a drug addiction. "The authorities will not associate with the men after 5:00 p.m. and the gong sounds," Norris said, "so the slave associates with his peers. They come here and spend twelve months in a pen and have no association with the war, so they create their own little wars. The young guys will rebel against authority to a certain point in order to retain enough individuality to get through a tour. Blacks are very suspicious of anything involving whites … So we first have to deal with that. We hope that whites will join. We're trying to get people to associate when they have background hang-ups about it."

He said at Hickam Air Force Base in Hawaii in 1956, he and another black airman stood at opposite ends of a barracks with baseball bats and wouldn't let anyone out to join in a race riot that had started outside over an argument during a volleyball game. "I figured if I could keep them in that time," Norris said, "maybe I could help in other ways. I'm not trying to accomplish very much, but I'm trying to establish some respect for the air force with the younger troops. It's a race-relations thing. I feel if they educate themselves about blacks, we'll cease to have misunderstandings. A lot of blacks trace their origins to the Virgin Islands. The general opinion of science and society is that blacks originated in Africa. Since that was thrown at them for so many years, they decided to fool society and go along with it."

The workshop was in two one-story barracks across from the base gym. One of the barracks housed a lecture hall and conference room; the other was a game and reading room with a bar and coolers of beer and soft drinks. "There is an NCO here twenty-four hours a day," said Norris, a former staffer at a San Antonio (Texas) Boys Club, "and if somebody doesn't pass the test with the kids, we'll use somebody else. If a kid has a headache, there is somebody here who'll talk to him about it. The air force is paying us to listen."

Norris added, "Senior NCOs have no respect for the young guy and what he has to say. They're more concerned with what he looks like. A book can have shabby edges and contain some of the most important information in the world."

He said, "A lot of us paid a lot of dues, and a lot of us want to make sure the old stuff [racism] doesn't ever happen again. The races are polarized in the service, always have been. I'm trying to pull 'em out of this. There's a lot of things whites don't know about blacks. If they come here, they'll understand what we're doing ... I'm hoping to make the commanders' jobs easier and reestablish credibility between the older NCOs and the young cats. Everybody on this base is my friend. I hope to teach black and white airmen how to cope with their environment."

Norris said he hoped to encourage drug addicts to use the workshop and talk about getting help. "They think they've got problems," he said. "I tell them the things I had to overcome to get where I am today. I want to use myself and my life as an example for them … I wish I could tell you [the depth of] the drug problems here. When I leave this place, I'll have a helluva lot to say about it. I'm going to tell it all."

"I grew up in south Chattanooga [Tennessee], one of eleven kids," Norris said, "and I was accustomed to being pounced on by whites for no reason at all." He said he was implicated in a basketball scandal during his junior year at Booker T. Washington High School in Chattanooga after his team won fifty-two straight games over two years and then lost a tournament game to Cleveland Sweetwater High by twenty points. School officials and classmates suspected the game was fixed; Norris's father stopped talking to him.

"We did our best and just lost," he said. "My friends snickered when they saw me. I couldn't stand it." He later was exonerated but found the incident impossible to overcome. He enlisted in the air force to find a new life. He also had the heartbreak of having his daughter die in 1971 at sixteen months old due to a rare heart disease. He had another daughter, Ayra, who turned four in March 1972. "Everywhere I go," he said, "I put myself to some useful purpose. The things in my life have fortified me for this. It's the baby of all the black GIs at Cam Ranh. Seventy of us have worked diligently to put this thing across."

Norris said he had been challenged and beaten up by militant blacks who accused him of being an Uncle Tom because he was respected by white NCOs. "It doesn't bother me anymore what they say," Norris said. "I know in my heart I'm doing the right thing. The world has decided that we're human beings. We need all the help we can get to bring that about. I've got an ear, and if you got a problem, you can share it with me. A lot of blacks don't even know their own history, so we have to reeducate ourselves about who we are, see who our heroes are. But I think I'd puke if I was labeled 'he was the first of his race' to do whatever."

Norris's commander, whom I can only identify as a Captain Howell, said, "The guys say nobody can rap like Norris. He's always available, always there; he teaches them to think straighter and get motivated. He really gives them direction. He's not afraid to chew 'em out, but he knows when to do it and when not to. He's sort of like a psychologist. Before, the gym was the only place a lot of the brothers could go for community. Here, they have a legitimate reason for coming. He's given them a helluva lot of work to do. He's begun a belief that they can help themselves."

"He's dedicated to people with problems," Sergeant Steven McCory said of Norris. "It's a twenty-four-hour type thing. He needs about thirty hours to do the things he does. Sleep isn't important to him ... We don't want guys going back home and telling kids skag [heroin] is great."

NFL USO Tour

In mid-February 1972, five NFL players made a USO-sponsored tour of South Vietnam: New York Jets defensive tackle John Elliott, Minnesota Vikings offensive tackle Grady Alderman, Buffalo Bills receiver Marlin Briscoe, Pittsburgh Steelers running back John Fuqua and St. Louis Cardinals defensive back Roger Wehrli. It was the seventh straight year that NFL players had visited US installations in Vietnam and elsewhere in the Pacific. I didn't have time to interview all of them but did manage to corral Elliott and Alderman for a bit.

"Some people say, 'Why do you want to go over there? Most of the guys are home,'" said Alderman. "But the fact is, there's still some here. Just because we're here doesn't mean we support the war. I just feel I have some sort of obligation to the men who are here. The league said no political implications come with it. They don't care if you're a hawk or a dove or whatever ... just go over and say what you want to say. Our country has been pretty good to most of us. These guys provide service for the rest of us, and the least we can do is show them that somebody cares about them. The main concern of the line units seems to be that nobody knows they're out there, nobody seems to care."

The players had visited the Third Field Hospital in Saigon and the Twenty-Fourth Evacuation Hospital in Long Binh and were headed to Da Nang, Qui Nhon, and a series of firebases in I Corps and II Corps. For Alderman, it meant talking to some men who did not know he was a twelve-year veteran who had missed only two regular-season games. "If some of the real Vikings fans don't even know who I am," Alderman said, "how can I expect these soldiers to know? It's not their fault. I don't mind. I'm just happy to be over here doing what I can. I said I would make another trip next year, but I hope to God I don't have to. I hope this thing will be over by then."

Among the patients the players met were a specialist fourth class from an artillery detachment with the First Cavalry Division who had a kidney infection, a civilian adviser with the office of public safety who had a malignant tumor in his stomach, and a master sergeant from Detachment 1, 374th TAW, who had hepatitis. Wehrli spent time with a specialist fourth class from Headquarters Special Troops in Long Binh who had a leg infection and a 101st Airborne Division troop from Phu Bai who had been injured by a booby trap.

Elliott at the time was only three years removed from the Jets' 16–7 Super Bowl victory over the Colts and brought Super Bowl film with him. He was twenty-seven and recovering from a right knee injury he'd suffered in the fourth game of the 1971 season. "I knew some other players who'd gone before," Elliott said, "and told [PR man Frank Ramos] if the chance comes up, let me know. When he asked me if I'd like to go, I said yeah ... I just wanted to see for myself what's happening. I have a lot of friends and relatives who've served over here. I ran into one guy from my old high school in Texas. Yesterday, I ran into a guy who lives forty miles from me ... It impressed me the way they move traffic around here. If they put half the motorcycles and automobiles that they have here in New York City, there'd be a traffic jam for four days."

PART III

AMERICAN UNITS

FINDING NEEDLES

One of the more interesting units I visited during my tour in Vietnam was the 483rd Field Maintenance Squad's nondestruct inspection (NDI) team in Cam Ranh Bay. Nobody is perfect, but when the eight-member team released an aircraft part after inspection, the crew could be pretty sure that the part was serviceable.

"We're dealing with people's lives," air force Technical Sergeant James H. Yarbrough, of Pine Bluff, Arkansas, said in early January 1972. "We make the last decision. If we have any nagging doubts about a part, we just don't release it until we give it a thorough going-over. We use a backup method. We check each other. Then we can be totally sure. We're confident in ourselves. We have to be, in this job."

The NDI laboratory in Cam Ranh Bay was the only one in South Vietnam. It operated on the premise that one did not have to take a piece of equipment apart or destroy it in order to inspect it. The technicians used many machines to detect cracks in helicopter and airplane parts, leakage in systems, malfunctions in electrical circuits, and so on. The men spent time in the field on temporary duty for as much as a month at a time before rotating back to the lab. "We don't know what's going to hit us tomorrow or what's going to hit us tonight," Yarbrough said. "Somebody's on standby here twenty-four hours a day."

In December 1971, Yarbrough and Staff Sergeant Michael D. Koflanovich, of Glen Lyon, Pennsylvania, spent several weeks at Bien Hoa Air Base, checking out twenty-six VNAF A-37 Dragonflies used to support operations in Cambodia. "That's when the responsibility really gets to us," Yarbrough said, "when it gets down to the nitty-gritty and we've got a colonel asking us if a part is cracked or isn't it, and we've got to tell him right away. We've got to be totally sure."

One of the basic tools of the NDI trade was a UM715 ultrasonic reflectoscope. It was as big as a stereo receiver with a green scope on the front that measured sound waves. A transducer was attached with a cord to the UM715. The transducer was made of a crystal and looked like a hearing aid. An NDI man applied the transducer like a stethoscope to a part. The transducer sent out an ultrasonic (above the range of human hearing) wave onto the part. The technicians had examples of sound patterns created by a defective part. They also had examples of the screen patterns created when a part was not cracked. They applied the transducer to the part and determined whether it was defective or not.

"It involves so much equipment," Koflanovich said. "It's really fascinating." He demonstrated an ultrasonic leak detector, used mostly to pinpoint oxygen leaks in helicopters. It was a Geiger-counter-like apparatus. He attached a contact probe (it looks like an ice pick) to the "microphone" of the detector. When he put the probe on his wristwatch, the sound of the detector came out loud and clear.

"Say a pilot comes to us," Koflanovich said, "and he's not getting any oxygen in his cockpit. The gauge drops, but he can't find a leak. A member of our team goes in and checks it out with this machine."

The team also used x-ray machines to check for missing or loose parts. "Say the area we want to check out is hard to get at," Koflanovich said. "Maybe there's all kinds of wires on top. So we take an x-ray of it. We can see everything on the picture. We can tell if a tiny cotter pin is missing or a rivet is loose."

Two NDI men, Staff Sergeant George E. Cole, of North Hollywood, California, and Technical Sergeant Percival S. Papia, of Tacoma, Washington, were in Da Nang, x-raying C-47s, the oldest cargo-carrying gunship in the air force's inventory, when I was in Cam Ranh Bay. Sergeant Larry C. Dahlman, of Meadowlands, Minnesota, also was in Da Nang, using an ultrasonic reflectoscope on Jolly Green Giant helicopters. His team checked rotor heads carefully because a cracked rotor head could cause the rotor to fall off a helicopter.

The other members of the NDI unit were Master Sergeant Jack R. Goodwin, of Georgetown, South Carolina; Staff Sergeant James Rister, of Warner Robins, Georgia; and Staff Sergeant Keith B. Anderson, of Newton, New Jersey. The men rarely saw each other together because they were constantly rotating assignments and picking up special jobs. "We're primarily air force," Yarbrough said, "but if the army or the navy calls, we help them too. Most of the equipment here has been duplicated in portable form, so we can take it out to the field … People on the base don't even know we're here, but we don't mind. We just do our job."

TESTING HIS METTLE

Harry Weddington dropped out of the straight life. But he didn't let his Afro grow wild, join the Black Panthers, or freak out on LSD. A US Army reservist, Weddington, twenty-seven, an African American, had a good job as a stockbroker and insurance salesman in Wilmington, Delaware. But he left his wife and three children, asked to come on active duty and volunteered for Vietnam. I met him in Bien Hoa in late January 1972.

"My wife understands why I came over here," he said. "I just got tired of the middle-class routine. One day, I looked at myself, and I didn't like where my life had come to. I decided to put myself through a little crap. Lots of Americans take too much for granted. I come from a ghetto. I've gotten a chance to see war and see poverty and people living in a lower standard than myself. I've gotten a chance to reevaluate myself ... I wanted to come over here, get with the Rangers, try myself at combat and see how I could do. I've been thinking about coming over here since '64. I just got around to it now."

Weddington arrived in Vietnam in May 1971 and was assigned as a cook with the 229th Assault Helicopter Battalion in Bien Hoa. Two months later, he volunteered for H Company, Seventy-Fifth Infantry, Third Brigade, First Cavalry Division, the last American Ranger outfit in Vietnam. He was one of only three men from a class of thirty-two who survived a rugged twelve-day training program. He was the honor graduate with a 99 percent classroom average. He was able to run five miles toting a full pack in forty-seven minutes, thirteen minutes under the requirement. "I just looked at the next man," Weddington said. "I told myself whatever he could do, I could do—and do it better."

He said his family was not hurting financially by his absence, since his wife was a college graduate and a registered nurse at a Wilmington hospital. "What I send home goes right in the bank," he said. "She makes more than enough to support the kids. When I first came, she worried. But she's become more confident in my abilities."

The buck sergeant team leader said he had been on twenty-five missions, fifteen of which he considered hot. "Yes, I have personal kills," Weddington said. "But I have a hang-up talking about them. It's not something I brag about to a lot of people. I just plan on being a little bit better than them."

The mission of the Seventy-Fifth was mainly intelligence gathering, to be ready to go anywhere at any time to patrol and look for trails, new bunkers, and evidence of enemy activity. Master Sergeant Robert Taylor, H Company's first sergeant, said Weddington was "one of the best. Squared away in the field. Knows what he's doing out there."

Weddington said on one mission his six-man team was dropped by chopper and quickly spotted four Vietcong soldiers. "They ducked into the brush, and we fired them up," he said. "We know we hit one because he left a lot of blood, but they all managed to get away. Once we'd lost the element of surprise, they lifted us out. See, what happens is that a box [area on a map] will come down from brigade. You know, an area they want us to work. We fly over the area, check it out, pick out a landing zone. We survey the area for trails and streams. Then we usually go to the nearest firebase for a briefing. Then we go back out and are inserted into the box. We usually stay out about five days. We have C rations for five days."

He added, "We can move about in the jungle so much more quietly than a line company of grunts. We can be sitting there monitoring the dudes, and they don't even know it. Our purpose is recon and setting ambushes. Charlie will duff from a line unit, but we can sneak up on him, and he'll be just sitting there talking, and we can grease him. We don't leave a trail. We can go in and come out, and Charlie will never even know we've been there."

Weddington, five foot seven and 160 pounds, carried eighty pounds of equipment, half his body weight, on missions. He used an AK-50 automatic rifle with a folding stock because he said M16 rounds were more easily deflected by bamboo. He carried a .45-caliber pistol, six fragmentation grenades, and six Claymore mines, plus food, water, and bedding. "Sure, we're in a dangerous situation," said Weddington, who was scheduled to leave Vietnam May 25. "But, like, you enjoy the challenge, you know. You enjoy going out against the dudes and coming out on top. We've had one guy wounded and nobody killed in the last eight months. We're good. Our job is not to get a hundred of 'em at a time, just to harass him, keep him off balance. We feel we're the best ... We don't see much difference in the Rangers' role. We're still taking the same chances they did in '68 and '69."

Sergeant First Class Robert Weaver said H Company had "32 percent of the brigade's kills" since March 1971. "Everyone's over here to do a job," Weaver said. "We've got some religious people in-country, but they consider it a job they've got to do. It's not really that they're bloodthirsty. I don't know how to explain it. Maybe a couple of 'em enjoy going out and killing, but the majority are not there just to be killers. They're just doing a job."

Weddington said, "The dudes are supposed to have some deal where they give a big reward to anybody that kills a Ranger. We've got a price on our heads. The dudes are smart. They know the jungle. But I think we'll always be able to outsmart them. Life's a gamble anyway. This just makes it more interesting." He added, "Some people think when you go to 'Nam, when you go back to the states you become a beast. But I've got a chance to see poverty, see war. I realized I've got a lot to be thankful for. I could understand how these people feel, but I think a lot of Americans are pretty soft."

I asked Weddington what his plans were when his tour was over. He said he majored in chemistry and spent three years at Rutgers University before dropping out. He also said he might want to teach. "I like working with teenagers," he said. "But I've thought a lot of times about being a professional soldier. This is war, and the only way I could prove to myself that I could be a professional soldier is to be in a war. I feel I have proved that to myself. And I feel it's an honorable thing."

THE MEN OF "BLUE MAX"

In the wild West, worried men slept with six-guns under their pillows. The AH-1 Cobra helicopter pilots of F Battery, Seventy-Ninth Artillery Battalion, at Plantation Army Base in late January 1972, could not even afford to do that. When they were on standby, they slept in their flight suits with their holsters on. The unit was called Blue Max; I never found out why. But the Germans awarded a medal that became known as the "Blue Max" to their World War I flying aces, and F Battery fliers certainly were daredevils.

"Sometimes, it's really funny," Captain Billy Causey said. "If you can imagine, one minute you're all asleep, and then you hear a siren blasting in your ears. Everybody starts running all over the place."

They ran because F Battery was the only aerial field artillery unit left in Vietnam, and its thirty-five aviators were on twenty-four-hour alert to provide gunship support for ground units of the Bien Hoa-based Third Brigade, First Cavalry Division, to which F/Seventy-ninth was attached. When American ground forces made contact with Communists in III Corps around Saigon, Blue Max usually was called in.

"We don't go anywhere without Max," said Specialist Fourth Class Tony Presciane of the Second Battalion, Eighth Cavalry. "If it wasn't for Max, the dudes would be walking all over us. When they know he's out there, they cool it. Max is just like our big brother out there."

The thirteen Cobras in Blue Max were equipped with an average of twenty-eight ten-pound rockets, twenty-eight seventeen-pound rockets, two thousand 7.62 mm minigun rounds, and a hundred fifty 40 mm grenades. The choppers worked in pairs, each saturating an area with ordnance and returning to rearm while the other bird took over. The process was repeated as many times as necessary.

On January 22, 1972, at about ten at night, I was told, Americans spotted twenty Communists in the wire at Fire Base Mace, thirty miles northeast of Saigon. Four and a half minutes later, four Blue Max Cobras had sprayed about 360 rockets, 6,000 minigun rounds, and 450 grenades in the area. The salvo routed the Communists, killing an unknown number of them.

I asked those involved to recreate the mission for me when I visited a couple of days after the incident. Captain Causey and Chief Warrant Officer William Presley said they were in Xuan Loc, ten miles northeast of the firebase, supervising guard duty there. Their Cobra was armed and ready to go. At about ten that night the radio operator in the orderly room where the aviators were talking was notified that Max firepower was needed. He yelled, "Fire mission, fire mission!"

Causey and Presley ran to their aircraft and were airborne in less than two minutes. They were briefed in-flight by ground forces. When they arrived at the site of the Communist infiltration after two and a half minutes flight time, they knew what to do. As directed by the ground commander, they shot two seventeen-pound rockets at the hillside. The ground commander radioed a slight adjustment in trajectory. Using code names, the aviators communicated with the ground commander and shot rockets all over the hillside.

Meanwhile, Chief Warrant Officers John White and Robert Knight prepped another aircraft at Xuan Loc. When the first team radioed that it had expended 50 percent of its ordnance, the second team cranked up and got airborne. It arrived at the site just as the first team was peeling off to rearm at Xuan Loc. The second team sprayed everything it had at the hillside. The first team then returned and dumped another full payload.

"They found a lot of blood trails later but no VC," Knight said. "I guess they'll think twice before they try that again."

In addition to flying combat assault missions, Blue Max provided escorts for VIP missions such as US Army Secretary Robert F. Froehlke's January 1972 visit. Also, one Max Cobra went up daily on a sniffer mission, escorting a Huey with a sensor device that could pick up Communist troop movement on the ground in the area around the Bien Hoa-Long Binh-Plantation complex.

"I've never seen anybody get off the ground as quick as we do," Captain Fred Bennett said. "It's gotten to the point where it's all just so natural. It's so coordinated. We play a lot of cards when we're on standby, and I've seen many a good-size poker game broken up in the middle with guys scrambling to get their birds up."

I was told the thirty-five Blue Max aviators had a combined eighty years of combat flight experience among them. Their pride extended to the maintenance section, run by Captain Skip Cleason. "He's got the highest availability rating of any unit in Vietnam," Bennett said. "Ninety-two percent." So on any given day, twelve of the thirteen Max choppers were ready to fly.

"We just sit around waiting for missions," Knight said. "The siren goes, phones start ringing, and people start moving. Lots of times we are all set to go out, and then at the last minute they bust it. But we're ready twenty-four hours a day. Ready for anything."

CAV. HATS

Soon after the First Cavalry Division was organized in 1921, one of its horse soldiers' most important jobs was patrolling the Mexican border to prevent smuggling of narcotics and liquor as well as cattle rustling and gun running. Horses were replaced by jeeps in 1943. In late January 1972, the Third Brigade (the last First Cavalry Division outfit left in Vietnam) relied on helicopter gunships and reconnaissance helicopters to help defend US installations in the Saigon area. Pershing rifles and sabers gave way to rockets, grenades, minigun fire, and machine-gun fire.

F Troop, Ninth Cavalry, First Cavalry Division, retained an important link with the past, though. Its enlisted men and officers wore black Stetson hats with crossed sabers and their rank on the front with their duty uniforms or civilian clothes. It was a symbol they were proud of. "It's like back in the states," First Lieutenant Dwight L. Jobe, of Tucumcari, New Mexico, said. "You don't mess with a guy's car or his woman. Well here, you just don't mess with a man's cav. hat. If you want to get into a fight, that's probably one of the quickest ways to do it … We're not a bunch of cowboys. That's a mistaken impression some people get because of the hat. But most of the troopers that wear the cav. hat feel they don't have to take it off for anybody."

F Troop, a scout company that flew light observation helicopters, was authorized to wear the distinctive hats. The only time most F Troopers took their hats off was when they went to bed. "I was at the Ninetieth Replacement Detachment in Long Binh last month, and some sergeant told me to take off my cav. hat," F Troop First Sergeant Franklin East said. "He said it wasn't authorized. I said, 'The commanding general has authorized the hat to be worn in Vietnam. I'm still in Vietnam, and I'm going to keep it on until I leave.'"

East added, "The hat's a great morale builder for us. I've been in the army twenty-two years, and I've never seen a unit with more pride and esprit de corps than this one." First Lieutenant Robert Kevan said, "Our people that go out [on recon missions] are driving. They want to get in contact. I haven't heard any of our people say, 'Why should I hang my ass on the line today if tomorrow we're going to go home? We're pullin' out of Vietnam, etc.' It's not really affected us. The cav. troop is still a driving force with a go-out-and-get-'em feeling."

The hats were ordered from a firm in St. Louis; delivery to Vietnam sometimes took as long as three months. Most troopers ordered three or four hats to make sure they got at least one. Once a hat arrived, it became a prized possession. "We went to an NCO club once," an enlisted man told me, "and we put our hats in a line up on the stage. The Rangers put their black berets down. Somebody put a boonie hat [worn by regular infantrymen] down, and our guy picked it off. So the grunt scrunched a cav. hat, and all hell broke loose."

Jobe said an officer had his cav. hat on an empty front seat in his chopper and two enemy rifle rounds went through it, adding, "He just kept wearing the raggedy thing. He wouldn't get a new one."

"Another man we had was killed," Jobe said. "And his family wrote several letters to us asking that we send his hat as something they could remember him by. We couldn't. It burned when his bird went down."

The only differences among cav. hats were the rank insignia and the color of the braids. Officers wore gold braids, warrant officers silver, and enlisted men yellow. Each man seemed to wear his hat differently. "The way he wears it becomes a trademark of the individual," Jobe said. "Some turn up the front like a pirate hat. Some turn up the sides like a cowboy. Some just leave the brim straight. No matter how we wear 'em, we just want to let everybody else know that we're the meanest SOBs in the valley."

The F Troopers' swagger sometimes sparked criticism from outsiders. But Jobe said, "We're the eyes and ears of the division. We're the first people to go into an area ... We've got guys from New York, Connecticut, Maine, Puerto Rico, just about everywhere. We're just as much army as any other group. We don't make our own rules and regulations. We don't do whatever we want. Gee, maybe we have conscientious objectors in the group, smack freaks and whatnot. But the cav.'s built up a tremendous tradition. More so than any other unit, we've acquired a fight-and-die attitude. You've got guys coming to the officers' club tonight knowing they might die tomorrow. We have our good, clean fun. A fight does evolve every once in a while. It's kind of antagonizing to other people; I'll grant you that."

PACKING

In mid-February 1972, all over Vietnam buildings were being dismantled, vehicles were being collected, and military equipment was being readied for shipment back to the United States. American officials were trying to salvage all the military hardware they could as they closed bases and withdrew troops. The extent of the pullout was evident at Cam Ranh Bay Air Base when a Korean contracting company took up a 10,000-foot-long, 102-foot-wide aluminum plank runway for shipment as parts to other bases around the world.

The project was designed and monitored by First Lieutenant Chris Doepke of the 483rd Civil Engineer Squadron, who said the removal would save the government $5.6 million. It was the first such project the air force ever had undertaken, he said, and the same method was being used to remove huge sections of runways at Phan Rang and Tuy Hoa Air Bases.

"We made up all the programming documents and got them approved at Seventh Air Force and Pacific Air Forces in Hawaii," he said. "The Koreans caught on very fast. I have to hand it to them. They had an assembly line going where they pulled up a whole section the width of the airstrip, then unhooked the clamps, cleaned the planks, and stacked them neatly on pallets."

Most of the forty thousand planks, which were two feet wide, two inches thick, and six to twelve feet long, had been sent by cargo ship to other US bases by the time I visited, Doepke said. The runway at Cam Ranh had been there since 1965. By February 1972, American strength at the base had dwindled to fewer than five thousand troops, and only one of the base's two parallel sections of runway were needed for combat and supply missions. The decision was made to remove the aluminum and leave the concrete section.

DEFENDING CAM RANH

I wrote a piece on defense plans for the sprawling American base at Cam Ranh Bay, and it never ran in *Stars and Stripes*; I guess because it was too specific. I interviewed Colonel Rolfe G. Arnhym, special assistant to the general for security, from Fairfax, Virginia. He told me that defense of the base included placement of 9,000 trip flares, 74 towers, 439 bunkers, 415 fighting positions, and 57,140 meters of concertina wire around the base. "As US forces draw down," he said, "the enemy runs out of places to hit, and bases such as Cam Ranh become more lucrative and vulnerable targets. So we have made a considerable effort to upgrade our defenses."

Those efforts took place between September 1, 1971, and January 15, 1972, he said. US officials reviewed and revised their defense plans, coordinated more with South Korean forces based at nearby Qui Nhon, initiated more alerts, and integrated the plans of the army and air force. The Second of the 327th Infantry Battalion patrolled the mainland to protect the base from incoming rocket attacks by not allowing the VC and NVA to set up within range. Navy personnel, meanwhile, patrolled the harbor to guard against swimmer/sappers and protect oil, gas, and ammunition storage areas from attack. The base had twelve jeeps that had mounted twenty-three-inch lights on them along with thirty-inch searchlights in towers.

"Because of the vastness," he said, "we have elements of the Second of the 327th and our own Support Command Infantry, four rifle companies of 160 men each, but they're short of men." Troops cleared brush from around all critical areas so that any attackers would be visible as they approached, he said.

"Oh, yeah," Arnhym said, "we're more prepared than we've ever been. Any place can be hit and penetrated. But the kind of defense we're conducting is acting as a very significant deterrent. It's a dynamic defense, not always patrolling the same areas, moving some of the towers, frequent inspections."

Arnhym told me a dud rocket hit the base on November 15, 1971, and that the last previous attack saw three rounds hit South Beach in July. So in the five months I spent at Cam Ranh, there wasn't a single live incoming round there nor a ground probe of any kind. "The key still is the individual soldier," Arnhym said. "He has to be properly trained and properly supported. But we still have a lot of things we can do. We're going into a critical period with Tet coming. We'll try to attain maximum possible readiness. It takes time because of the enormity of the task. But to accomplish what we have in four months is a significant effort in a short period of time."

It all seemed so important at the time. But after Saigon fell, Cam Ranh Bay became a deepwater port for the Soviet Navy.

NEW LOOK FIRE BASE

By late February 1972, the days of living in sewer pipes and using five-gallon cans for showers were over for members of A Battery, Twenty-First Artillery, at Artillery Hill in Pleiku. The thirty-eight members of the battery lived in comparative style. Their crews that handled three 105 mm howitzers lived in underground concrete-encased hooches at the gun emplacements. They had bunks with mosquito nets, electricity, coolers or refrigerators of ice-cold beer and soft drinks, dressers made of ammunition boxes, and maids to keep the place clean and do their wash.

"It's really beautiful," Specialist Fourth Class Don Hibben said. "No rats, decent food for a change, recreation, a swimming pool, craft shop, service club, books to read, PX, and hot showers. It beats the old water bucket, anyway."

The battery had been based at Fire Base Amy, eight miles east of Xuan Loc near Saigon, before being shifted to Pleiku to provide cover for ARVN ground troops, the aviation group and American infantry brought there on temporary duty for use as a quick reaction force in case of a Communist attack on US installations. That unit was Delta Company, First/Twelfth Cavalry.

Specialist Fourth Class William McCollum said, "It's beautiful, best firebase I've ever been on." Specialist Fourth Class Tom Pessagno, who had been at eight firebases on his tour, said, "We used to live in sewer pipes. Now we've got maids."

"We'd like to stay here," battery commander Captain Robert L. Stapleton said. "People here like us, and we like the job. We get to fire rounds every night, varying our times and our locations, and that keeps artillery guys happy. We feel like we're doing our job. We had to build the place from scratch, but the men didn't seem to mind. Most of them have bounced around to at least half a dozen firebases in the past few months. Each time, they have to start building from scratch. We have a good position because we're well dug in with a low profile.

"We're kind of on our own here. I guess the guys realize they've got it good and don't want to mess it up. There's a nonverbal understanding. I was an enlisted man for four years. I know what it's like, so I take care of my people. We have rap sessions. Morale is good. I don't hassle people. But they get haircuts, do their jobs well, and there's no trouble in the clubs."

The artillery rounds weighed about forty pounds, had a maximum range of about nine thousand meters, and contained high-explosive C-4. At least three men were at the three firing positions twenty-four hours a day, and three others were on duty in fire direction control. The rest took turns sleeping, swimming, or visiting the service clubs when they were not pulling details.

Specialist Fifth Class James Maciejewski said the battery's presence was merely for show. "There's never nothing [enemy] around here," he said. "We're not really supporting anybody. It's a psychology thing that they have artillery here, in case Pleiku's overrun. But as far as a firebase, this is unbelievable. We have refrigerators plugged in ... It's not your average firebase."

Stapleton added, "There's a lot of pride about firing [the howitzers] right. It's very competitive with guys yelling back and forth to each other. They all want to be the closest to the target." On one mission, he said, the unit dropped rounds only yards from a target more than three miles away while supporting a US recon patrol. "That's pretty good shooting in anybody's book," said Capain Robert Robertson, who saw the rounds hit from his OH-58 light observation helicopter while flying as a forward observer.

HAVING IT EASY IN PLEIKU

In late February 1972, boredom had set in among US troops near Pleiku City in the Central Highlands. The men of D and E Companies, First Infantry Battalion, Twelfth Cavalry, Third Brigade, First Cavalry Division had been moved to Artillery Hill in mid-January. Their previous duty station had been Fire Base Gibraltar, forty miles east of Bien Hoa near Saigon. Their new mission was to provide a quick reaction force if the Communists decided to attack the key South Vietnamese provincial capital.

In the beginning, the men enjoyed the luxury of the service club, craft shop, PX, and the enlisted and NCO clubs. But the good life got old, and the men said they wanted to go back to work. "They told us Tet was going to be really heavy," Sergeant Starr Eckholdt of D Company said. "They told us Pleiku and Kontum were going to be hit hard. The mountains were supposed to be swarming with dudes. But nothing happened. We haven't even had one patrol. We have been taking it easy, but it gets boring going to the service club, drinking beer, watching movies. We all wish we were back in the bush because time goes by more quickly and you don't spend any money."

Captain Thomas Dombrowsky, D Company commander, said, "You take dirty boots. That's a status symbol for a grunt. The dirtier, the better. And some guys would wear the same fatigues their whole tour if I let them. It's like a badge. They just want to show people they've been in the bush. But we can't have them looking like bums when we're in garrison. We have hooch maids to take care of the boots and uniforms, so there's no excuse for being sloppy. I don't think it's hassling them to ask them to look like soldiers."

The GIs were grumbling about repetitive classroom training and mock combat assaults on American bases in the area. "It's just like basic and AIT [advanced individual training] all over again," Eckholdt said. "A lot of guys expected to go on active patrols, but that never came off."

Dombrowsky said, "Whether we choose to accept it or not, we are here just to be ready to go in by helicopter, foot, or vehicle to any compound that is hit or about to be overrun. We were handpicked for this job. Our company has been actively in the field since the war started. But I admit a cav. company is just not organized for this type of situation [being in the rear]. We are very anxious to get out in the field."

At Fire Base Gibraltar, a normal cycle was five days at the base, fifteen in the bush for sixty days, followed by three days of rest and relaxation at the beaches of Vung Tau on the South China Sea. "They told us when we go back to the bush, we can go back to Vung Tau," Private First Class Jerry Baranczyk said.

Dombrowsky tried to keep the troops busy by filling sandbags, training, and improving fighting positions but said the men were getting rusty. "I guess we are kind of losing our combat edge," he said. "But we have done a helluva lot of work to tighten up our defense here. And we've worked out a reasonable series of plans for getting into these compounds in the event they are penetrated by sappers. Just let us go in and police them up. That would be a real mission."

In the meantime, it was movies, beer, basketball, and sandbags. "We've got a joke," Private First Class Charles Pettijohn said. "We can go to Israel and become professional sandbag fillers with our experience."

For Sergeant Robert J. Griffin, a veteran of sixty-three months in Vietnam, being in the rear was torturous. "It's not that I'm a warmonger or a sadist," he said. "But I wish it was the way it used to be when we would just be out in the field doing our job. I don't like the rear. I believe if we're going to be in Vietnam, we should be doing our job. If they're going to hold us back in the rear, why not pull us out altogether?"

He added, "We expected to get active patrols when we got here. We like to make patrols. Why let the Communists come to us? Why not take the initiative?"

Dombrowsky said, "I know how they feel. But I have to follow my orders. This stuff about the guys all being a bunch of peace creeps and potheads is a bunch of bull. They're just as anxious as anybody to go out and do the job. All the stories you read back in the world about drugs and [widespread] disciplinary problems are a bunch of bull. I have a lot of respect for these guys. They are good soldiers, and they know their job. But if I'm told to keep them on this hill, that's what I've got to do."

YANKS IN KONTUM

The most incredible part of covering the Vietnam War was the contrast between what life was like on a US base and what it was like in the field or in a neighboring village. Nowhere was this more evident than at the MACV compound in Kontum. I spent a few nights there in late February 1972, hanging out with the air traffic controllers that ran the airstrip, and as a favor to them I wrote a story about how good they had it.

Their compound had not been rocketed in more than two years, they said, although the city had been rocketed three times that month. "We're concerned about being here," Lieutenant Barry Shearer said, "but we're not scared. An hour after the rockets went over last week, we were out there taking pictures of where they hit."

During a card game in the stereo lounge between single rooms that the enlisted men enjoyed in their barracks, they drank and talked about how their worst worry was that their wives and parents were being misinformed. "If they read that a rocket hit Kontum," Sergeant John Grange said, "they immediately think it hit in Kontum City, MACV compound, room number 5. My wife has enough to worry about with rent to pay, a baby coming, and taxes to figure out. I don't want her worrying about me."

Shearer said, "My fiancée wrote after the rocket attack in town on February 7 saying she read we 'got bombed.' I guess it's human reaction to paint a far-bleaker picture than what really exists."

Specialist Fourth Class David J. "Crash" McDowell said, "This is where the war's supposed to be, and it does scare you when the rockets land in town because you know the bad guys are close. But with F-4s in Da Nang, B-52s at other bases and the carriers [with their tactical aircraft] plus the gunships at Pleiku, you have a sense of security."

"We can take care of ourselves even if they do come," Grange said. "We've got a lot of bunkers, and we're well armed. The other day, we were sitting in the daily afternoon briefing, and the ARVNs started dusting off the perimeter with artillery rounds. We didn't know what it was, so we ran to our rooms, grabbed our M60s, and hit the bunkers. We all know what our responsibilities are."

Jerry French Dunn, the deputy senior US provincial adviser and a retired army colonel, said he did not think the Communists would try to overrun Kontum (he was proven wrong). "If they did expose themselves to all the firepower we have at our command," he said, "it would hasten their finish as an effective fighting force in this province."

SAIGON MPS

A US Military Police jeep moved slowly through the twisting, rutted backstreets of a sleeping city in early February 1972. I was a rear seat passenger. Sergeant John A. Niebuhr, a burly young man with dark-rimmed glasses, was driving. He was twenty-seven days short of being discharged and had patrolled Saigon's streets for seventeen months with C Company, 716th Military Police Battalion, the only one in Vietnam's capital city. In the right front seat was Lieutenant Jim Horn, on his last working night and two weeks from finishing his tour.

Horn was the duty officer, responsible for monitoring four walking patrols, fifteen other jeeps and twelve static posts. There were three companies and about seven hundred troops in the 716th, and each worked eight-hour shifts patrolling the city and suburbs. Horn's company was pulling the 11:00 p.m.-7:00 a.m. shift. "Not much happening lately," Horn said. "Not since the elections. It's been very quiet, just routing stuff." He sounded like Jack Webb from *Dragnet*. "We check a lot of documents and vehicles. We've been finding a lot of falsified IDs and documents. The other side can get anything for a price."

A few minutes after midnight, the MPs spotted a GI sitting on a cyclo (small motorcycle with a sidecar) on a dark side street. They talked to him and sent him on his way. "I just advised him not to travel this way," Horn said, "because it's a good place to get your head kicked in. This section is believed to be harboring a number of AWOLs."

In an alley off Plantation Road, the MPs heard some loud arguing. They left the jeep and ran to investigate. "No sweat," Horn said. "This civilian was living with this girl and her mother came home and wanted to throw him out. He didn't want to leave. We have no jurisdiction over

97

something like that, so we just let 'em hash it out themselves ... A lot of guys head to the massage parlors and then go back there and get a piece cheap. When they do, a lot of 'em end up getting rolled. We call this '100 P [Piasters] Alley.'"

There was a 1:00–5:30 a.m. curfew for Vietnamese people and American servicemen, who were not supposed to be on the streets during that time. Vehicular traffic, except of an official nature, also was banned. The MPs spotted a GI walking down a side street away from Tan Son Nhut Air Base with no hat on and his khaki shirt hanging sloppily out of his pants. They told him to get in, and we drove him back to his billet at MACV Special Troops Headquarters.

"He said he was looking for a taxi," Horn said. "Yeah, sure. Obviously he was just walking up the road to stay at his girl's house. I could have gotten him for a curfew violation, but he was cooperative with us, so I gave him a break."

Niebuhr drove the gleaming jeep toward Alpha Six checkpoint at the entrance to Tan Son Nhut. MPs there were detaining two GIs in civilian clothes. Horn got a report. "Apparently these two guys left Camp Alpha without authorization," he said. "I don't know how the heck they got out of there. They were supposed to be waiting for an R&R flight. We'll just take them back and send a report to their unit. Their commanding officer may take action against them, or he may not. It's up to him."

The men said they responded to a terrorist attack on September 15 at the Tu Do Night Club but that it had been very quiet lately. "A charge was set inside with a timed fuse," Horn said. "We were twenty feet from the front of the building. We had some trouble with a civilian and a taxicab driver. I was watching people go in and out, and then the glass breaks, and metal and everything goes flying around. We had to seal off the area. You never know when something's going to happen. We're kept busy, but we really don't want to have a lot of trouble."

Horn said he had little respect for the Vietnamese police (Quan Canh). "I can't stand those guys," he said. "They'll leave you high and dry. You want to go in a club or a house to pick up an AWOL GI, and they won't come in. Either they're on the take, lazy, incompetent, or afraid of the consequences. Our guys don't understand the job of the Vietnamese police or the customs of the city, but our guys want to be out on the road. The Vietnamese don't seem to give a damn about their duty."

Not much happened the rest of the shift. Somebody was arrested for impersonating an officer. There were three reports of robberies, three traffic accidents, two AWOL GIs arrested, one alleged assault, one GI arrested for possessing a couple of vials of heroin and a host of lesser violations.

"I told you," Niebuhr said. "Nothing much happens after curfew these days. It's not like it was last September. It's been quiet lately. I hope it stays that way. Twenty-seven days, man. Twenty-seven days."

THE RED BARONS

In mid-February 1972, the name *Red Barons* brought to mind a brilliant German World War I flying ace, Snoopy, and the one-hit wonder group the Royal Guardsmen. You thought of dogfights and the rat-tat-tat of machine-gun fire. The song went: "Ten, twenty, thirty, forty, fifty or more, the bloody Red Baron was rolling up the score. Eighty men died just to set men free from the bloody Red Baron of Germany."

The 201st Aviation Company at the army's Camp McDermott in the coastal city of Nha Trang, two hundred miles northeast of Saigon, was nicknamed "the Red Barons." But its fixed-wing aircraft and helicopter pilots were anything but bloodthirsty killers. "We don't have any combat heroes here," 201st commanding officer Major Hubert S. Williamson said. "Anyone who comes here and wants to get some combat time, I'll help him get transferred someplace where he can get it. Hell, I'm all for it. But I don't want any combat heroes in my unit."

The 201st's job was flying civilian and military VIPs around the II Corps region in its four U-21s, ten OH-58 Kiowas, and ten UH-1H Hueys. "The war is over for us," said Warrant Officer James Hudkins. "We're just here to spend our year. We're not going anyplace where we'll have a chance to get shot up."

"I'm a very peaceful person," said Captain Rick Mason, a U-21 pilot. "A VIP gets in, we take off, get up to ten thousand feet as quickly as possible, stay high as long as possible, come down, and let 'em off. The reward comes from just knowing you got the people to where they wanted to go on time."

Mason, in his second Vietnam tour, said he "blew up trees, set booby traps, and cleared landing zones" with the 101st Airborne Division in his first tour from 1968 to 1970. On this tour, he said, he felt more like he was working for an airline than for the army. "Once in a while, you'll get shot at," said crew chief Sergeant Isidro Pena, who had been in-country thirteen months, "but there's no real threat. It's like R&R. You're working hard, but it's not like it used to be. It's a nice change. The average mission time is about an hour."

John Paul Vann, senior adviser in II Corps, had one of the Red Barons' OH-58s on standby twenty-four hours a day for use in flying from his Pleiku headquarters for meetings with Vietnamese and US officials throughout the region's twelve provinces.

"There's nothing much to our job except hauling big wheels," OH-58 pilot Captain William C. Smith said. Smith, five months into his second Vietnam tour, said he flew O-1 Bird Dogs in 1968–69 and had been shot down twice. "We go to a lot of small hamlets flying two thousand feet off the ground. Nha Trang's nicer than any place [in Vietnam] I've ever been. You can go shopping downtown. I've never been any place before in Vietnam where you could do that."

"The pilots are all officers," Hudkins said. "A good portion of us are on our second tours and like to fly something where we don't get shot at. I got shot at on my first tour."

Another pilot, Captain Vince Aberle, said he had been shot down three times flying O-1s in 1967–68. "It's a lot different now," he said. "We're kept busy every day, but the missions aren't dangerous. Oh, we'll talk about what it was like in the old days, sure. But I'm sure nobody wishes it was 1968 again. We're happy with the mission here. I haven't heard anybody complain."

Williamson said, "We provide professional air support. We need a guy who does what he's supposed to do: get a guy where he's going without taking any chances. No combat assaults, that's what we try to preach to them all the time. Don't fly at low level unless it's absolutely necessary. Most of our guys want to be here. They never lived this good."

"The beach is here," Mason said. "We have hot showers. The restaurants are excellent. We have good people … It's a fat job, probably the fattest in Vietnam. This is sort of an old folks' home, a reward for services rendered."

BASIC TRAINING

Private First Class Jorge Colomes had a dream when I met him in mid-March 1972. It was something he thought about while on night patrols east of Saigon. "Someday," he said, "and I know it is coming, my countrymen and I will return to Cuba and overthrow Castro. Then we can go back to our homes."

Colomes, twenty-five, said he had escaped from Cuba in his brother's fishing boat in 1961 with fifteen friends and family members. He said there was one tense moment in the trip. Somehow the boat turned around and was heading back into Havana harbor before somebody noticed the mistake. "We were lucky nobody saw us," he said. "We turned around again and made it to Key West in about twelve hours. We had to get out of Cuba, man. They were executing people for nothing. You never knew whether you'd be the next one."

The five-foot-nine, 128-pound soldier was in the middle of his first trip to the bush with Charlie Company, Second Infantry Battalion, Eighth Cavalry, Third Brigade, First Cavalry Division, when I spent a few nights in the field with the unit, which was based at Fire Base Melanie, twenty miles east of Saigon. It worked the so-called "rocket belt" to the south looking for Communist guerillas.

"My wife and my mother were upset when I enlisted," he said. "But my father was proud of me. He knows I will need training. Someday, it will pay off. My uncle writes me that things are getting worse and worse in Cuba every day. No food, no clothes, everything is rationed … we've got to get rid of Castro and the Communists. Vietnam is the best place for me to get training."

Colomes's nickname in his unit was "Columbus." He arrived in Vietnam on February 25, 1972, fresh out of basic and advanced infantry training at Fort Hood, Texas. He said six months before I met him he had left a $130-a-week job as a serviceman in a Los Angeles cosmetic factory and left his twenty-one-year-old wife, Maria, sobbing.

"I write her letters now," he said, "and tell her not to worry, I'm not in much danger. But I'm learning to live out in the bush. The weather is a lot like Cuba, and the banana trees sure remind me of home. It's something I just have to do. I want to go back to my country and am ready to fight to do it."

FIRE BASE MELANIE

"A hot area, a hot area," a restless grunt growled. "Every time you go somewhere, they tell you you're going into a hot area. It's a bunch of junk. The VC don't want to meet us. They're just waiting for us to leave."

It was mid-March 1972, and I was visiting the Second Battalion, Eighth Cavalry, Third Brigade, First Cavalry Division, one of seven US combat battalions left in Vietnam at the time, at Fire Base Melanie about twenty miles east of Saigon. Its men patrolled the rocket belt to the south, searching for Communist guerillas.

Since the Americans took over the base in December 1971, it had not been hit. "We fired up two individuals in the bush the day after we got here," an officer said. "I guess the word went back not to mess with Melanie."

When I visited, the troopers had been involved in only one contact in the previous month, and they were bored and becoming careless. "Sometimes, I think the men believe we're out here on a camping trip," said Lieutenant William N. Norton, twenty-three, a platoon leader in C Company. "You drill into them to be quiet out here and get serious. But there's no way they're going to believe there's VC out there unless they see for themselves."

C Company had not had a man wounded in nine months and had not killed a Communist since December 28. The highlight of the next three months was on February 29, when the company blew up a VC ammunition cache. Only a handful of the men knew what it was like to have been in a firefight.

"Sure, everybody's been a little lax," said Specialist Fourth Class Jerry Cupp, twenty-five, a radio telephone operator from Piqua, Ohio. "Back when I was here the first time, there were dinks all around. You couldn't afford to get careless. Now you don't see any. But we'll do all right if we get into contact. When you get shot at, you get down. You shoot back."

Charlie Company's commanding officer, Captain Leonard T. Hale, twenty-six, from Clearwater, Florida, was a wiry little man with dirty-blond hair, whiskers he liked to grow long in the bush, and a yen for action. He was in his third tour in Vietnam. "I've been in one or two contacts," he said, smiling. Hale said he worked closely with his thirty-man second platoon on his last patrol because only half those men had spent more than eight months in-country.

"Most of them can't tell what a hot trotter [trail] is," he said, "or what the signs of a bunker complex being near are. Our guys walked right into the middle of one the other day before they knew where they were."

Hale said the platoon pulled back quietly, and he sent a ten-man patrol of his most experienced troops up a steep hill to check out the bunkers. The men saw a shirt on the outside of one bunker, so they knew there were enemy soldiers there. Hale ordered them to withdraw, and Cobra gunships were brought in. Hale said the helicopters spotted a dozen fleeing VC and saturated the area with rockets and minigun fire but got no confirmed kills.

The point man on that patrol was Specialist Fourth Class Jesse Johnson, twenty, from Jackson, Mississippi, who had eight months in-country, including time with the Americal and 101st Airborne Divisions. "I wanted to take the hill," he said, "but they told us to pull out. We're here to fight. A couple of new guys were a little shy about getting into contact, but I think we've squared them away. Only thing is, every chance we get to have a contact, the VC split on us."

Hale said Charlie Company stayed in the VC bunker complex—they found eleven log-covered holes—for a night and ran patrols from it the next day before blowing it up. They followed blood trails for a few hundred yards, but then the trails ended, and there was no sign of the enemy. "I think I know where they've gone," Hale said. "We'll find them yet. It wasn't a big thing really, blowing the bunkers, but they had beer, wine, and lawn chairs there. They were taking it easy, like on R&R. And we went in and destroyed three months of their work in one day. That gives you a little satisfaction."

"Yeah," Johnson said, "but it would have been better if we'd had a chance to get some of them. That's the reason we're out here."

CONVOY MAN

Twice a day and once on Sunday Lieutenant Donald E. Curry drove in a jeep behind a convoy of supply trucks back and forth between the rear headquarters of Second Battalion, Eighth Cavalry, at Bien Hoa and Fire Base Melanie, twenty miles east. "The war is something I'm really out of touch with," said the roly-poly, twenty-five-year-old First Cavalry Division officer from Youngstown, Ohio.

As the officer in charge of resupplying the firebase, Curry logged 650 miles a week over paved and bumpy dirt roads in the thirteen convoys. He never got a day off because regulations said an officer must ride in every convoy. "It's a pain in the backside," he said, "but it's necessary because we don't have the blade assets [CH-47 Chinook cargo helicopters] that we used to."

Although part of the route to Melanie was through "unsecure" territory, convoys had no contact with Communists between December 19, when Second Battalion took over the base from the Thais, and late March, when I visited. The only trouble Curry said he had was getting flat tires. "My jeep had one the other day," he said, "but the convoy doesn't stop. We had it fixed in five minutes, and then we caught up to the convoy. We keep to a strict schedule every day. It's a little risky going the same way at the same time every day, but the men have to get supplies."

Doc Holliday

US Air Force Captain Kenneth D. (Doc) Holliday had been flying C-7 Caribou cargo planes by the seat of his pants to some of the most treacherous and remote areas of the Central Highlands for ten months when I interviewed him in early March 1972. For the ten thousand Montagnard tribesmen of Dak Pek and Dak Seang in northwestern Kontum Province, Holliday and a dozen other C-7 pilots of the 457th Tactical Squadron at Cam Ranh Bay were their only link to the outside world.

I Iolliday said he had logged seventy-five supply missions to the outposts and taught most of the other pilots the tricks of landing on the 1,500-foot, steel-matting, restricted airstrips. "Some of our pilots," he said, "when they take one look at those airfields, don't want to go back. At Dak Pek [ten miles east of the Laotian border and fifty-five miles northwest of Kontum City], there is an unbelievable crosswind—about twenty knots—which hits you on the final approach. It's like hitting a brick wall … I approach at 8,500 feet, cut the power, and fall as fast as possible."

During the descent, he said, he took his aircraft on a series of rivet-popping twisting turns that made it difficult for Communist gunners.

The Dak Seang strip, about fifteen miles south of Dak Pek, also was difficult to negotiate. "Although it's in the open," Holliday said, "the crosswinds are fierce here too. During one landing, a strong gust hit my bird, and the brakes went mushy. I managed to stop about five feet from the end of the runway and the edge of a minefield … A couple of years ago, we had three Caribous shot down over Dak Seang. When you fly up there now, you know there's still a war going on. We land [a loadmaster and a co-pilot complete the crew], slide the cargo out the back, turn around, and take off again. Meanwhile, the Montagnards are out there with oxcarts hustling the food and ammo away."

Holliday said the Montagnard radio operator at Dak Pek, Ky Niem, presented him with a knife he made out of a mortar casing with a carved wooden handle. "It'll make a great story to tell my three little boys," Holliday said.

TANKS FOR THE MEMORIES

The Second Squad, Eleventh Armored Regiment, the last American tank outfit in Vietnam, stood down in early March 1972, and its tanks, armored personnel carriers, and most of the men were shipped home. No more breaking brush, all-night recon patrols, or mad minutes. But some of the Second Squad troops just missed getting drops off their one-year tours and were reassigned to the First Cavalry Division. They were waiting for orders at the Combat Training Center, where three thousand in-country transfers and newly arrived troops had filtered into the cav. in a two-month span. I was there looking for a story and got one.

"I had a pretty important job," said Private First Class Robert M. Lewis, nineteen, of Lockport, New York. "I liked it quite a bit. We provided security for the grunts and gave them most of their intelligence. We kept the Communists on the run. They don't wanna mess with tracks. Now, I don't know what's gonna happen to our people."

The Second Squad had worked mostly in Tay Ninh Province and more recently in Binh Duong north of Saigon with more than a hundred vehicles. The two staples had been the Sheridan tank and the APC. The last few days of February had been hectic. The unit had gone on all-night recon patrols several times a week, changed night defensive positions a couple of times each night, and fired up a lot of jungle searching for Communist gueril(as.

"We didn't get much sleep," Lewis said. "We were having mad minutes—when everybody fires at once—every hour. Any unit, when it starts standing down, likes to play games."

"People kept telling us we weren't going to stand down," said Specialist Fourth Class Rod Easter, nineteen, from Muskogee, Oklahoma. "But we knew something had to be up. They probably wanted to give the Communists one last blast."

The cutoff date for drops in the unit was September 27, 1971, meaning that if a trooper arrived after that date, he would have to finish out his tour. Easter's DEROS date was October 5, so he was being reassigned probably to Second Squad, Eighth Cavalry, at Fire Base Melanie, twenty miles east of Saigon. But since he had taken shrapnel in his leg, he could not be used as an infantryman. "No way," he said. "I'll just be filling a hole somewhere until another drop comes down."

Another tank driver playing a waiting game was Specialist Fourth Class David Healey, nineteen, of Kansas City, Missouri, whose DEROS date was October 8 and who also had just missed a drop. "You're free in the bush," he said. "Nobody hassles you, and you just do your job."

"Yeah," Easter said, "but it wasn't always good. You'd be breaking the bush, and a tree would fall on you, and these red ants would crawl all over you. You couldn't get them off. I guess we don't have to worry about them anymore. And another thing—the chow. I'm gonna have to get used to using silverware again. They gave us plastic silverware in the field, and the meat was always so tough you couldn't cut it. The cooks did their best, I guess, but the chow we had brought out to us by chopper was really bad."

Members of the unit said they had lost only two men since the previous April. One had been their commanding officer, who had been killed January 10 when he'd been hit by AK-47 fire while checking the body of a Communist he had killed. Easter said he himself had killed four Communists with tank fire on a January 19 patrol. No one knew how many kills the squad had totaled in recent months.

A normal patrol by the unit involved seventeen vehicles, including a half-dozen Sheridans. The men usually smashed through the jungle, firing rounds in all directions and hoping to smoke out the enemy. "We really had a lot of pride," Healey said. "I wish I could be back in the field with the guys again instead of being in the rear, as long as I have to be in Vietnam." He said he expected to receive orders shortly assigning him to the US Army Garrison at Bien Hoa.

"I've learned a lot," Lewis said, "gone through a lot of stuff, and came through in one piece with only one buddy killed. Now, I'm just waiting for a drop. I'm sick of war. I just want to go home."

PEACOCK HILL

When I visited the US air base on Peacock Hill outside Pleiku City in early March 1972, the VNAF had been running its own show since January 1 at the 921st Air Control and Warning Center, monitoring and assisting via radar and radio 120 VNAF aircraft that flew in and out of the base daily.

Most of the unit's 120 airmen had been trained in the United States, the Philippines, or Okinawa. For several years, Americans of Detachment 2620, 620th Tactical Control Squadron, had handled the operation, but by the time I visited, only a few dozen Americans were left to handle US aircraft while the Vietnamese handled theirs.

"When we have problems," Captain Tran Quoc Ban said, "we handle them by ourselves. Sure, we had difficulties in the beginning because any time you learn new jobs you're going to have them. But not anymore."

Ban, thirty-one, had ten years of experience in his field. He had attended an eight-month weapons control school at Tyndall Air Force Base in Panama City, Florida, in 1963 and had taken a couple of months of English classes at Lackland (Texas) Air Force Base. He had advanced training in Okinawa and spent five years as a training officer in various "dark rooms" in Vietnam tracking aircraft.

The VNAF and American airmen at Peacock Hill tracked helicopters and fixed-wing aircraft and gave them navigational assistance, weather information, and advice on the tactical situation in the area. Ban said civilians from Lockheed Aircraft Corporation were installing a T2T4 simulator device in his shop. Operated by eight men, the device simulated the actions of a pilot on a tactical airstrike.

MEDICS

The combat medics of the Second Battalion, Eighth Cavalry, Third Brigade, First Cavalry Division, were not being called upon in mid-March 1972 to perform any heroic feats or save lives in the bush because contacts between GIs at Fire Base Melanie and Communist guerillas were few and far between. But the medics did have work to do.

"Sure, the number of battle casualties has dwindled to almost nothing," said battalion surgeon Captain William Osheroff, twenty-eight, of Virginia Beach, Virginia, "but a medic on a firebase still has to treat all of the common maladies our men are prone to in a tropical climate. We get people coming into the aid station twenty-four hours a day. The emotional strain of always having to be ready for anything is really tough."

Osheroff supervised thirty-two medics in the battalion and was training a half-dozen infantrymen to be medics because of a shortage. He said the most common ailments were skin diseases; non-battle injuries such as cuts, bruises and broken bones; extractions of grenade fragments; ankle and back sprains; and fevers. He said his men handled eight hundred to a thousand patients a month and treated up to seventy men a day on sick call.

"We've been getting a lot of sprained ankles and backs lately," said Specialist Fifth Class Jimmie A. Keeton, twenty-five, a medic from Colorado Springs, Colorado. "Some guys don't know how to jump correctly off a chopper on a combat assault. Another guy went into post-accident trauma. He'd been in an accident in the states in his car, and his blood pressure dropped. He had a concussion and just collapsed. And at midnight last week, some guy had an epileptic seizure and started shaking and then became unconscious. We took care of them all night and medevaced them out in the morning."

FIRE BASE BUNKER HILL

Fire Base Bunker Hill, the home of the First Battalion, Twelfth Cavalry, Third Brigade, First Cavalry Division, in late March 1972, was so named because Bunker Hill was the name of the first American firebase in Vietnam in 1965. Due to President Nixon's troop withdrawal plans, which projected only forty-nine thousand troops left in-country on July 1, the new Bunker Hill figured to be the last new US base built during the war.

Members of three engineer units had been at work for almost a month when I visited to observe that Bunker Hill was one of the best firebases every built. "It's gonna be really great," said Specialist Fifth Class Frank Cox, nineteen, a squad leader from Chicago. He and the other infantrymen there were living in sewer pipes and culvert hooches until they could move into their underground Conex-enclosed hooches in the berm of the firebase, about seven miles northeast of Bien Hoa. Conexes were metal storage containers.

"They finally wised up," Cox said, "putting the bunkers underground. That'll relax a lot of the hassle you have on a firebase. Before, you'd have to scrape for a place to sleep. And during the rainy season, being underground will be cool. It's gonna be a nice place to come back to after being out in the bush."

The base was one of only four large fortified camps from which the four remaining combat battalions in the First Cavalry Division patrolled the "rocket belt" east of Saigon. It sat on a hill overlooking the Dong Hai River. "It was just a grassy pile of dirt before we got here," said Staff Sergeant Matt H. "Big G" Gross, twenty-eight, of Taylorsville, Kentucky. Gross was the enlisted man in charge of the earth-moving 557th Engineer

Company, which had four bulldozers, five dump trucks, and a dozen other vehicles moving dirt twelve hours a day for four weeks.

"We've been kept very busy," Big G said, "and my equipment has been standing up real well. It'll be a damn good firebase when we get through."

Members of the 501ˢᵗ Engineer Company were building the bunkers while men of B Company, Ninety-Second Combat Engineer Battalion, handled the hammer-and-nail construction of the underground mess hall and tactical operations center. Huge cranes were lifting Conexes into the berm, where they were covered with at least three layers of sandbags, waterproofed with a mixture of tar and gasoline, and padded with dirt on all sides.

Bulldozers were used to clear fields of fire in all directions along the slopes of the hill, scraping away vegetation and trees and eliminating gullies that could cause erosion problems. "The drainage will be good," Lieutenant Richard Peters said, "but we've got to make sure the water drains off evenly during the monsoon season so that nature will not create a place where the VC could sneak up on us." Peters was the officer in charge of the earthmovers.

The firebase also was to have portable showers and prefabricated latrines. "We'll probably get it all built," said Specialist Fourth Class Lindell Bradbury, twenty, of Oklahoma City, Oklahoma, "and then we'll have to turn it over to somebody else. We helped the engineers build Fire Base Gibraltar [twenty-five miles east of Saigon] and then had to turn it over to the Second of the Fifth and were sent to Tuy Hoa to be green-line guards. We'd like to stay here a while." As it was, it was only a few months before the base was abandoned.

XM3

Some GIs in the bush around Bien Hoa in late March 1972 worked with scout dogs. The members of the Twenty-Sixth Chemical Detachment at the base went one step further. They used an electronic bloodhound called an XM3 personnel detector to smell out Communist guerillas. The GIs and their "sniffer" flew daily helicopter missions at treetop level while a gunship cruised above, waiting to strike.

The XM3 was about a yard long, eighteen inches wide, and eighteen inches high with a vacuum-cleaner like hose that was attached to the skid of a helicopter. It picked up smoke, dust caused by movement of an unseen enemy, and human sweat at a range of more than five hundred yards.

The way it was explained to me, particles were drawn into the hose and magnified by a photomultiplier, which changed the light from them into electrical current, which registered in amperes on a gauge. I flew with the men on a sniffer mission.

"We're flying into an area where we should get some readouts," Sergeant First Class Louie Langford said as he loaded an XM3 aboard our chopper. But when the aircraft got to the area of operation about twenty miles southeast of Bien Hoa, he was disappointed. Artillery had fired up the jungle there on the previous night, and curls of smoke drifted skyward like Indian smoke signals all over the place. It was a good scenario for a Smokey the Bear commercial.

"No use flying here," Langford said. "You get a max readout all through the area. Maybe we'll get lucky later."

The chopper flew to an area twelve miles northeast of Bien Hoa near the Dong Nai River, escorted by a Blue Max Cobra gunship. The men got clearance for a reconnaissance by fire, which meant they could fire M79

115

grenades, M16 rifle rounds, and M60 machine-gun bullets indiscriminately through the trees in hopes of smoking some Communists out.

One trooper fired a few rounds near the bank of the river, where Communists liked to camp during the dry season. The door gunners, Specialist Fourth Class Roger McKenzie and Specialist Fifth Class Sam McCraw, fired their M60s. "It's the only low-level Huey mission left," one of the men said after we touched down. "It's a worthwhile thing, too, because you'll find things a pink team [OH-6 Cayuse light observation helicopter and Cobra] won't find. They'll be searching an area all day and not find anything. We'll go in and get a reading on our machine. It'll even pick up cigarette smoke or the smoke coming from a cooking fire in an underground bunker."

"We fired so many chunker [grenade] rounds," he added, "because the machine doesn't pick up anything unless the guy is moving. So if we fire down there, the dude might say, 'Wow, I've been spotted,' and start running. Then we'll catch him. Also, it gets monotonous just flying back and forth dodging trees. So you fire up the area. It gives the mission an element of danger that most missions now don't have."

STANDING DOWN

The last US Army unit at Phu Loi, a once-thriving post fifteen miles north of Saigon, was withdrawn on April 1, 1972, and in the first ceremony of its kind, the base was turned over to South Vietnam's Ministry of War Veterans for use as a job-training and resettlement center.

Pham Van Dong, fifty-four, a retired major general and minister of the Ministry of War Veterans, accepted a symbolic key to the post from Lieutenant Colonel Lewis J. McConnell, commander of the 520th Transportation Battalion, the only US unit left at the post. The base at one time housed 6,000 GIs and supported some 1,200 aircraft. The 520th stood down on April 1.

After the ceremonies, Dong announced privately that he hoped to turn Phu Loi into an industrial complex that would serve as a pilot project for the retraining of disabled and demobilized war veterans. He said at the time there were 216,000 Vietnamese war veterans, 65,000 of them disabled. He said his office paid them a pension and gave stipends to families of disabled and deceased veterans. Dong said there were 350,000 war orphans, 90,000 war widows, and 90,000 parents of war dead.

They were being cared for by members of Dong's 1,200-person staff and a budget of $50 million—10 percent of the national budget. Dong's ministry was to have moved its vocational training center from Cat Lai on the outskirts of Saigon to Phu Loi. Dong said he planned to set up a farm that would support three hundred families, plus a weaving factory, a banana-drying plant, a sawmill, and an animal-feed factory to provide jobs for an additional five hundred families.

DEADLY FIRE

Two weeks into the Easter Offensive in April 1972, US chopper pilots said they were facing heavier and deadlier antiaircraft fire than at any time in the war.

The most effective weapon the enemy was using in the Central Highlands was the .51-caliber machine gun, which sat on a tripod and could easily be moved by two men, according to members of the Cobra helicopter company based at Camp Holloway in Pleiku. The other weapon frequently used was the 37 mm World War II vintage antiaircraft gun. It was more cumbersome because it was towed by a vehicle and less accurate because its rounds were preset to explode at certain altitudes.

"It used to be that our Snakes [AH-1 Cobras] would come back once in a while with some small holes in the tail section," said Warrant Officer Kenneth Wright, twenty-five, of Norwalk, California, assistant maintenance officer of the 361st Aerial Weapons Company. "Now, they are coming back with .51-caliber and small-arms holes, most of them around the cockpit, almost every day. There is not a bird on the line that hasn't been hit."

None of the unit's choppers had been downed by Communist ground fire in the first two weeks of April, but at one time half its Cobras had been grounded because of battle damage. "These birds have been around a long time and have a lot of hours on them," Wright said. "Number 803 has got freckles; it took thirteen hits in one day. But they were easy to patch up. Just skin damage. As long as none of the machinery or fuel lines are hit, we can get them flying again in no time."

Lieutenant David Messa, twenty-three, of New Orleans, said a .51-caliber round smashed through the back of his seat as he leaned

118

forward to sight his minigun. Warrant Officer Dan Jones, twenty-eight, from Tucson, Arizona, had Plexiglas fragments removed from his face after an AK-47 round smashed through his canopy. "A cheap Purple Heart," he said. "These guys realize they can't knock a Cobra down unless they hit a strategic place. They are going for the pilots."

Recalling Tet of 1968, Jones said, "We are taking more and better antiaircraft fire now than we did then." Although the pilots would not reveal their secrets, they said they employed several tricks to avoid the deadly fire. At Fire Base Delta, two Cobras dodged fire from six different locations. The pilots said they probably knocked some of them out during strafing runs. "It's not hard to get [kill] people manning the gun," Jones said, "but most of the time three more will jump into the hole, throw out the bodies, and start shooting again."

PATROLLING THE
PLEIKU BUSH

Staff Sergeant Harris T. Little had seen his share of combat. He had been with the Twenty-Fifth Infantry Division in 1966 and the First Infantry Division in 1968–69, operating in dense jungle north and west of Saigon. But since September 1971, on his third tour in Vietnam, he had been fighting another kind of war when I caught up to him in mid-May 1972: a war against boredom. While serving in Germany, he'd volunteered for Vietnam and been assigned to the 101st Airborne Division at Camp Evans near Hue. He had sent his wife and three children to live in his hometown of Jessup, Georgia.

The 101st stood down in December 1971. Little, twenty-seven, was made sergeant of the guard of an infantry company pulling bunker guard duty at Cam Ranh Bay. Then he was transferred back to the field as a platoon sergeant with Delta Company, Seventh Infantry, the only American infantry unit left in II Corps, covering the Central Highlands provincial capitals of Pleiku and Kontum. Its mission was to provide an early warning for Camp Holloway, the big Pleiku helicopter base, in the event of a Communist ground assault.

The unit had not made any contact since it began patrolling in early May 1972, and most of his men, drawn from various grunt units that had stood down, doubted that they would ever see a Communist. "No," Little said, "I don't like it here. It's not the same war we used to fight. Too many restrictions. I'd rather keep on fighting like we used to than be doing this."

Little's men patrolled slices of territory between South Vietnamese areas of operation and wondered why the ARVNs couldn't handle the whole show. "I don't believe we need Americans out here," Little said, rigging a shelter out of two bedspreads. "There are ARVNs all around us. They should send us a little farther out, but they can't, because we have no artillery support. I'd rather be here than in the rear, but I'd rather be home than anywhere."

Many of D Company's men either just missed drops or had them canceled. Most had not done anything more dangerous than pulling bunker guard duty at night. Now they were living in circus-type tents at Holloway and sleeping on the ground; they'd go out on six-day patrols and come back in for three.

I went out on a daytime patrol with Little's company. It seemed like little more than a romp in the woods until Little spied a series of bent-over bamboo sticks along a trail. "Everybody down," he said, inching forward to check them out. "Never seen anything like this before," he whispered. "Looks like trail markers of some kind." Little radioed the command post at Holloway a few miles away. "Before I do anything," he said, "I'm going to check with the South Vietnamese and see if they know anything about this."

The patrol walked to a nearby ARVN compound where an interpreter told them they had found animal traps. "I figured they wouldn't be booby traps," Private First Class Cooper R. Allen, twenty-one, of Houston, said. "The Montagnards run cows through here all the time, and they would have set them off by now."

"Okay," Little told the South Vietnamese. "No sweat. Just checking. We leave tomorrow. See you later."

"Oh," the interpreter joked, "VC come here tomorrow."

"Good," Little said. "We see you in about two weeks. Bye now."

The company walked off laughing. Another walk in the meadow and no contact. "The only thing we have to be afraid of is the ARVNs," one GI said. "They fired mortars at us one night. They thought we were VC, I guess."

Pfc. Steven J. Parker, nineteen, of Hartford City, Indiana, said he had been in Vietnam eight months and had been in four contacts with the 101st near Phu Bai. "Nothing heavy," he said, "just ambushes, sniper fire, people taking shots at you. I hate it. There are too many men working this area. What the hell am I out here fighting a war for? GIs have no reason to be out here. The ARVNs should be handling everything. It's low-cut, nice walking, like a picnic around here, but if a GI gets killed, he dies for nothing. It's a sorry outfit as far as I'm concerned. Nobody wants to be here."

THE MEN OF MACV-SOG

There was beer on the grizzled sergeant's breath as he spit the words into my face. "These bastards from MACV are gettin' to be a pain in the ass," he said. "Well, I'll tell you this—we ain't leaving our 'Yards. We'll die with 'em right here, but we're not running out on them. Way it looks now, there's no contingency plan for evacuating them. And we ain't gettin' on no choppers and leavin' 'em behind."

The sergeant toted a carbine. Bandoliers of ammo were slung over his shoulders. He belonged to the top-secret elite force known as Military Assistance Command, Vietnam—Studies and Observation Group (MACV-SOG). I don't know how many of them were in Vietnam in the spring of 1972, and I don't know exactly what they did. But I met about a dozen of them. All said they were US Special Forces Green Berets, but they wore black caps because there weren't supposed to be any Green Berets left in Vietnam.

Most of those I talked to said they had been in-country for multiple tours. They were big, strong, and seemingly fearless. In early May 1972, in Kontum, the fuzzy-cheeked, red-haired, wiry commanding officer of the MACV-SOG troops told me, "We're prepared to defend this compound to the last man if that's what they want. I feel sort of like Custer at the Little Bighorn."

MACV-SOG personnel had trained and fought with more than a hundred Montagnard commandos for more than five years. Most of the Americans seemed to be societal misfits: from broken families, divorced, separated, etc. They seemed to love being in the field, and they did not seem to mind killing. It was their job. They all had stories to tell, and late at night at the club in besieged Kontum, lubricated by liquor, the stories flowed.

"If you've ever heard a 'Sioux' [another nickname for the Montagnards] say, 'You die, I die,'" the old sergeant said, "then you'd know how we feel about them. There's not a one of us here who hasn't had his life saved at one time or another by a 'Yard. I know I'd die for my 'Sioux,' and they'd do the same for me. They'll set up an ambush, charge, surround the enemy—anything you tell them to do. Their devotion is unequaled. They act like machines, automatically. They assault, withdraw, set up, and blow Charlie away. Best jungle fighters I've ever seen. Your average 'Yard has five years' experience."

He added, "We may have to escape and evade out of here to Pleiku on foot, but if that's what we have to do, we will."

One of the Montagnards I interviewed, twenty-one-year-old Rahlam Peo, said he had worked with Special Forces troops for five years. He said he did not think the Communists would try to overrun Kontum for a few weeks. "We're afraid," he said, "but if the VC come here, we're ready for them. We'll listen to the Americans. If they tell us to stay and fight, that's what we'll do. If they want us to leave, then we'll leave."

The MACV compound near Kontum City was almost deserted except for the handful of MACV-SOG advisers and their protégés. The Montagnards manned perimeter bunkers at night. Flares bathed them and their weapons in an eerie glow every few minutes. The Montagnards imitated the Americans by wearing patches that said "Maine Airborne" or "Texas Rangers." The advisers wore bracelets and other trinkets signifying brotherhood with the tribesmen.

Another buck sergeant, who did not want his name used, said, "You may not believe this, but some day—and it won't be long, believe me—the 'Yards is gonna rise up and take over this country. When they do, I'm gonna be here fighting with 'em."

A few days later, I learned that the sergeant had been killed in the crash of a Nationalist Chinese troop transport plane used by MACV-SOG. Six Americans and a few dozen Montagnards died in what the U.S. Command described as a "clandestine mission" near the Laotian border.

THE EIGHTY-SECOND
WEIGHS IN WITH TOWS

A top-secret group of GIs from the Eighty-Second Airborne Division left the Central Highlands for Bien Hoa in May 1972. They had been teaching ARVN soldiers how to use TOWs, which were tube-launched, optically tracked, wire-guided missiles mounted on jeeps. About sixty of them arrived in Vietnam earlier in the year wearing First Cavalry Division patches and on temporary duty orders, so they would not constitute a technical reintroduction of US ground troops. Some were stationed in two-man teams near Pleiku and others near Kontum. The TOWs were designed to pierce the hulls of NVA tanks, which were threatening the provincial capitals during the Easter Offensive.

I saw the troops in the field working with the ARVNs and caught up to some of them in Bien Hoa on their way home. "It wasn't a bad couple of weeks," a squad leader, who would not give his name, told me. "A few of the guys wanted to stay here. Not me, though. I want to get home. Everything was hush-hush. Nixon doesn't want it known that he's bringing troops back. They never even told us we were coming to Vietnam. But since they gave us malaria pills, we had a pretty good idea it was 'Nam." The GI said he had confidence that the TOWs could do the job against NVA tanks. But he said the Eighty-Second had not destroyed any during their deployment. Another said his team had fired at one tank near Kontum and believed they scored a hit. "But the tank limped away," he said, "and was gone the next day." They turned the weapons over to the ARVNs and left.

Members of the unit were proud of the fact that according to congressional investigators, of tanks inspected among four army divisions stateside, theirs was the only one whose tanks were in satisfactory fighting condition. "Damn," one trooper told me, "since we're so damn good, they'll probably send us to Korea next."

Specialist Fourth Class Barry L. Flipse, nineteen, of Littleton, Colorado, who had spent five months in Vietnam and was on one of the TOW teams, said, "I think they should take everybody out, let the ARVNs do it all." Norm Barber, nineteen, a specialist fourth class from Winooski, Vermont, said, "I'd just as soon stay up in Kontum and Pleiku than be down here. They're on your ass all the time here ... A REMF [rear echelon mother fucker] hat, shined boots, starched fatigues—that's not gonna cut it." Ron Kremer, nineteen, a specialist fourth class from Arpin, Wisconsin, said, "All our buddies are going home who taught us everything in the bush. It's good to see 'em going. We seen there was a war going on. We saw NVA all over the streets ... got a good look at it."

Private First Class Charles Mays, nineteen, of Covington, Tennessee, who served at Fire Base Bunker Hill with the First of the Twelfth Cavalry, said, "You feel like you're leaving something back there. We were filling two thousand sandbags a day to get that place squared away. All I'm waiting for now is a drop [off the usual time served]. I hate this country. There ain't nothing over here for me. I'm against this war. There's already too many GIs died over here. They should send 'em all home right now."

DELTA WAR

In the cozy safety of Charlie Troop's officers' club in late May 1972, First Lieutenant Michael King, twenty-two, a scout pilot, drank cold soda with his left hand. His right arm was in a sling. The Sixteenth Air Cavalry officer had been hit in the forearm by fragments from a Communist AK-47 rifle round while assessing results of a B-52 strike in his little OH-6 light observation helicopter. "It's just like the rest of the country," King asserted. "There's as much activity down here as anywhere."

Charlie Troop was the last American chopper unit flying combat missions in the Mekong Delta. There were about 2,500 Americans left in the southernmost military region (IV Corps) in South Vietnam, and most were at Can Tho Army Airfield where C Troop was based. King was hurt just southeast of Can Tho in Chuong Thien Province, one of the hottest areas in the Delta at the time.

"It was the first time in two weeks that any of our birds has taken a hit," the Hartsville, South Carolina, native said. "We know there's a war going on down here, if nobody else in the Delta does. Our scouts [light observation helicopters] have been taking heavy fire for over a month."

"The Delta's supposed to be pacified," King said, "but only from two thousand feet. I went down on a BDA [bomb damage assessment] and took fire from a hundred different directions." The AK round that hit King had deflected off the armored vest "chicken plate" that all chopper pilots wear, and fragments had lodged in his forearm. Another bullet had torn through the floor and left through the top of the chopper.

SMART BOMBS

The commander of the only US Air Force fighter-bomber wing in Thailand that was using "smart bombs" said at a Saigon press conference on June 28, 1972, that the chances of inflicting civilian casualties had been greatly reduced by the use of the guided bombs.

Colonel Carl Miller, commander of the Eighth Tactical Fighter Wing at Ubon Royal Thai Air Force Base, said laser- and television-guided bombs used by his F-4 Phantom jet pilots were 90 percent effective. Miller said Soviet-built MIG fighters were the most dangerous Communist threat to US pilots and that the North Vietnamese pilots were getting better. He said the Communists had an adequate antiaircraft artillery system three months into their Easter Offensive but that their surface-to-air missile capability was significantly less that it had been early in the offensive.

"We've not yet seen the effects of what we've done," Miller said, "but we hit one [storage] facility and destroyed six million gallons of fuel near Hanoi with one flight of aircraft. Practically every bridge in the northwest and northeast of North Vietnam has been hit. The trucks and the tanks are still rolling south of the DMZ, but sooner or later they've got to run out of fuel."

Miller said 75 percent of the missions flown by his unit used smart bombs. He said a laser-guided bomb cost $5,000, and a television-guided bomb cost $11,000. The bombs were the conventional World War II type either with the laser system fixed to the front or the television system on the tail. Miller said OV-10 Broncos and AC-130 Spectre gunships sometimes were used to shoot laser beams at a target as the bombs from an F-4 homed in on them. Some F-4s were equipped to shoot their own lasers.

Miller said the bombs were locked onto targets before their release and were able to make in-flight corrections. "With a conventional bomb," he said, "it's very hard to figure where to release it, allowing for wind velocity at different levels. With a smart bomb, it might be blown in three directions on the way down but still find its way to the target."

He said the bombs could be guided into tunnels in hillsides and had delayed fuses so they could hit and bounce into a tunnel before exploding. He said the bombers were equipped to conduct night missions as easily as day missions. He said the only time a smart bomb was inaccurate was when it was dropped on a water target, such as a ford in a river used as a truck crossing, because water reflects laser energy. It all sounded good on paper, but the North Vietnamese almost weekly were complaining of civilian casualties from US bombing runs. So I took the comments with a grain of salt.

UP HIGHWAY 13

It was a slow day in early July 1972, after the NVA's Easter Offensive had been blunted, and I decided to see how far I could drive up Highway 13 toward An Loc, a provincial capital about sixty miles north of Saigon that had been virtually leveled by airstrikes during fierce fighting a few weeks before. The first thirty miles, as far as Lai Khe, was uneventful. Then I had to tool my air-conditioned Rambler station wagon around shrapnel and spent shell casings on the two-lane asphalt road.

About fifteen miles north of Lai Khe, I came to the town of Chon Thanh. Blown-in roofs and shattered windowpanes in houses on either side of the road reminded me that Vietcong mortars and rockets still were a constant threat. But I kept driving along, going about thirty miles an hour, past the parked military vehicles, around the Hondas and oxcarts, heading north. About eighteen miles north of Chon Thanh and twelve miles from the rubble of An Loc, I dropped in at a firebase along the highway.

I wheeled the wagon onto a dusty dirt road, waved at an incredulous Vietnamese gate guard, grabbed a bundle of *Stars and Stripes* newspapers as a peace offering, and strode briskly into the command bunker. "Morning, sir," I said, shaking hands with a surprised African American captain who was talking into a field telephone. The bunker shook as an ARVN howitzer began pumping shells at a nearby suspected enemy position. "Care for a paper? Name's Jim Smith, *Stars and Stripes*. Just wanted to check in and see how far it was safe to go up the road."

"You're already farther up than you should be," Captain Bill Moon, thirty-two, of Chicago, said. "What the hell are you doin' here?"

"Just wanted to get a situation report, sir."

"Oh, yeah, well, wait a minute."

130

Moon switched channels and called TRAC forward headquarters in Lai Khe. "I got a Jim Smith here who says he's from *Stars and Stripes* and wants to talk to me. What am I supposed to do with him?"

"Smith," a voice on the field telephone crackled. "Yeah, he's all right. He checked in with us. Give him what he wants—you know, nothing specific, the general scoop about what's happening."

"Roger that."

"Excuse me a moment," Moon said. He was in contact with a US Air Force light observation plane marking Communist positions with smoke so fast-moving bombers could drop their deadly payloads on them.

"Cut off the artillery," Moon hollered to his South Vietnamese interpreter. The battery of 105s fell silent. Seconds later, two F-4 Phantoms unleashed a couple of hundred pounds of napalm bombs, and they impacted with the fury of a lightning bolt. Then everything was silent again.

"Okay," Moon told the interpreter. "Turn on the artillery."

Moon was one of more than a hundred American advisers connected with the ARVN effort to reopen the highway and eliminate the Communist suicide troops who had refused to abandon their bunkers south of An Loc. Four advisers died and several were wounded in this area from April through June.

"We average about ten or fifteen rounds of incoming a day here," Moon said between field telephone conversations. "Sometimes, we don't get any, but other times they really hit you. We took fifty-one rounds of 82 mm mortar between five twenty and five thirty in the evening on July 1." Moon would not comment on when he thought the road might be reopened, nor would he give an opinion on how the ARVNs were doing. He could not figure out why I'd want to do a story on him.

"Actually, sir," I said, "I've got to get a story up today, and you seemed like an interesting one."

The field telephone crackled with the news that seven A-1 Skyraiders had put in bombs on Communist bunkers. Moon reported that they "did them a job."

It was midafternoon. Moon leaned back against the wall of his sandbagged bunker. Having flown 0-1s on his first tour in Vietnam in 1967–68, he knew about directing airstrikes. He had volunteered for his present assignment. "I don't know why," he said. "There's just a job here that's got to be done. I'd rather be here than in the rear."

C rations were on the menu for supper—or maybe rice eaten with chopsticks and hot tea with his South Vietnamese counterpart. Then he planned to write a letter to his wife and go to sleep. He said his slumber often was interrupted by the pop, whistle, and thud of incoming. "I slept right through it last night." Moon said. "After a while, it doesn't bother you."

"Well, very good, sir," I said. "I think I'll head on out of here before today's fireworks start."

Bill Moon returned to his field phone, and I drove back down the road.

BATTLE TACTICS

The introduction of Soviet-made SA-7 heat-seeking missiles during the North Vietnamese Army's Easter Offensive of 1972 forced American chopper crews to change their battle tactics. They began flying right on the deck almost exclusively. The thinking was the lower they were, the less time the Communists had to line them up for a missile shot, because the time they actually were in view of ground troops was limited.

"The only thing that's destroyed when we go out on a search-and-destroy mission is us," Major John P. Kennedy said. The thirty-one-year-old commander of F Troop, Eighth Air Cavalry Regiment, at Marble Mountain outside Da Nang on the northern front, said he lost more than a dozen aircraft to Communist ground fire between April 1 and the end of July in 1972.

"In the old days," he said, "we'd locate the enemy and respond with a whole American brigade of troops on a combat assault. Enemy soldiers were told not to fire at our scout birds, because they knew the consequences. But now the threat of [massive ground troop] retaliation no longer exists, so we're getting ourselves fired up."

F Troop was supporting the ARVN First Division and was charged with the defense of the old imperial capital city of Hue. Their mission in late July in a winding-down war mainly was intelligence gathering. Where was the enemy? What was the battlefield terrain like? What were the results of a B-52 strike? Which trails showed recent use? Those were the questions F Troopers were asked to answer.

"Once you venture past known friendly lines these days," Kennedy said, "you are engaged. What we do is employ heavy fire teams [AH-1 Cobra helicopter gunships] to shoot our way into an area. Then we bring in the 'Loaches' [smaller helicopters] to recon the area. We shoot the enemy up and try to provoke a response. Then the friendly [ARVN] troops move in, and we leave. Our job is done."

On June 12, Kennedy said, F Troop lost two of its tiny light observation helicopters (LOHs) and had five crewmen killed by ground fire. The next day another Loach was shot down, and two more crewmen were killed. "The day after that," Kennedy said, "I had five guys outside my door volunteering for LOHs."

Kennedy said some of his aircraft crew chiefs had gotten up a petition they wanted to submit to *Stars and Stripes* at the beginning of the offensive. "I told them they could send whatever they wanted to," he said. "I figured it would just be griping about something. But one of the kids said. 'Hey, sir, don't you want to read it?' I did. It said that the North Vietnamese had attacked the south and no matter what happened in the war before, this was wrong. The men said they were fighting to defend the freedom of South Vietnam and that they felt what they were doing was right."

The men of F Troop swaggered like modern-day cowboys. In fact, they wore black cavalry hats with crossed sabers on them, Custer-style. They were as cocky as bantam roosters. They laughed at death and thrived on excitement.

"We're flying missions now that we used to envision for the next World War," Kennedy said. "They're conventional war missions. We're flying into every sophisticated piece of equipment the Soviets have made, we're surviving it, and we're doing a good job."

EAST OF QUANG TRI

I got more foolhardy near the end of my tour, figuring that since I'd never ridden in a chopper that had taken fire, I was leading a charmed life and there was no bullet with my name on it. The last mission I flew in late July 1972 began as if it was going to be a waste of time.

I was in a command and control (C&C) bird on a hunter-killer mission over the rolling sand dunes east of Quang Tri City, just south of the Cua Viet River. It looked like Cape Cod in the summertime. Two hummingbird-like Loaches hovered over brush and tree lines, exposing themselves to ground fire and looking for enemy supply caches and troops, trying to smoke Communists out of bunkers.

Above, two AH-1 Cobra gunships waited. The C&C bird was on the deck because of the SA-7 threat—the NVA were using shoulder-fired, heat-seeking missiles. "If they can't see you, they can't hit you," said the officer in charge, Captain Jim Voorhees. "The enemy has missiles and all kinds of antiaircraft guns up here. But he has got to see us to hit anything. By flying low, we minimize the chance that he'll see us."

That morning, two helicopters from F Troop, Fourth Air Cavalry, had been shot at five miles south of the Cua Viet and within sight of battered Quang Tri. At least a dozen US Navy ships were offshore with guns blazing away at NVA positions. Inland, huge clouds of black smoke billowed as sortie after sortie of tactical air and B-52 strikes went in around the provincial capital.

We had burned half of our fuel when a silver streak plummeted from the sky and crashed into the sea about a half mile offshore. The Loaches and our Huey swooped to that location. We saw two orange-and-white parachutes dropping slowly. The captain told two young army

135

rescue experts, Sergeant Richard Dyre and Specialist Fourth Class Mike Remington, to strip to their shorts and be prepared to make a "feet-wet" rescue. But two navy destroyers steamed to the scene. We breathed a collective sigh of relief when the fliers hit the water and scrambled aboard the two yellow-and-orange life rafts, which automatically had inflated on their way down. We were close enough to see the men wave. The Loaches pinpointed the rafts' position with purple smoke grenades and hovered above them until the downed airmen were pulled aboard lifeboats.

Between June 10, when F Troop moved from Phu Bai south of Hue to Tan My near Quang Tri, and July 20, the unit covered four ARVN combat assaults with gunships. Two Loaches from the unit rescued five US Marines and an ARVN soldier after Communist gunners shot down three troop transport choppers during one of the assaults. The troop had rescued twenty downed airmen in the previous month.

JOLLY GREEN ANGELS

The field radio at Da Nang Air Base crackled. An F-4 Phantom jet was having hydraulic problems. The message: get a Jolly Green cranked.

"It'll probably be nothing," US Air Force Staff Sergeant Doug Wilson said over his shoulder as he ran to his camouflaged rescue chopper. "We get these all the time. Ninety percent of them are false alarms." Moments later the five-man crew got the word: the Phantom made it home okay; turn off the engine.

In late July 1972, I was standing by with the men of the Thirty-Seventh Aerospace and Recovery Squadron who flew HH-53 Super Jolly Green Giant helicopters. The unit had rescued 17 downed airmen in the previous two months and pulled 129 American troops out of Quang Tri City on May 1 when it fell to the Communists.

The big, dual-rotor, slow-moving, vulnerable aircraft were escorted by A-1 Sandy planes, which shot up landing zones with machine-gun fire. OV-10 Bronco light observation planes popped smoke to mark the spot. And on missions north of the DMZ, F-4s tagged along as insurance against missile-firing Soviet MIGs.

The Jolly Green crewmen I spoke to told me they relished their role. "We mean a lot to the pilots," said Captain Dave Mullenix, who commanded the first Jolly Green that flew into Quang Tri to rescue US troops. "They know they can stick their necks out, and if they get shot down, we'll go in and get them. We'll do everything we can to get them out, even if it takes a couple of days."

The Thirty-Seventh lost one helicopter and a five-man crew between March 30 and July 30, 1972. The Jolly Green was hovering over two downed fliers who were surrounded by an estimated NVA division west of Dong Ha and just south of the DMZ on April 6.

"Shot up, yes," Sergeant John Stephens said. "Go down, no. We've taken hits beaucoup times, but it takes a lot to knock one of these big birds down."

Stephens was a member of the air force's elite, three-hundred-man pararescue force. There were two PJs—short for parajumpers—aboard every Jolly Green with the pilot, co-pilot, and flight engineer to assist in making rescues. They were heavily armed and often waded into dense jungle searching for injured fliers.

Stephens and his boss, Master Sergeant George Schipper, were involved in a rescue where a VNAF chopper had gone down west of Hue, pinning crew members underneath it. Stephens and Schipper were put on the ground and scrambled through bamboo only to find three dead men. "We could see the bad guys coming up on the other side of the hill," Stephens said. "We just got out of there in time. That's one of the things about being on the ground: you never know what to expect."

NIGHTHAWK

Da Nang was a beautiful city at night. From 2,500 feet above, in a windswept helicopter, the twinkling lights reminded me of home, where all was calm and safe. But sometimes, the Da Nang nights were not so beautiful. They were interrupted by the thunderous impact of Communist-fired rockets. The shellings supplied the city the nickname "Rocket City."

From the middle of May 1972 through mid-July, when I was assigned to look for stories on the 7,500 American army troops and airmen stationed in South Vietnam's second-largest city, we all slept a little easier because the amount of shellings decreased. Part of the reason for that was patrols by Nighthawk, a combined army-air force mission that consisted of two UH-1H army helicopters and an air force AC-119 Stinger gunship. The aircraft scanned the area south of Da Nang from dusk until dawn and had clearance to destroy anything that moved outside of villages. A Vietnamese interpreter rode with the helicopters to prevent friendlies from being shot up.

"We've stopped between 60 and 75 percent of the planned attacks from coming in," said Lieutenant Colonel Tom A. Teal, commander of the Eighteenth Special Operations Squad. "Captured documents showed that the enemy was ordered to put maximum pressure on this base. It was supposed to be 'obliterated.' But they haven't been able to do it. And when we do get rockets [the last shelling was three weeks before I arrived on July 8], we don't get as many as we used to."

The choppers were provided by either Delta Troop, Seventeenth Cavalry, or F Troop, Eighth Cavalry, both based at Marble Mountain Army Air Base outside Da Nang. One low bird flying at treetop level was equipped with a high-powered xenon searchlight, a minigun, and a machine gun. The other chopper, the high bird, popped magnesium flares and was the rescue ship in the event the low bird was shot down.

When a low bird took fire, which it often did, or spotted Communists setting up rockets, it opened up on them and then moved off, and then the Stinger moved in to use its powerful guns on the site. The Stinger was equipped with infrared sensing devices that picked up enemy troop movement and directed the choppers to it. Several alternating Stingers stayed up all night, every night. The helicopters varied the sites and times at which they flew, each flying three missions a night and hoping to catch the VC and NVA off guard.

On the night of July 13, 1972, the Nighthawk mission engaged Communists five miles south of Da Nang. At ten o'clock, the low bird spotted a Communist soldier in a blue uniform under a tree. The crewmen began firing at the individual, and other Communists began running in all directions, some shooting at the chopper. The low bird killed thirteen Communists and destroyed about two dozen 122 mm rockets, which exploded in flames. Then they called in the Stinger.

The airplane's guns killed thirteen more enemy troops, and its fire resulted in ten secondary explosions. South Vietnamese troops later moved in on four armored personnel carriers and captured two dozen more rockets, killed five more Communists, and captured five others. "We spoiled their little party that night," a US Army officer said. The chopper and Stinger crews on the operation were presented with Vietnamese Crosses of Gallantry.

On another mission, there was a report of a platoon-size enemy force (about forty troops) about six miles south of Da Nang. Since the range of a Soviet-built 122 mm rocket was six miles—eleven miles if it had a booster—those troops were within range of the city, whose population was swollen by an influx of refugees to five hundred thousand.

At about 2:40 a.m., the low bird took fire from two huts outside a tiny village. The high bird, which I was invited to fly in for the story, popped flares, illuminating the area. The low bird's machine gun rat-tat-tatted into the wooden frames that probably concealed fortified bunkers. There was no more fire at the chopper. I couldn't see much from the high bird, but I took the crew's word for it: Da Nang slept peacefully. There was no incoming that night.

PART IV

SOUTH VIETNAMESE AND SOUTH KOREAN UNITS

'KIT CARSONS'

The GIs called him "Smiley," and it was easy to see why. When Nguyen Van Lau, Kit Carson scout extraordinaire, cracked a smile, his gold front teeth glittered in the sun. But Lau was not smiling a lot in late March 1972. He realized that the Second Battalion, Eighth Cavalry, Third Brigade, First Cavalry Division, would soon stand down along with the other three battalions of troops stationed east of Saigon.

"When GI go home," Smiley said during a patrol with Charlie Company, "maybe work for ARVN. But not so good as now. GIs have beaucoup everything—food, clothes, ammo. ARVNs have maybe *tee tee* [a small amount]."

Lau, twenty-nine, a former Vietcong mail carrier who *chieu hoied* (surrendered) in 1967, was one of about 150 Kit Carsons (KC) employed by the cav., which had as many as 300 KCs before Vietnamization. To keep him and others working after American infantrymen left, a thirty-man platoon of the best scouts was formed. It was to have been supervised by Lieutenant Michael Jones, twenty-four, of Dallas, the platoon leader; Staff Sergeant Richard L. Cramer, twenty-five, of Coloma, Michigan; and radio telephone operator Specialist Fourth Class Roy Holland, twenty, of Portland, Oregon.

"It would be a shame not to use these highly trained scouts," said Major Mitchell Leeds, who had come up with the idea for the Kit Carson platoon. "We're going to run these men through ARVN airborne training, and we feel they'll be a big asset to the Vietnamese later."

Smiley said, "I'd like to try it." He said he had worked with American units since September 1968. According to Charlie Company's commanding officer Captain Leonard T. Hale, Lau was one of the best scouts in the

143

brigade. "I wouldn't trade him for anybody," Hale said. "I've only got a few old-timers in my company, so I rely on Smiley more than ever. I break in all my point teams with him. He squares them away on how to read trotters [trails] and find dudes in the jungle." The troops were called "Kit Carsons" after the famous American mountain man, wilderness guide, and army scout who helped open up the American West.

The KCs made eighteen to thirty dollars a month and were paid by the Americans. According to Captain Chesley Durgin, who handled their administrative affairs, 75 percent of them were said to be former Vietcong, 20 percent former North Vietnamese Army regulars, and 5 percent former Cambodian soldiers. The scouts were recruited by Durgin from chieu hoi detention centers around the country.

"They are very hungry and very poor when they fight for the Communists," said Sergeant First Class Nyugen Tien Binh, twenty-four, an ARVN interpreter at Fire Base Melanie. "When they're sick, there's no medicine. They don't want to die in the jungle. Many cut off their fingers or toes so they'll be left behind and can give themselves up to GIs."

Leeds said twenty Kit Carsons were up for awards for valor. Le Van Dinh, a battalion chief scout, was given a Silver Star by President Richard Nixon. Leeds said that during his tour, there was only one Kit Carson who returned to the Communists. "When a man becomes a Kit Carson," said Ly Menh Ngoan, twenty-eight, another battalion chief scout, "he's not going to go back. He's had enough of everything. We come to love the GIs as brothers. When we are on an operation and one of them gets wounded, it's just like somebody in our family getting hurt."

Some Kit Carsons tried to go home and resume lives as farmers, but after they left American employ, they were eligible to be drafted by the ARVN. Most preferred not to work for the South Vietnamese, who viewed them with suspicion because of their former association with Communists.

Lam Tuc, twenty-one, was training to be a member of the all-KC platoon, which was scheduled to begin patrols in April 1972. He had worked as a KC for three and a half years, most recently with the Second Squad, Eleventh Armored Cavalry, which stood down in March. "I've never jumped out of a plane," he said, "but if they tell me to jump, I'll jump. I don't like being in the rear. When the cav. pulls out, I'll either work for the ARVNs or go back home to Loc Ninh and be a farmer. If they draft me, they draft me. No sweat. Fighting is what I do best."

Chau Sam Uon, twenty-one, a Cambodian, said he had worked for GIs since October 1968. "I'm going to stay in the army until the war is over," he said. "We'll be doing the same things in the bush the GIs were. If I have to work for the ARVN, I will, but it won't be the same. With the GIs, you get resupplied every few days."

Uon said Communists kidnapped his mother in 1969 because they needed someone to cook for them in the field. He got the news when he returned to Lai Khe after a patrol with the First Infantry Division. "I've got a score to settle," he said. "I'm gonna fight until the end. The parachute training doesn't bother me. The only bad thing would be if it doesn't open."

Nguyen Van Chuc, thirty-two, said he chieu hoied after seven years of fighting for the Vietcong, in 1969. He said he was scared by B-52 bombers that pounded a VC area of operations eighty miles north of Saigon. He said the reason he wanted to make it into the all-KC platoon was that his family was at Lai Thieu, fifty-five miles north of Bien Hoa, and if he went home and tried to be a farmer, he figured the ARVN would draft him and send him to the northern part of the country, away from his family.

Another trainee, Nguyen Dac Cau, twenty-four, said he had worked for five years with the Eighty-Second Airborne Division, the Marine Corps, the Third Division, the Fifth Division, and the 101st Airborne Division, with whom he had been a chief scout until it stood down in Hue in early 1972. Cau said he made 12,500 piasters or about thirty dollars a month with the 101st. He hoped to get a job with the cav. "But for 7,500 p. I would quit very quickly," he said. "An ARVN PFC [private first class] makes 15,000 a month. This is a great idea forming an all-KC platoon, but they should give us a raise, don't you think?"

Abandoning Fire
Base Charlie

The Dak Poko River snakes through Kontum Province in the mountainous Central Highlands, bending at Dak To and flowing southeast of what the American advisers called "Rocket Ridge," a fifteen-mile-long barrier of jagged, forested cliffs guarding the approach to Kontum City (population thirty thousand in 1972).

When I visited the area in mid-April 1972, I was told that ARVN soldiers had found diaries on the bodies of NVA troops whose opening page read, "The Poko River must rage away to sweep the enemy from the Highlands and liberate it." But according to the advisers I interviewed, a natural disaster is about the only way the Communists could break through a series of seven base camps on the ridge and sweep into Kontum.

On April 14, the South Vietnamese abandoned Fire Base Charlie on the ridge in the face of a massive human wave assault by elements of the Sixty-Fourth and Forty-Eighth NVA Divisions. An adviser estimated a thousand Communists died in the engagement. Another adviser told me losing Charlie was not a crushing defeat for the ARVN because "The ridge is still ours. And they're not going to haul any tanks along that road near Charlie as long as we keep the other bases."

The Communist forces, estimated at thirty thousand, were well supplied from what they called their Base Camp 609 in the area where the borders of South Vietnam, Cambodia, and Laos met. "The prisoners we catch seem healthy," the adviser said, "and they're not short on artillery. They get enough supplies to do the job."

A South Vietnamese officer said, "The airborne troops at Charlie suffered heavy losses in Cambodia, and when they arrived here in March, they were not at full strength and were fighting under very poor conditions. They really took a beating at Charlie. I cried when I saw the faces of the wounded at the airfield when they were brought in for treatment."

Charlie had withstood two previous Communist assaults, repelling one on April 8 with the aid of VNAF and US Air Force fighter-bombers. Two days later, about 350 Communists died in close fighting in another attack. "I think those two NVA regiments were seeking revenge for the heavy losses they suffered in the previous attacks," the ARVN officer said.

Why did the Communists pick Charlie? "They had to pick one of them," a US adviser told me. "It wasn't a citadel ... but it did fill a gap, blocking a road, and was technically sound. You want to fight the war as far from home as you can, and the ridge dominated the whole valley [northeast of Kontum]. You control the ridge, you control the road into the valley. And we've still got the ridge."

An ARVN officer told me field commanders believed they had the ability to defend Kontum City but said the Central Highlands always had been a vulnerable area. US advisers said they felt the NVA goal was to raise their flag over Kontum to demonstrate they could take a provincial capital. The adviser said he believed the NVA could not do that "unless they've got more people in the area than we think they have. I think the ARVN is going to see a lot harder combat in this military region, but I'm confident they can hold." As it turned out, the city did hold.

CAPTAIN LE VAN PHUC, MAN IN THE MIDDLE

"I don't know, Smith," the little bald-headed South Vietnamese captain told me. "I seem to be—how do you say?—the man in the middle. I try to do the best I can to help the foreign correspondents, and the Vietnamese journalists criticize me. They sit at their desks in Saigon and expect me to give them all the facts before I give them do you. Then they write in their newspapers, 'Our correspondent in the field reports from Pleiku …'

"It is I, Captain Phuc. I am their correspondent in the field. They don't know what the field is. And if I don't help the foreigners, then *they* criticize me for not being fair. They say every journalist should be treated equally."

Captain Phuc, who I think was in his early forties, was the II Corps ARVN information officer whom I dealt with during my many visits to Pleiku in the Central Highlands in 1972. All my friends in the press corps agreed that Phuc was the best information officer in Vietnam. He made mistakes. His sources sometimes were erroneous. But he tried to get you the news. He'd give you the official war news at his daily 5:30 p.m. briefing, and after he'd finished reading the notes typed for him at headquarters, many times he would say, "Now, gentlemen, not as a spokesman but in the nature of a heart-to-heart talk …" And he would provide some useful tidbits of information about battlefield action.

DELTA'S SPORADIC WAR

I walked through the streets of the bustling Mekong Delta city of Can Tho (population 160,000) wearing a helmet and flak vest, and the shopkeepers looked at me and laughed. In late May 1972, the Delta region (IV Corps) was the only one of South Vietnam's four military regions that had not erupted into flames during the Communists' Easter Offensive.

For most of the almost seven million residents of the country's most populous area, life went on as usual. None of the major population centers was threatened. But there was another kind of war in the Delta—not a conventional war with tanks, heavy guns, and Stinger missiles but a guerilla struggle of midnight sapper raids and shellings.

"The enemy has had limited success in a few areas," a high-ranking American official said when I visited. "He was trying to spoil our pacification program and keep ARVN units tied down here so they couldn't be used as reinforcements [up north]. But we've been holding our own. We haven't lost a provincial capital yet or a district capital."

The high point of Communist activity in the Delta came on April 6–7, the official said, coincident with their drive across the Demilitarized Zone in the far north, with 140 enemy-initiated skirmishes in the Delta's sixteen provinces. In the days before my arrival, the number of clashes was about twenty a day and few involved large forces.

After Major General Ngo Quang Troung was rushed from the Delta to I Corps following the fall of Quang Tri, Major General Nguyen Vinh Nghi, forty-two, former commander of the ARVN Twenty-First Division, was appointed IV Corps commander on May 3. Soon after he assumed command, Nghi began removing Popular Forces (PF) and Regional Forces (RF) militiamen from the more remote and less strategic of the more than five thousand government outposts in the Delta. A US source said about a hundred bases, most manned by only a squad of soldiers, were abandoned or overrun.

Nghi also inserted regular ARVN troops into areas infested with NVA regulars and made his Rangers patrolling the Cambodian border more mobile. The results by the time I arrived had been good. According to Nghi, almost 7,500 Communists had been killed, and nearly a thousand weapons had been captured in the first three weeks of May. He termed his own losses as "less than a thousand" men.

According to Nghi, there were forty-six thousand Communist soldiers in the Delta or just across the Cambodian border. Arrayed against them were two ARVN divisions, the Seventh and the Ninth, twelve battalions of Rangers, more than two hundred thousand PF and RF militiamen, and two hundred thousand People's Self-Defense Forces (PSDF). There were three main areas of concern in the Delta: Chuong Thien Province, the Ha Tien region, and the Parrot's Beak area.

Chuong Thien Province was just east of the U Minh Forest and west of Can Tho. American sources told me two NVA regiments began moving out of the U Minh in early May, hoping to seize the provincial capital of Vi Thanh and use it as a springboard to other operations in the Delta. But in a series of heated battles, American sources said, the NVA were driven off with heavy casualties.

The Ha Tien region was in the extreme west section of the Delta near the Cambodian border. An ARVN spokesman said in recent operations there and in adjacent Chau Doc Province, almost 300 Communists were killed while government troop deaths were put at 45 killed, 228 wounded.

The other hot spot was where the provinces of Kien Phong, Kien Tuong, and Dinh Tuong met, about fifty miles southwest of Saigon. According to a US military source, 1,000 NVA regulars from the Parrot's Beak region of Cambodia moved south in early April to join 2,500 NVA and VC troops already operating from a forested base camp. In a dozen major clashes between April 7 and May 24, I was told 203 Communists were killed and government losses were negligible. The source said 766 enemy had been killed in Dinh Tuong Province since the beginning of April and government losses were 132 killed, 389 wounded.

In June 1968, just after the Communist Tet Offensive, Civilian Operations and Revolutionary Development Support (CORDS) officials said 2,106 of the Delta's more than 4,000 hamlets were controlled by the Communists and 984 were contested. Four years later, according to the Hamlet Evaluation System and CORDS figures, about three-quarters of the Delta's districts were controlled by the government, and less than 1 percent of all hamlets in the Delta were rated as Communist-controlled. (CORDS was a joint pacification program of the Americans and South Vietnamese; its aim was to gain support from its rural population for the South Vietnamese government.)

CLOSE TO THE ACTION

I took more chances, flying and driving closer to the action, in May, June, and July of 1972 as the Easter Offensive went on. My girlfriend had written me a Dear Jim letter saying she'd met somebody at Fordham University and wouldn't be waiting for me, so I figured "What the heck?" In late May, UPI stringer Matt Franjola (whom I always thought was a CIA spook) and I followed an ARVN patrol up Highway 14 near Kontum. We meandered off onto a winding dirt road through tall grass, filled our canteens at an ARVN water truck, and snapped photos as we went. We walked calmly into a bivouac site and watched the ARVN Fifty-Third Regiment soldiers dig foxholes, eat C rations, and fool with their weapons.

"You see those two tall trees there," a South Vietnamese officer told me in perfect English. "Well, there's a battalion of NVA thirty meters behind them. And over there, to the east, are twenty or thirty NVA bodies. Don't go over there. They stink very badly. We killed them a few days ago."

As he spoke, 105 mm artillery rounds whistled over our heads and impacted like rolling thunder near the suspected Communist troop location. "We tried to move ahead yesterday," the officer said, "but took heavy fire and had to move back. Today, we're staying put and hitting them with artillery." The regimental commander, Lieutenant Colonel Phung Van Quang, said his men had killed sixty NVA troops on consecutive nights when a tank-spearheaded attack on Kontum failed. He said he expected another attack shortly. "But," he said, pointing to his field map, "last night we had a B-52 strike here, here, and here. We think we destroyed their main elements. We just can't figure out exactly where they are."

Kontum was taking sporadic mortar and rocket fire. But in the MACV compound, a half-dozen GIs played cards on the hoods of their jeeps, equipped with TOW antitank missiles, and waited for a call to action. From my standpoint, it was good to see the South Vietnamese seemingly in control of the situation and the Americans not in harm's way.

OPTIMISM REIGNS

Just outside Cheo Reo, a Central Highlands city of tin-roofed shacks and grass huts, stood what Lieutenant Colonel Nguyen Van Nghiem hoped one day would be Phu Bon Province headquarters. The empty building sat in late June 1972 in the corner of a huge, dusty, plowed rectangle crisscrossed by neat dirt roads.

"All I need is peace," said Nghiem, the province chief. "Then we can develop. We must worry about security now. But someday Cheo Reo will be a model city for all of Vietnam."

Before Nghiem could move into his model city and before other buildings could sprout up around the headquarters, local Communist forces had to be eliminated. Nghiem knew that would be a long, hard struggle, made more difficult by the fact there were no regular ARVN soldiers in the landlocked little province of seventy thousand people, 84 percent of whom were said to be semiprimitive Montagnards.

Regional Forces and Popular Forces militiamen, about six thousand of them, defended the province. They were hard-pressed during the Easter Offensive as NVA troops filtered through Phu Bon on their way to base areas in coastal Binh Dinh and Phu Yen Provinces and Vietcong guerrillas increased their terrorist activity.

The RF and PF soldiers fought well, Nghiem's American advisers told me. One example came on June 14, 1972. Communists had occupied the hamlet of Ban Biech, about twenty-one miles southwest of Cheo Reo, the previous evening. The advisers said Nghiem assembled five companies of militiamen for a counterattack. In fighting that they said lasted from six thirty in the morning until midnight, the militiamen killed twenty-nine enemy and drove the VC out of the hamlet. The advisers said the militia lost three men killed and sixteen wounded.

"We don't need regular troops," Nghiem said. "It is more important to have them elsewhere. Our soldiers here fight well. I have requested twenty medals for the men in that battle and asked that two of my captains be promoted. We are not afraid of the NVA. On March 29, my men surrounded a battalion of them heading to Phu Yen, killed eighty-three and forced them to leave Phu Bon sooner than they expected."

The senior US adviser in the province, Lieutenant Colonel R. F. Spinks, forty, of Columbia, South Carolina, said the Communists' objective in Phu Bon was to destroy the government's pacification program. "He [VC] was successful in five hamlets in early April," Spinks said, "but the GVN [Government of Vietnam] was back in there two weeks later. We gathered up the 4,400 people involved, moved them out of the hamlet, went in and killed the VC, and then let the people come back in."

He added, "We don't make TV like Kontum and Pleiku, but ours is a continuous, small-level fight every day. No massive invasions, just hard fighting every day. We don't get any B-52s, because there are other priorities. We had tac. air the other day, but it was diverted to Kontum. All we have is the militia, and these kids have done well."

Communists had closed Highway 7B running east from Cheo Reo (population fifteen thousand) to Tuy Hoa, so goods and arms were being transported from the seaport of Qui Nhon west to Pleiku via Highway 19 and then southeast about fifty miles over bumpy dirt roads to Cheo Reo. "The potential here is unlimited," Spinks said. "Cheo Reo is in a fertile valley. We've got mountains all around us, but we've got good land here."

"Right now," he continued, "the people live for themselves. They just grow enough rice and raise enough livestock to feed themselves. But we'll have big farms and plantations eventually. The Delta has all this miracle rice. We just planted our first shoots of it the other day. The Montagnards have been set in their ways for hundreds of years. It's a long process to bring about any significant changes."

During the previous year, with money from Saigon, Nghiem built the province's first dam in Phu Tuc District. A second dam was under construction; its cost was $175,000, about six times that of the first, and Nghiem said it would irrigate six hundred thousand acres of land. Other projects in the province involved building roads, improving sanitation, rebuilding homes, and constructing schools. Nghiem said sixteen thousand Montagnard children in the province were attending school, compared with three thousand in 1966. Several hundred attended a recently built agricultural school.

"We build a dam each year," he said, "build one school here and one there. We will be a rich province someday. We're not developed yet, but the day is coming."

THE BROWNS

Walking down the flight line at Lai Khe one afternoon in late June 1972, I saw some heavily armed South Vietnamese soldiers in brown camouflaged fatigues lounging in the shade under some helicopters. I decided to talk to the Americans who were reading books and magazines nearby and found out that the Vietnamese were a twenty-two-man unit called "Browns" who worked and lived with the men of F Troop, Ninth Cavalry, in Bien Hoa. The ARVNs were experts at rigging downed helicopters for extraction by huge twin-rotor Chinooks.

"I've worked extensively with Vietnamese units here," said Sergeant Bruce Barney, twenty-five, of Wyandanch, New York, an adviser to the group who said he had spent more than three years in-country. "I'd say these guys are the best I've seen. They're a cross section of volunteers from the best units the government has. Their mission is to rescue the aircraft, not engage the enemy, but let me tell you that if they get into contact, they won't have any problems."

The Vietnamese platoon leader was Second Lieutenant Tran Van Ra, twenty-two, who said he'd been a Ranger for the four years he had been in the army. "This is my country," he said, "and I want to go out and kill NVA and do all I can to end the war." Ra said his men had killed about twenty Communists in the fourteen months they had worked with US helicopter recovery teams. He said none of his men had been killed or wounded. "My men are very good, better than the NVA," he said.

An American door gunner, who did not want his name used, said of the Browns, "They don't understand much English, but you tell them, 'Do here,' [simulating a jump] and they know that you mean rappel." When a Brown rappelled, he lowered himself by rope from a hovering chopper into dense jungle at a crash site. Barney said, "Each of them has a job when they go in. They set up their security around the bird, get that nylon sling around it, and the whole thing only lasts a few minutes. They live with us, and they're just like part of the family. Everybody respects them because they know how good they are. They're always ready to jump when they get the word."

"WE ARE HERE EVERY
DAY" (VNAF)

It was lunchtime on July 1, 1972, in Lai Khe, and several VNAF helicopter pilots were relaxing inside their aircraft. One read a few lines from a paperback book out loud, and everybody laughed. While the well-groomed officers in neat zip-up flight suits chatted, their door gunners, wearing camouflaged boonie bats, tinkered with their M60 machine guns.

"Where are the Americans today?" one aircraft commander asked me. I told him American choppers were being used elsewhere and wouldn't be flying that day into the previously besieged provincial capital of An Loc, some thirty miles north. "They're lucky," the officer said. "We are here every day. We've flown every day since the offensive started. You come back tomorrow, and we'll still be sitting right here."

A couple of dozen VNAF UH-1H Hueys were on standby daily at Lai Khe. They flew resupply, troop lift, medevac, and rescue missions around An Loc, which was still being harassed by pockets of Communist troops. The VNAF crews realized that if they were shot down and landed in a Red troop concentration, they would probably not be taken prisoner as American fliers usually were. "If they get to us," an officer said, "they will kill us. Right away."

US sources told me that seven VNAF birds had been shot down in the previous week but all their crewmen had been rescued. "We have strict orders," an officer said, "that if anybody goes down, the others immediately go down to cover him and get his crew out."

Nevertheless, one Vietnamese Chinook flier carried no ammunition on his pistol belt, only the six rounds in the chamber of his weapon. "That's all I need," he said. "If they shoot me down, I will kill myself."

"I think that guy was only joking," a Huey crewman said. "Most of us will try our best to escape. And we will fight as much as we can to stay alive."

The gunships were standard Hueys equipped with Cobra-type rocket pods and miniguns. "I think it would be better if we had our own Cobras," an officer said, noting that the VNAF had no Cobra gunships in its inventory at that time. "We could give our men better cover and have more firepower. If we ever get Cobras, I'd like to fly them."

One officer who had been born in a village near Dong Hoi in North Vietnam said one of his gunners had been injured the previous week when he'd been hit by .37-caliber antiaircraft artillery fire at four thousand feet. "They can hit us at any time," he said. "They shoot antiaircraft guns and SA-7 missiles. If I ever get hit by a missile, I won't know what to do."

"I hope I make it through until this An Loc fighting is over," the pilot added. "Every day, we receive sad news that somebody is shot down. I just want to fly safely and not get killed myself. Two crews have gone down, but nobody was hurt. They were lucky. Maybe next time we won't be so lucky."

The VNA choppers were not used exclusively to provide low-level fire support for troops in combat. Tactical airstrikes and B-52s did most of the damage as the ARVNs broke the siege at An Loc and were battling to reopen Highway 13. But the choppers braved enemy fire daily to extract troops, fly combat assaults, drop supplies, and pick up the wounded. The choppers were based at Bien Hoa, fifteen miles south of Lai Khe, and staged out of Lai Khe.

"We know the Americans call it 'Indian Country' up there," the Vietnamese officer said. "That's what it is. The VC are still shooting at us." Just then, the men got the word to start cranking: another mission over An Loc. "Excuse me, please," a pilot said, lacing up his boots and zipping up his flight suit. "I'll see you again."

THE ROKS

In July 1972, I visited the Republic of Korea (ROK) base at Qui Nhon on the central coast, where I was assisted by South Korean Sergeant Yoon Seung Joong in reporting and writing an article that *Stars and Stripes* did not run; I wasn't given a reason why and didn't ask for one. I offered it to *Newsday*, and it passed too. It's ironic because the ROKs treated me like a dignitary and gave me a plaque commemorating my visit, something I never got from my own army.

At the time, President Nixon had announced that US troop strength would drop to thirty-nine thousand by September 1. It appeared likely that the thirty-seven thousand ROKs left in-country would be going home as well. But until they got the word, two ROK divisions continued to patrol a section of the coast. Here are excerpts from the article.

"We will stay here and accomplish our mission first," Major General Yun Hung Jyong told me in Saigon, "then worry about going home. And when we do return, we will do so with great honor." At the time, only eleven thousand ROK troops had been withdrawn since their peak strength of forty-eight thousand in 1967. Those troops, including the elite Blue Dragon Marine Brigade, were pulled out between December 1971 and March 1972. "Some people in our country—minority political parties and newspapers—talk about pulling out," Yun said, "but we don't care about such talk. If there are enemy out there, we will meet them and destroy them and not avoid battle ... We will help the Vietnamese by keeping our area secure."

South Korean forces arrived in Vietnam in 1965 and were assigned to secure a populous strip of the central coast from Cam Ranh Bay north to Qui Nhon. Some 870,000 people lived in the ROK-controlled area, or

5 percent of South Vietnam's people. Their mission was critical. "If there were no Korean forces in this area," Yun said, "the enemy could take Qui Nhon, Nha Trang, cut Highway 1, cut Highway 19, and Vietnam would be divided into two parts."

According to figures from ROK command in Saigon, the ROKs had killed 40,182 Communists in the war through June 30, 1972, while suffering 3,673 men killed and 8,121 wounded. They hurt the enemy so badly, captured documents revealed, that the Communists were ordered to avoid contact with them. "The only time they can get contact is when they [ROKs] surround them," said Lieutenant Colonel Carthel L. Sands, forty-one, Checotah, Oklahoma, senior liaison officer to the Tiger Division based outside of Qui Nhon. "There are three thousand NVA and VC between here and Phu My [thirty miles northwest], and they avoid the Koreans like the plague."

Sands had worked for nearly a year with the Tiger Division and said the unit's headquarters had received only five rounds of 122 mm rockets during that time. "No Korean base has been attacked up here by ground troops except for one raid of five sappers—and they killed all of them," Sands said. "There's never been any enemy inside a Korean compound. These soldiers have experienced tyranny firsthand and have come over here to help a fellow Asiatic country. They're here to kill Communists, and they've done a fine job. I'd like to command a battalion of them."

"I've seen Koreans sit on an ambush site for three days and never make a sound, never smoke a cigarette," said Lieutenant Colonel Thomas W. Wilkie, forty, of Michigan City, Indiana, liaison officer to the ROKs' Twenty-Sixth Regiment. "Their discipline, persistence, and aggressiveness are such that the NVA cannot compare with them." Sands said ROK troops taught camouflage techniques to South Vietnamese Regional Forces and Popular Forces ("Ruff-Puffs") militiamen. Binh Dinh, of which Qui Nhon was the capital, was the most populous and least secure of Vietnam's forty-four provinces with little more than two regiments of regular army troops, so it had to rely heavily on the ROKs and local militia. "One time last month," Sands said, "the ROKs were being used as a blocking force as RF troops went into a hamlet with camouflage on their helmets and uniforms like ROK troops wear. The VC thought they were Koreans and ran away into an open field. Vietnamese [helicopter] gunships just slaughtered them."

From March 30 to July 1, the Koreans fought only one major battle with the Communists, April 11–26, when ninety-seven Koreans died and 164 were wounded in a bloody clash to clear the Communists out of fortified positions in the An Khe Pass, forty miles west of Qui Nhon. ROK spokesmen said 705 enemy soldiers were killed by Tiger Division troops. The White Horse Division was based at Nha Trang and handled the southern portion of the area.

First Lieutenant Lee Kim Sun, twenty-six, from Seoul, was a platoon leader of a forty-man element assigned to guard a bridge from a bunkered minibase about twenty miles west of Qui Nhon. "We haven't had any contacts since we got here a week ago," he told me, "but if the enemy comes, we are ready for him. It is a great honor for me to be a part of the security force on such a key supply route. I will do my best there."

Like all the other ROK officers and most of the enlisted men, Lee volunteered for Vietnam. "I am young and ambitious," he said, "and I need combat experience so I can get promoted." One reason ROKs enjoyed serving in Vietnam was a subsidy the US government paid them. A first lieutenant would have made $85 a month in South Korea; he made $135 in Vietnam. A buck sergeant made $50 at home and $107 a month in Vietnam. "And the duty is easier here," a soldier told me. "It's harder working on the demilitarized zone in Korea. We have a hundred twenty miles of fortified positions, and you've got to be ready because you never know what the enemy will do. In Vietnam, the enemy doesn't even want to meet us. And when we do meet him, we can defeat him."

In the Tiger Division, every soldier below the rank of staff sergeant pulled three hours of guard duty every night and engaged in tae kwon do self-defense classes for an hour a day. "Why are the Koreans here?" Sergeant Woo In Kyoo said. "I am a sergeant, and this is beyond my knowledge. I was ordered to come here, and I did. I guess we came for the same reason US troops did—to help the South Vietnamese defend their freedom, just as many free world forces helped us defend our freedom in the Korean War."

"There are forty thousand Americans in Korea to help us," Lieutenant Colonel Tong Hwi, forty-one, of Kwang Choo City, said, "and we came to help the South Vietnamese. By helping them, we help Asia, and we help ourselves."

The ROKs, however, were viewed with suspicion by many Vietnamese civilians and with jealousy by ARVN soldiers. "Before," said a Korean secret agent in Qui Nhon, "the people didn't want anybody here—Koreans or Americans. But since the NVA attacked the South in April, they have changed. Now they greatly appreciate the fact that we are here. The ARVN are still a little jealous of us, though. We operate with the same equipment and facilities they do and get better results in terms of enemy killed and area pacified. They're jealous of the combat wage we get from Americans too. But what do they expect, to be paid for defending their own country?"

One criticism of the ROK system is that too much emphasis was placed on an individual commander. When a battalion leader was killed or wounded, sometimes a unit could become paralyzed. "During the Korean War, I had such an experience," Major General Yun said. "I lost a company commander, and his company didn't know what to do. The commander has a very strong influence on his men in our system. The second in command has very little influence. But I hear that is one reason why the ARVN lost Quang Tri. Some of their leaders were killed or evacuated, and soon, all the soldiers were withdrawing. So this is a problem not only of Korean forces. But we are working to overcome this. One thing about our system that is good is that we do not have any drug problem or any hippies. Our system is simple. A man is told to do something, and he does it."

General Yun said of the two Koreas, "Logically, a single place and a single people should be unified. But emotionally, we cannot do this. Kim Il Sung, the prime minister of North Korea, is a criminal. He dispatches assassination groups to Seoul, sends saboteurs to destroy our facilities, so I cannot believe anything he says."

US officials said South Koreans' hatred of North Korea motivated them to fight against the NVA and VC. "The young Korean soldier was not fighting in the Korean War," Sands said, "but their parents told them about it. It's something their people can never forget."

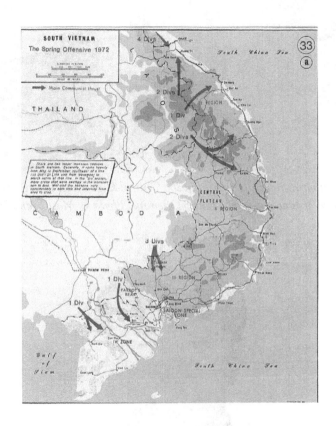

Map courtesy of The Department of History, United States Military Academy at West Point.

The author at Kontum Airfield in the Central Highlands, where he spent a lot of time during the Easter Offensive. Photo by Matt Franjola

The author's Stars and Stripes head shot. Stars and Stripes photo

The author, wide awake and ready for duty. Photo by Matt Franjola.

The author, looking foolish in a REMF headband. No credit.

An overview of Cam Ranh Bay Air Base, where the author spent the first five months of his tour. Photo by Jim Smith

The author between fellow clerks and barracks mates Red Irwin and Richard Ledford in Cam Ranh Bay. No credit.

The author, rear left, at a dinner with the Stars and Stripes staff. No credit.

The author relaxing on leave in Bangkok. No credit.

The author in khakis with girlfriend Loan. No credit.

The author between chopper flights in the field. Photo by Matt Franjola

Correspondents wait out a rocket attack in a bunker;
Peter Arnett is at right. Photo by Jim Smith

John Paul Vann, II Corps senior adviser, was killed in a helicopter crash June 9, 1972. Photo by Jim Smith

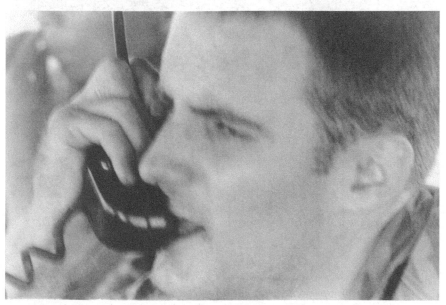

Former Army football star Lynn Moore calls in an airstrike. Photo by Jim Smith

U.S. advisers brief each other on the situation in the field. Photo by Jim Smith

Ly Tong Ba, who helped foil the Communist drive on Kontum. Photo by Jim Smith

*II Corps information officer Capt. Le Van Phuc, left,
respected by correspondents. Photo by Jim Smith*

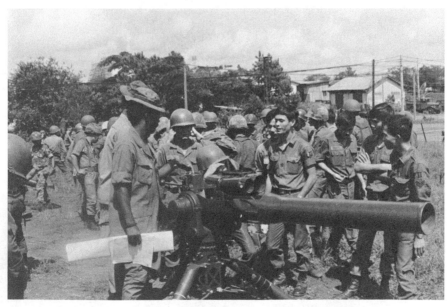

*U.S. advisers teach ARVN troops how to use tank-
killing TOW missiles. Photo by Jim Smith*

A familiar scene: Americans moving from one base to another as the U.S. presence dwindled. Photo by Jim Smith

A dead Vietcong troop near the perimeter of Fire Base 42 in the Highlands, where a friend of the author was killed. Photo by Jim Smith

*Anguish on the face of a refugee fleeing the Communist attacks
in the Central Highlands.. Photo by Jim Smith*

*A helicopter view of a U.S. ship rescuing two downed American airman
in the South China Sea off I Corps in July 1972. Photo by Jim Smith*

*An airstrike goes in just outside the wire of an American base
in the Central Highlands. Photo by Jim Smith*

*A wounded South Vietnamese troop is helped after being
medivaced from the field. Photo by Jim Smith*

*The author posing with a captured Russian tank in Kontum, just before
a rocket attack had him scrambling. Photo by Matt Franjola*

*Captured North Vietnamese tanks and weapons on
display in Kontum. Photo by Jim Smith*

South Vietnamese troops examine the damage after a rocket and mortar attack at Pleiku Air Base. Photo by Jim Smith

A Vietnamese officer huddles with American advisers during the Offensive. Photo by Jim Smith

A South Vietnamese radio operator smiles at a reporter while giving a situation report. Photo by Jim Smith

An American adviser comes home from the field. Photo by Jim Smith

SOLDIER OF FORTUNE
COMBAT VETERAN

INTERNATIONAL LOVER
WORLD TRAVELER

SgT James S. Faulkner
(SILVER DOLLAR)
UNITED STATES ARMY
VIET NAN
ORGANIZER OF REVOLUTIONS AND LARGE ORGIES

WARS FOUGHT
GOVERNMENTS RUN

O - DENS EMPTIED
VIRGINS CONVERTED

FIGHTER BY DAY LOVER BY NIGHT STONED ALL THE TIME

The card carried by Ranger Sgt. Jimmy Faulkner. No credit

THẺ BÁO CHÍ
PRESS CARD

Số I2I0   BC

VIỆT-NAM CỘNG HÒA
BỘ THÔNG TIN

THẺ BÁO CHÍ

TÊN JAMES R. SMITH

CƠ QUAN STARS_STRIPES

Trân trọng yêu cầu các giới hữu quyền
hành chánh, quân sự dành mọi dễ dàng cho
đương sự thi hành phận sự.

Saigon, ngày 22.6.1972

KT   Giám Đốc Nha Báo Chí
QUÂN-ĐỐC   O-CHI

VŨ-KHÁNH

*Stars and Stripes reporter Mark Treadup enjoys a
card game at our Saigon office. No credit*

*American troops stave off boredom at a base; the South Vietnamese
did the brunt of the fighting. Photos by Jim Smith*

Group shots of American troops relaxing in the rear. Photos by Jim Smith

PART V

VIETNAMESE PEOPLE

RICE WINE

I had a friend in Kontum named Bud Cavanagh. He was in his early sixties and an engineer for Pacific Architects and Engineers, a contacting firm. Cavanagh lived downtown with his common-law wife and several adopted little boys. We often met for drinks at the bar at the MACV compound. Bud always helped me out with story ideas. I checked in with him before I went anywhere in Kontum Province. I could get more information from him than from official sources.

One day, he invited me to his house, and two of his neighbors stopped in while we were talking. It was the last week of April 1972, just after Tan Canh had fallen. Kontum City was in a state of confusion. Refugees were streaming in from the northwest battleground. Kontum residents were fleeing to Pleiku, Saigon, or the coast. But I was relaxed. I wasn't going to believe Kontum would fall until I saw it. I was caught up in the arrogance of the Americans I wrote about.

Le Ba Luc, fifty-one, was born in Kontum and said he'd lived there most of his life. He said he was leaving for Saigon right away. "Things are very bad here," Luc said through an interpreter. "They've taken Tan Canh and Dak To easily, and they're on their way south. If I was sure that ARVN troops could stop them, I would stay. But I don't know if they can."

A former city chief, Luc and his wife of twenty-seven years were living in a three-room home made of concrete blocks with a tin roof. They drew rent from three nearby houses they owned. Luc said he knew a lot of other people also planning to flee. He said many of his friends with automobiles would have driven south already if Highway 14 to Pleiku hadn't been cut in several places.

"I know what the VC would do to us if we stay," Luc said. "When they were here before, they destroyed houses, power plants … everything they could. I heard that this time they have tanks. I don't have a military mind, but I know we must leave. The NVA wants to make a town of NVA [Communist provincial capital] either here or at An Loc or Quang Tri, so that all the world will know they control all over. We will leave as soon as we can."

Meanwhile, Nguyen Khiet, forty-four, the other neighbor, said he was born in Qui Nhon but had lived in Kontum since 1954. He said he was spending up to eighteen hours a day as a local leader of Popular Forces militiamen. He had been married twenty-six years and had twelve children, nine living at home.

"There is no way I will leave," Khiet said. "This is my home, and I will stay here. The biggest battle anywhere in Vietnam is coming right here. I think the ARVN and the American air force can stop the NVA before they reach Kontum. If we lose Kontum, we've lost the whole Highlands. We can't let that happen. You can't blame Luc for leaving. He's retired, old, rich … He has relatives in Saigon. And he's an administrator, not a fighting man. He wouldn't be of much help to us."

Khiet said one of his sons was fighting at Vo Dinh, a few miles north, with an armored cavalry unit. "We wouldn't leave while he is still fighting," Khiet said. "My family could probably get out, but they want to stay here with me. I will stay here if the NVA come right into town. If you don't believe me, just come back after they attack, and you'll see me fighting with my men, right here in the streets."

The next trip I made to Kontum, I asked Cavanagh about his two neighbors. He told me Luc had gotten an Air Vietnam flight out the day after I talked to him. And Khiet, the self-proclaimed patriot, left a few days later, a month before street fighting began in the city.

"I can't believe that," I said. "Khiet was supposed to be at the barricades."

"That was the rice wine talking," Cavanagh said. "Couldn't you smell it on his breath?"

"WE THINK THEY'RE DEAD"

Watching Vietnamese refugees flee the Kontum City area daily, I couldn't help but feel their pain. With the help of a translator, I interviewed some of them in May 1972. Mrs. Ngo Thi Bu was seven months pregnant. She fell several times on the road while fleeing from North Vietnamese Army troops who had captured Tan Canh Village. "I had to help her get up," Mrs. Nguyen Thi Hue told me. "We couldn't stop walking. We walked two days and most of one night to Vo Dinh [north of Kontum City]. We don't know where our husbands are. We think they're dead."

Mrs. Hue, thirty-one, whose husband worked for an American contractor, said she last had seen her husband a few days before she and the other women and children had fled Tan Canh. She figured her husband still had been inside the command post when it had been overrun. "The VC didn't kill any civilians or fire at them," she said. "But they took thirty or forty of the men prisoner and marched them away."

During the long walk to Vo Dinh, Mrs. Hue said, "Many small children died because they could not keep walking and had no food or water." She said the refugees kept moving because they were afraid of the Communists. She said she knew they were North Vietnamese because of the dialect they spoke. Once the women arrived at Vo Dinh, they were trucked to a refugee camp in Kontum City where I spoke to them.

Mrs. Bu, twenty-five, said her husband was a lieutenant with the ARVN Forty-Second Regiment stationed inside Tan Canh, and she feared he had been killed by the NVA. The only possessions the women had were the clothes they wore—blue shower shoes, black pants, and faded white blouses. "Why do they come?" Mrs. Bu said. "I don't know. Why don't they stay in the North? All we want is peace. Why don't they leave us alone?"

"I Can't Go Home"

"I no can go home anymore," little Hueng Yeng said. "If I go my village and VC see me, they kill me. They know I live with Americans. They know my hands have shake with GIs. They would cut them off."

Yeng, fourteen, was one of three Montagnards I met in Pleiku in early May 1972 who had done most of their growing up with Americans in Kontum City in the Central Highlands. The others were Lee, thirteen, and Lang, twenty, who gave no last names. The boys had been cared for during the previous year by Staff Sergeant Earl L. Hendershot, thirty-three, of Canton, Ohio, and had been evacuated from Kontum in the face of a Communist attack.

"They wouldn't even be accepted by their own people now," Hendershot said. "They've been around Americans too long. But GIs have taken good care of them over the years. They are good boys. They don't smoke, drink, or cuss. They've got good manners, and they do what they're told."

The dark-skinned boys had their own rooms in the MACV compound at Kontum and made themselves useful by cleaning up the after-hours club, traveling with Hendershot to Pleiku on PX runs, and doing other odd chores. They wore fatigues and carried carbines, and Hendershot said they were good marksmen. Lang went on several overnight patrols with US troops. The boys were soft-spoken, never seemed to be in the way, and were eager to find a way to help out.

Lee said he had spent three years in America with relatives of an American air force officer. When the officer had been killed in Vietnam in 1968, Lee had been deported. He said he had returned to his village of Mang Buk in northeastern Kontum Province and soon hooked up with an American advisory team. He had been cared for by Americans ever since.

"I happy to stay with advisers," Lee said. "VC kill my father, and I live with my mother for a while, but we have nothing. With Americans, I have everything."

Lang said he hoped to return to his village on the outskirts of Kontum City and rejoin his parents and be a rice farmer.

Hendershot enrolled Lee in elementary school in Pleiku and arranged for Yeng to begin classes at a military academy in Pleiku in June 1972. "Our people don't like us," Yeng said. "They don't want to play with us. But we don't care. We have American friends, and that is all we need."

NEWSPAPER PIONEER

On a visit to Can Tho in the Mekong Delta in early June 1972, I met Le Dinh Hai, publisher of the only one of South Vietnam's forty-three dailies that was being published outside of Saigon. The paper was called *Torch of the West*. Hai, its founder, copyeditor, layout man, advertising director, and sometimes reporter, said he had lost about $20,000 on the project since he opened for business four months before. He said he expected to lose $10,000 more before he would break even.

"I'm a rich man," he said, "but I can't go on losing money forever. Now I've got another problem. Seven of my typesetters are being drafted into the army next week. I may have to shut down for a while until I can train replacements for them."

Hai, fifty-four, said he was losing money because 60 percent of his papers were being exchanged by customers for higher-priced Saigon papers that arrived later in the morning. *Torch* was available for twenty piasters (about a nickel) at six in the morning every day except Monday. "The [vendors] are poor," he said. "When the late papers come in, they take my paper and ten more piasters and trade for a Saigon paper. I only get money for the total of papers they tell me they sell. I will accept their terms now, but later I will dictate my own. I will be very tenacious."

Hai said he also was losing money because he distributed free papers to establish a readership. He had seven delivery trucks, and one of them traveled from Can Tho to Saigon, sprinkling free papers on the way. Despite the handicaps, Hai said he had hired more than a hundred men and boys as deliverers. His paperboys wore basketball jersey sweatshirts with the paper's name printed on the front. Most of his employees were in their teens. He had seven reporters, all of them students, and stringers in all the Delta's sixteen provinces who called in nightly with war notes and feature stories.

"There are seven million readers in the Delta," he said, "and I hope to get twenty thousand or thirty thousand of them eventually if times are not hard and they have money."

Hai said he fled in 1954 from Hanoi, where he was born, after the French were defeated at Dien Bien Phu. "We [he and his wife had eight children] came with only the clothes on our backs," he said. A series of shrewd investments in the clothing industry and a travel agency, he said, enabled him to accumulate a fortune. He was a career journalist and published a weekly magazine while traveling all over Vietnam to write stories for several Saigon newspapers.

"Everybody knows me in Saigon," he said, "and they are prejudiced against what I am trying to do. Several years ago, some of my colleagues from France and America asked me why it was that Vietnam had no local newspapers. That's when I got the idea that I could start one. I invested a lot of money and did a lot of planning. If I succeed, I hope it will be the first of many local newspapers in Vietnam."

WAR BRIDES

I had a romantic relationship with a Vietnamese woman for the last five months of my tour. I considered marrying her and investigated the procedure for doing so. But when she gave me her passport, she turned out to be thirty-three years old, not twenty-three as she had told me. My friends laughed that she was trying to play me for a sucker. I was sad and relieved at the same time. I really wasn't ready for marriage anyway. So I put aside those thoughts and just enjoyed the sex and the comfort of living with her part-time in her two-room Saigon apartment.

I did, however, write a story, which appeared in *Newsday* on May 7, 1972, about how the army was stonewalling many GIs who were attempting to bring home war brides. "I've already paid close to a thousand dollars under the table," a GI on his fourth tour in Vietnam told me, "and if something goes wrong now and the paperwork doesn't go through, I'm going AWOL until it does. I love my girl, and I'm not going back to the world without her."

The soldier said he had been in-country fifty-four months and had known his fiancée for four years. He said he realized that when he went home this time, it would be for good, so he was starting to climb the tortuous cliffs placed in front of him by the army. The red tape deliberately made it tough for Americans to marry Vietnamese. The theory was that only the most serious would persevere.

From 1968 to 1972, there were nearly 1,500 military marriages. In 1971 alone, there were 560. Many more were expected before the last troops left. There were two ways for an American to bring a Vietnamese woman to the United States. The easiest was to obtain a K visa issued by the consular section of the American embassy. Under terms of that visa, the GI pledged to marry the woman within ninety days of returning to the states. If no marriage took place, she had to return to Vietnam. The advantages of that method were obvious. The woman would have a chance to meet the man's parents, see what America was like, and decide whether or not a marriage would work.

The alternative was in accordance with MACV directive 608-1: marrying first. This process took four to six months, but the government paid for the bride's plane fare to America if they married in Vietnam and her husband was at least an E-5 (buck sergeant). The directive applied to all US servicemen in Vietnam. Its announced intention was to "protect both parties from the possible disastrous effects of an impetuous marriage entered into without a full appreciation of its implications and obligations."

Going through channels, a serviceman first had to obtain permission to marry from his commanding officer. Then he was counseled by a chaplain and by a legal assistance officer. Then he had to apply to the US command for permission to marry. He had to provide birth certificates for himself and his bride-to-be. If either was under twenty-one, they needed a notarized statement of consent from a parent or legal guardian. The woman had to provide a chronological record of all her residences. In a turbulent country embroiled in a war, that was no easy matter. The woman also had to prove she had not been married before and get a certificate from the police that she had committed no crimes. She also had to obtain a certificate attesting to her good conduct from officials in the district in which she lived.

The soldier had to get a statement from his personnel officer proving that his records did not indicate a previous marriage or divorce. He had to agree to the terms of directive 608-1 and agree to support his wife. Applicants below the rank of E-4 (corporal) with fewer than four years' service had to list their assets. Both parties had to undergo a thorough physical examination, including x-rays. Then a packet containing all the above documentation was submitted to the command.

It usually took about ninety days for military intelligence to check the applications. If the couple checked out, they were given a letter of introduction to the consular section of the US embassy. Only then could the woman apply for a passport and visa. The red tape drove some GIs to take desperate risks. "I'm going to go through one of those agencies and get it through as soon as I can," a twenty-one-year-old private first class told me.

The GI said he was going to see Phan Van Ro, sixty, who owned a marriage license office on Cong Ly Street and knew all the places to apply grease. He charged $365 to arrange all the details of a marriage. There were a dozen such agencies in Saigon, but embassy officials said they were a waste of money. "Tell them to come to us," said Naran S. Ivanchakov, a vice consul. "We're swamped, but we'll help them."

Some GIs had problems going through normal channels. Specialist Sixth Class Jimmy Bennett, twenty-six, of West Memphis, Arkansas, said he had known his fiancée, Mai, twenty-two, for three years. The woman had worked as an interpreter for the army. "Every time I filled out the paperwork, I got transferred," Bennett said. "And then once they lost it all. So I said the heck with the army way. I decided to do it by K visa. It ran me 60,000 piasters, graft and all. But my girl's brother is a policeman, and we took him with us to the Ministry of Interior to help us push the paperwork through."

PART VI

CLOSE CALLS, INDISCRETIONS, AND UNCONFIRMED REPORTS

UNDER FIRE

I was under fire only twice during my tour. The first time was on the morning of May 25, 1972, when I was sitting in the Air Vietnam terminal at Pleiku Air Base with UPI stringer Matt Franjola, my best friend in the press corps.

Arthur Higbee, UPI's Vietnam bureau chief, was coming in from Saigon on a noon flight. Since I had nothing better to do, we drove down to pick Higbee up in a jeep we had been "watching" for an NBC correspondent who had left town. We had been waiting for a half hour when I heard something whistling overhead.

"Incoming!" Franjola yelled. "Get down!"

Booom! A rocket impacted about a hundred yards from us on the tarmac. We crouched behind a service counter, bracing ourselves against a wall, as Vietnamese soldiers, women, and children scrambled out of the concrete building and into bunkers outside. A second Soviet-made 122 mm rocket crashed like thunder into a VNAF chopper flight line. And a third.

"Here's your picture, man," Matt whispered. "The fear on the people's faces, the women clutching their children, the soldiers cowering in bunkers."

We went outside, but another rocket whistled overhead, and I dove behind a revetment, catching my fatigue trouser leg on some barbed wire. Across the airstrip, ARVNs in jeeps drove toward the impact area in case they were needed to fight a fire.

"Geez, look at that," Franjola said. "Here's your picture. I wish I brought my camera with me."

But by the time I untangled myself and stood up to take a shot, the truck had moved out of my view. I had nothing in the foreground, and the fragments of earth and concrete were drifting away. Snap, snap, then I ducked behind the revetment. Two photos, both bad.

"You're too slow, man," Franjola said. "You missed the picture. Geez, I wish I had my camera."

"Fuck you!" I shouted. "I guess I'm worried more about myself than about making page one."

"You'd never be on my team," Franjola said. "When the stuff starts to fly, *you've* got to fly."

The rockets had begun coming in at 10:40 a.m. We counted seven, two of them being duds. One struck near an ammo dump, another crashed into a supply shack, and one blew a hole ten feet across in a revetment in the middle of the VNAF chopper pad. Remarkably, the only damage to the chopper was some blown-out side-door windows.

"Here," Matt said, "shoot these guys checking out the hole. No, from over there. That's it. Come on; let's hurry up. They might be shooting some more in here."

I snapped the photos, picked up a piece of shrapnel, and put it in my pocket. I sent it home with my baggage and kept it as a war souvenir.

Walking down the street toward the mess hall after the shelling, an ARVN sergeant asked Franjola in Vietnamese what happened.

"A lot of incoming," Matt told him, "but I didn't have my camera."

The sergeant said something in Vietnamese, and Franjola laughed.

"What did he say, Matt?" I asked.

"He said I should have hit you over the head and taken yours. Maybe I should have."

The other close call I had came in mid-June 1972. It was a few days after the North Vietnamese troops that had penetrated Kontum City had been driven out. Franjola and I hitched a ride from Pleiku to Kontum. An occasional round of incoming rockets or artillery fire into ARVN positions showed that the Communists weren't far away. After getting briefed by our U.S. sources, Matt and I decided to stroll up the highway. Neither of us was armed. We never were. Matt had a canteen, a small knife, pistol belt, first aid pack. We both wore sweaty flak vests. I had my army helmet on. Matt preferred a boonie hat.

We walked a couple of hundred yards up highway 14, the two-lane asphalt highway that squirmed through the Central Highlands. ARVN soldiers on trucks waved to us as they headed toward the front. A couple of tanks and armored personnel carriers carrying troops rumbled by. I snapped a bunch of photos.

Matt pointed to a ditch where he said that he and a US adviser had been pinned down by NVA machine gun fire for more than an hour the previous week while I was slow-dancing with a Thai whore in a psychedelic nightclub in Bangkok on R&R. We followed the ARVNs to the east, taking a dusty foot path into high grass. The company commander there told us there was a "battalion" of NVA 200 meters away. We hoped not.

We watched as ARVN artillery pounded the suspected enemy position. Huge clouds of ugly, black smoke billowed and tons if earth flew, We were convinced the NVA actually were there when we heard the crackle of their AK-47s from the bushes. We decided to get out of there. But on the way back to the chopper pad we saw a captured Russian tank sitting in the middle of the South Vietnamese compound, its drab green hull turned brown by layers of caked mud.

I jumped up on it, handed Matt my camera, made a mean face and clenched my right fist as he took my picture. Then he gave me his camera, jumped up on the turret and I photographed him. Just then, I heard something whistle overhead."

"What the hell's that," I said, trying to focus on Matt.

"Incoming," he said. "Hurry up. Take the picture."

But I was too slow and too scared and didn't get a picture off before a 122-mm rocket slammed into the earth 50 yards away, just in front of a half-dozen US troopers who were operating a TOW missile system. I hit the ground, breaking my glasses at the nose bridge and damaging the lens on Matt's camera.

Another round whistled in, impacting 100 yards behind us as we crouched in the shadows of the tank. We ran into some bunkers with the ARVN troops and they laughed when they saw us scramble. A third round hit 50 yards to our right, damaging an old barracks building. A fourth hit short, just on the other side of the road. An ARVN made a sweeping motion with his hand, indicating the flight of the rocket. "Boooom!" he screamed into my ear. I jumped and everybody chuckled. But the barrage was over.

   We trotted down the road to the chopper pad and an hour later, we exchanged our sweat-soaked fatigues for bathing trunks and were swimming in the officers' club pool at Camp Holloway in Pleiku.

WHAT A DUNCE

After a couple of trips to the Highlands, where a real war was in progress, I decided to cool it and work around Saigon a while. One morning in late May or early June, I drove up to Lai Khe, thirty miles north of the capital, with my *Stars and Stripes* colleague Hal Drake and Paul Harrington, a *Stripes* reporter-photographer. They were a team based in Tokyo, who had been reassigned temporarily to do some war stories.

We stopped at the US advisers' headquarters and met some of the key officers. Drake and Harrington introduced themselves, and I told the officers who I was.

A crew-cut major said, "Hey, Smith, you work for Jimmy George down there, huh?"

"No, sir," I said, stupidly. "I work for myself."

It was one of my biggest mistakes in the seven months I worked for *Stars and Stripes*. It turned out that the major was our key source of tactical information in Lai Khe, and he'd served on a previous hitch in Vietnam with my editor in chief of the *Stripes* Saigon bureau, Captain James George. I had to make myself scarce for a month and hope that the major didn't torpedo me.

MISTAKEN IDENTITY

Another time, I flew up to Kontum with UPI stringer Matt Franjola and did a story on how the pressure was off up there. We spoke with the commander of the ARVN Twenty-Third Division, Brigadier General Ly Tong Ba. While we were in Kontum, we heard about the Cathay Pacific jetliner that had crashed on June 15 and decided to try to drive south to the crash site.

After breakfast, we were standing outside another general's office waiting for the rain to stop. He came bustling out to his official car, raincoat flapping in the breeze. "Hey, General," Franjola quipped, "where'd you steal that Aussie raincoat?"

"I didn't steal it," the general mumbled. "Bought it in Bangkok." And off he went. I barely took note of the incident. Matt and I tried to get to the crash site by jeep, but the closest we could get was six miles away. The next day, we flew there by chopper. I smelled the stench of death, saw bodies in body bags heaved onto a truck, talked to the Green Berets and their men guarding the area, and took some pictures. While the troops were flinging the body bags into the truck, they were whistling "Whistle While You Work." I'll never forget their casual attitude around death.

When I got back to Pleiku, I was informed that the general had passed the word down that he wanted me out of II Corps. He said I'd made some fresh remark to him that morning (I hadn't said a word) and that I was taking notes on who was entering and leaving his office. Although the misunderstanding later was cleared up, my immediate boss, Sergeant First Class Frank Castro, thought it best that I left. Matt and I flew back on a midnight cargo flight. I was shocked but pretty glad too, because I figured I'd spend the rest of my tour in Saigon and be able to see more of my girlfriend. But I was wrong. To keep me out of trouble, Castro sent me to the Delta.

"[FRIENDLIES] FIRED
AT US FOR KICKS"

I hitched down the road from II Corps headquarters to Camp Holloway in Pleiku for lunch one day and stopped in at the C Troop operations office. "Here's a story for you," an officer said. "Our troop commander was shot down the other day in a Loach and killed. We used our slicks [Hueys] to lift ARVN Blues [infantry] into the area where the fire came from. We put the little people on the ground, and they just sat there, refused to move out. They said they weren't going anywhere without an American adviser who could direct airstrikes for them. We went back at six o'clock, picked them up, and took them back to camp. Here we are, using men right and left for them, and they won't even go out and recover the body of somebody who died helping them. It makes me sick to my stomach."

The men of C Troop, based at An Son in coastal Binh Dinh Province, were moved to Pleiku in late February 1972 to combat an enemy offensive that was in the making. "We had six hours' warning," the lieutenant said. "They threw all our personal possessions aboard a couple of Chinooks and told us to move out. We don't know how long we'll be here, but we're pulling missions every day and finding little concentrations of enemy all over the place, closer to Pleiku than you'd think."

"But the ARVNs are really something else," another officer said. "One time recently, they fired at our lift birds that had just dropped them into a hot AO [area of operations]. Our Cobras wanted to go in and fire them up, and they would have if they hadn't gotten a direct order not to do it. This happens all the time. I guess these guys are so frustrated and tired of fighting that they've got to take it out on somebody. They fired at us for kicks. It really makes you wonder what this war is all about."

VC PSYOPS

One afternoon in April 1972 at the officers' club in Kontum, I was allowed to sit in on a classified briefing with the proviso that I didn't write anything about it for *Stars and Stripes*. A major in starched fatigues droned on for a few minutes, using a pointer to show the position of contacts with the Communists in the previous twenty-four hours. After giving the casualty reports, the major looked the full-bird colonel province senior adviser in the eyes.

"And here's an unusual report from the village of Mang Buk—here, sir," the major said, pointing to its location on the map. "Agent reports say that last night a battalion of VC surrounded the village and talked to the people with bullhorns or loudspeakers of some sort.

"'Why do you fire your weapons at us?' they asked. 'They will be ours very soon. Why don't you surrender? There is no escape from us. Send out your women and children. We will not harm them. We will not harm anyone who surrenders to us. You had better surrender, because when we take over your village, our battalion commander will come not in a jeep but seated on a lawn chair.'"

There previously had been no recent reports of substantial VC activity in the area, which was northeast of Kontum City. The colonel asked of the VC psyops, "What the hell are we doing about all this?"

"Well, sir, we dropped a whole lot of leaflets in that AO [area of operations] yesterday."

"Well, goddammit, we got to try and get some air in there soon."

"Yes, sir."

Since I was ordered out of Kontum a few days later, I never found out what happened at Mang Buk. But the name of the village never appeared in any of the official press communiqués I saw in Saigon. Who knows? Maybe it was one Communist with a bullhorn. Or maybe the agent who reported the incident was high on rice wine.

RIGHT OUT IN THE OPEN

I was sitting on a bench at the chopper pad near II Corps headquarters in Pleiku one May afternoon in 1972, hoping to get a ride up to Kontum. That morning, Pleiku Air Base had taken a half-dozen 122 mm rockets. I wasn't concerned about my own safety, even though I was only a half mile away. The enemy had the air base zeroed in and were trying to damage aircraft on the ground. They never seemed to hit anyplace else in Pleiku.

About one thirty, though, I heard a nearby explosion. My first reaction was to hit the dirt. *Holy jeez,* I thought, *they wouldn't hit us again, would they?* There were a few more incoming rockets about a mile off to the west. Then I saw huge clouds of smoke billow as a Vietnamese Air Force A-37 Dragonfly dropped bombs on what I figured was an enemy position.

The next day, back at the air base, I was waiting for my C-130 flight back to Saigon after ten days in the field when I met an old Vietnamese friend from my first trip to the Highlands. He was an operations officer at the Peacock Hill air traffic control center. He was putting his parents on the Saigon flight because he feared the Communists would soon attack and overrun Kontum and then advance on Pleiku.

"Hey, how about that action yesterday afternoon?" I said.

"Oh, you mean out there?"

"Yeah, like what was that plane bombing?"

"Oh, one of our men was on his way to another mission when he spotted a VC on the ground. He figured it was the one who fired the rockets [at the air base]. Right out in an open field. He dropped a couple of hundred pounds of bombs on him."

MYSTERY PLANE

In late May 1972, I was at Pleiku Air Base waiting for a flight to Saigon when I met two friends from Kontum whom I previously had interviewed. They were air traffic controllers (ATCs) who directed allied aircraft into the beleaguered Central Highlands city despite daily shellings that left their 3,600-foot runway looking like a polka-dotted handkerchief.

"You want a story?" said Sergeant John Grange, the NCO in charge of the ATCs. "Well, how about this one. We've got a VNAF Bird Dog [O-1 light observation plane] marking positions for the dinks. He's been around for about a month. At first, we didn't think about it, but then a pattern developed. Shortly after he'd fly over an area, we'd start taking incoming. We figure he was helping the gunners make adjustments."

Grange said the ATCs counted more than three hundred rounds of incoming artillery, rocket, and mortar fire on and around the airstrip in April and May. Three VNAF C-123s, a C-130, and a Cobra gunship were destroyed during that period as they sat on the strip. Another C-130 crashed, Grange said, as its pilot tried to take off hurriedly during a rocket attack after unloading only a portion of its cargo. Many Vietnamese civilians were killed or wounded in the daily barrages as they awaited Air Vietnam flights.

One day, Grange said, the mysterious O-1 swooped less than a hundred feet over the ninety-five-foot-wide runway and fired a white phosphorus smoke canister only two hundred meters from the heavily sandbagged control tower.

"Twenty minutes later," the long-haired enlisted man said, "we started taking incoming. We know there's something strange going on. I've told all the officers in Kontum about it, but I don't think they believed me. They

210

won't let anybody shoot at him, because they're not sure who he is. But I'll tell you this: I'm damn sure he's working for the enemy."

There were other reports of an O-1 landing on the airstrip at Polei Kleng border Ranger camp, twelve miles west of Kontum, after the camp was overrun by human wave assaults in early May. An O-1 also was reported to have landed on Highway 14 north of Kontum, Grange said, taking cover beneath trees.

"When he flies over," Grange said, "we try to call him on every frequency we know, but he doesn't answer. Sometimes, he flies only about fifty feet over us. We've seen the VNAF markings on the side of the aircraft. Hell, it could be some supposedly friendly pilot working for the bad guys."

Grange and a dozen other ATCs worked three-man, twelve-hour shifts at the airstrip through the height of the Communist shellings. They proudly flew a tattered American flag from the top of their twenty-foot tower. "The closest rocket landed about a hundred feet away," Specialist Fifth Class George Furnage said. "But there's no one that can knock us down."

An average of twenty C-130 cargo planes daily flew into Kontum "blacked out," meaning without lights, during the early stages of the Easter Offensive. "They stopped coming during the day," Furnage said. "Every time they did, they'd get fired up."

Often, Grange said, the mysterious plane flew over the airstrip at low level, seemingly to assess the damage. "Chinooks have chased him," Grange said, "but he just disappeared to the northwest."

I spent a few afternoons at Plei Mrong border Ranger camp, twelve miles southwest of Kontum, watching airstrikes go in during early May. Once, some strange white smoke rose from the ground in the distance as an American forward air controller (FAC) guided fast-moving F-4s a few thousand yards outside the perimeter to drop their payloads on suspected Communist troop locations.

The FAC radioed to the US adviser at Plei Mrong that the FAC had not popped the white smoke. The adviser radioed back that there were no friendly troops operating in the area. Conceivably, the mystery plane could have popped that smoke in hopes the bombers would unload on the wrong target. Since the American FAC, in his own light observation plane, was low on fuel, he couldn't check it out. "It all fits," Grange said. "All I know is, somebody's got to get rid of that guy and do it soon."

I filed a story on the incident to my office in Saigon, and the editor teletyped it to the Tokyo bureau with the advice to hold it until we could come up with some official corroboration. But when I never was able to get high-level acknowledgement of the existence of the mysterious plane, the story was killed. Saigon officials told me, "We have no evidence whatsoever of any aircraft flying missions for the enemy."

But I had known the ATCs for a couple of months. I drank with them, watched movies with them, and listened to tapes with them in their hooches. They impressed me as intelligent, willing, capable soldiers who were not given to making rash statements. I believe what they told me about the Bird Dog, and I feel American officials intentionally withheld information from me to avoid adverse publicity.

THE BRIEFING

Every afternoon at four fifteen in Saigon, representatives of more than a hundred foreign and domestic newspapers and wire services gathered in the National Press Center on Tu Do Street for daily briefings on the war from the American and South Vietnamese commands.

ARVN spokesman Lieutenant Colonel Le Trung Hien or a substitute read any late additions to the daily communiqué in Vietnamese, and an aide translated into English for the benefit of foreign correspondents. Everybody knew the communiqués often bore little resemblance to the truth. Many times, reports delivered at the briefing were contradicted in the next day's newspapers by dispatches from the field.

For instance, Hien reported one day that most of Quang Tri City had been retaken from the Communists in July with little or no resistance from the VC. But UPI and AP, with correspondents near the battlefield, reported bloody clashes between marines and airborne troops and dug-in Communists until the city finally was cleared on September 19.

Sometimes the communiqués stretched the truth. I was at the base camp of the ARVN Forty-Fourth Regiment one afternoon as the troops sat around eating and cleaning weapons about a mile north of Kontum City. As they relaxed, US artillery and tactical airstrikes pounded Communist positions a few hundred yards north. I wrote a story, which never ran, about my trip to the front and flew back to Saigon that afternoon. The next day, I went to the briefing and saw an item that read, "An element of the 44th Regiment engaged the enemy yesterday a mile north of Kontum City, killing 44 and suffering light casualties." There was no mention of artillery or tac. air.

I raised my hand, was recognized, and said, "Isn't it true, colonel, that the kills were all due to artillery and tactical airstrikes?"

Hien said, "We have no further information to report on that." There was chuckling in the crowd as reporters realized why we called those sessions "the Follies."

INVITED GUESTS

THE BOB HOPE
CHRISTMAS SHOW

Somehow, I was among eighteen GIs from my unit, the 518th AG Personnel Services Company, chosen to represent it at Bob Hope's ninth annual Christmas show at a packed twenty-five-thousand-seat amphitheater in Long Binh near Saigon. About a hundred of us from various Cam Ranh Bay units were awakened at three thirty in the morning on Christmas Day 1971 and scrambled at five fifteen into the belly of a C-130. We sat shoulder to shoulder, on the floor, packed in tight. "As for safety procedures," an airman told us, "there are none. Not with this many people. You can hang it up if we go down."

We flew into Bien Hoa Army Base, were bused to Long Binh by seven, and arrived at the stadium by eight thirty. We had to sit out in the blazing sun until the show started at one thirty. It was hotter than I'd ever felt it in Vietnam. Other troops were flown in from all over the country in what was dubbed "Operation Jingle Bells." They filtered into the arena right up to show time. Snack wagons sold ham-and-cheese sandwiches for sixty cents, cans of Coke for a dime and giant cellophane bags of popcorn for eighty cents. Military police (MP) poked with their clubs into lunch bags and coolers, checking for weapons and drugs. They asked troops to unfurl rolled-up bedsheets, checking for obscene language. Some GIs threw popcorn and garbage down on officers seated on folding chairs near the stage. A Frisbee started circulating, cooling things down. Troops began passing marijuana cigarettes. Every time an American woman walked down an aisle, even if she was as ugly as sin, she got an ovation. Wounded soldiers wearing blue bathrobes and sitting in wheelchairs got a huge ovation when they rolled into position near the stage. A "freedom bird" (747 returning to the United States) flew overhead and was cheered.

The MPs missed some great banners: "Merry Christmas, Nixon—Wish You Were Here"; "Welcome, US Army Mortuary"; "Where is Jane Fonda?"; "Freeze Nixon." The show included Oakland A's pitcher Vida Blue, Jim "Gomer Pyle" Nabors, Miss World and USA Brucene Smith, Martha Raye, Suzanne Charny, Jan Daly, all-female singing group Sunday's Child, and the Hollywood Deb Stars, who danced in a chorus line in short skirts. But the star of the show was Hope. His monologue was funny and well received. In a Hawaiian shirt and top hat and swinging his signature golf driver (he later switched to a fatigue shirt with unit patches and a military cap), Hope cracked these jokes:

*"It's so hot here, the thermometer went over the hill."

*"Ah, Long Binh: Reno with salt tablets."

*"Santa Claus slid down the chimney in one barracks and went flying back up faster than he came down. I don't know what they were smoking in there, but …"

*"Many of the men have been taking home exotic souvenirs; others have been more careful."

*"Here I am back in Vietnam. Don't look so surprised. It was either this or play golf with [Vice President Spiro T.] Agnew. This is less dangerous."

*"You know, according to the papers, the war is over. Somebody forgot to tell the Cong."

*"You know, there are 160,000 troops here. But that's a military secret. I got it from a little old lady in black pajamas behind the stage."

And then came his line that drew a standing ovation: "I hope this is our last show in Vietnam." On a nearby hill, a couple of longhaired GIs unfurled a banner that said, "Vietnam is like a Bob Hope joke. Where is Jane Fonda? Peace, not Hope."

The only troubling part of the show was near the end when Raye, clad in fatigues, boonie hat, and boots, said, "Remember, you may not hear much about them, but there are people back home that love you. And these characters, these protestors you read about, could never even shine your boots [there was murmuring in the audience]. And don't you forget it." Raye expected to be cheered, but she got mostly silence because she was out of touch with us. She failed to realize that many of us would join

218

those protestors when we got home and that many of us were in Vietnam against our wills.

Hope added, "Take a look at these peace protestors; what have they ever done for their country?" A handful of soldiers clapped, but again there was mostly silence. The entertainers had to get political and spoil things. They didn't really understand who they were talking to.

FROEHLKE GETS THE BIG PICTURE

During his January 1972 tour of US bases in Vietnam, Secretary of the Army Robert F. Froehlke visited Camp Holloway in Pleiku. Spokesmen said Froehlke first got "the big picture" during meetings at MACV headquarters and the US embassy in Saigon and at United States Army Republic of Vietnam (USARV) headquarters in Long Binh. He also saw the USARV drug treatment center in Long Binh. Then he flew to Da Nang to tour two firebases and talked to officers and enlisted men from the 101st Airborne Division, the 196th Infantry Brigade, and Da Nang Support Command.

I caught up to him in Pleiku and wrote a short piece on his trip for my second published *Stars and Stripes* story. He was briefed by ARVN Lieutenant General Ngo Dzu, the II Corps commander, and met with officers of the Fifty-Second Aviation Battalion, the army's last large combat support unit in the Highlands. Froehlke met with twenty-five enlisted men, asking them questions and listening to their gripes. He was heading for his helicopter to leave when he saw Chaplain (Captain) George Gudz standing at the entrance to the post chapel with the doors wide open.

"Are you telling me I should go to church?" Froehlke asked.

"That's what we tell everyone, sir," the chaplain answered, giving Froehlke a copy of the New Testament.

"Keep up the good work," Froehlke said.

Before he left, Froehlke told me something that wasn't published, referring to eventual peace talks: "My own theory," he said, "is to go out there and beat him out there, and then maybe he'll come in here [to the negotiating table]. But if you wait for him to come in here …"

A USO BAND THAT
WAS FAR OUT

"I hear cosmic sounds in my head," the young man who called himself "Gypsy" said, running his fingers through his flowing brown hair and leaning against the wall of a sandbagged bunker in mid-May 1972. "I have rarely listened to radios because they just confuse me."

The leader of an American rock group called Lite Storm looked older than his twenty-one years. "That's what everybody says," he confided. The lines around his eyes; the long, curly hair; mustache and full beard made him appear to be a middle-aged guru. His smile was warm and friendly. He spoke in parables with a simple wisdom.

"I only started playing lead guitar a year ago," Gypsy said between shows at Camp Holloway in Pleiku, "but it's easy if you let the cosmos move you. All the instruments have little spirits in them. They will express themselves. All you have to do is move your arms and legs."

My first reaction was to think that Gypsy and his bandmates, who were making a four-month US-sponsored tour of American installations, were put-ons. But he said, "We're all yogis. We meditated together on a name for the group and came up with Lite Storm. Everybody got good vibrations from it."

I asked him if he was on drugs.

"No," he said and introduced me to the rest of his group. "We never touch anything. We're high on love."

Gypsy's wife, Sui-San, nineteen, played organ and sang. Her twenty-year-old high school friend Kala-Su helped with vocals. Mate, twenty-three, was the skinny bass player. Silver, twenty-two, handled the drums. "We really don't care about ages," Gypsy said, "or last names."

He added, "While we've been in Vietnam, we've tried to explain to the guys that not everybody that looks like us happens to be a doper. We've been offered bags of stuff by GIs and just give it back to them. We talk to them about love. We are what's happening today. They'll listen to us. When we tell them we're not hung on stuff, they really think it's far out. They wish they could be like us."

Lite Storm had a dream for removing the barriers between nations. "After we make a few albums and get a name," Gypsy said, "we want to play for free—for donations to the Village."

The Village was something he said the band planned to start on the West Coast—something he called a "truth and realization city." They planned to adopt children from all over the world and select "young and aware" couples to be parents. They planned to build "bubble houses" for each family, purchase land that could be farmed, and build a school and a hospital. The model, self-sufficient community would be an example to the world of the ability of all men to live and work in peace and harmony.

"We're going to try our best to do it," Sui-San said. "If we fail, then maybe someone else will take up the cause."

The group was to begin its money-making crusade in mid-May after returning to Hollywood, where the members lived. "Vietnam was a great tour," Sui-San said. "We've made a lot of people happy, and that's why we came."

The group was paid $4,000 a month by an American agency that had booked them through the USO. "We lost a lot of money coming over here," Gypsy said. "We had a whole tour lined up with [American group] Ballin' Jack on the coast and would have been taking in $5,000 to $7,000 a concert. But we wanted to come here and play for the guys."

He added, "Where is love best taken unless it's everywhere? People in the Green Machine don't want war any more than we do. We came here for all the people who are here and don't want to be here. We figure there's not too much love given to them in the Green Machine, so we'd try to bring them some."

Gypsy said the group was almost sent home before the tour began. Its music was screened in December 1971 by a USO committee in

Saigon. "We got a standing ovation from the guys who had dropped in," Gypsy said, "but we flunked the audition. Apparently, our music was too thought-provoking."

Silver said, "We want to express our own feelings, not simply copy someone else's."

The band members were vegetarians, refusing to eat animals because they did not believe in taking life. They believed in the power of meditation. Before coming to Vietnam, they said they visited yogi Suthya Sai Baba in a village outside Banglor in southeastern India. "Baba is one of the physical examples of godlihood," Gypsy said. "He brings people back from the dead … He materialized these beads I'm wearing for me."

The group said they were ribbed by inebriated NCOs about their appearance during some of their gigs. "Some of them hassled us," Gypsy said, "because we are what we are and we don't change for them. But when they talk to us, they are surprised because they find out that we are real people. It's time that everybody started opening their eyes and that there was no prejudice against someone just because he has long hair or is black or pink or green."

He concluded his monologue by saying, "The only reason we play is to get some money for [the Village]. Our whole being is cosmic sound and love because everything has got to come down to love in the end."

The group planned a Vietnam album with a cover featuring pins and patches they gathered while traveling to shows from the Delta to the DMZ. They said the songs would be about GIs, the war, drugs, boredom, Vietnamese women, bars, and love affairs. They said musical spirits would play a big part in helping to produce the album.

"Would you like to meet them?" Kala-Su said, seriously. "Well, there's Zeko in my keyboard, Chee in the lead guitar, Bruno in the bass, and Toga in the drum."

I asked her if she was serious.

"What do you mean do I really believe that?" she asked. "If I didn't, I wouldn't say it."

The group said it had $10,000 worth of instruments and equipment stored in a friend's garage in Los Angeles. They had been together for only one year, but Gypsy said they had written more than two hundred songs and recorded about sixty of them through the label Divine Mother. Much of their show was improvised, consisting of long musical breaks and jokes told by each member of the group.

"A lot of times, we don't even know what we're going to play until we play," Sui-San said. "We're together mentally to such a degree that we can do that."

She said often during the tour, drunks in the audience made lewd remarks to her and Kala-Su. "We know they are drunk," Sui-San said. "Many times, guys would come on over after the show and apologize. But we didn't get uptight or anything. We're just something they used to take out their frustrations on. We didn't mind."

The group said it rented an apartment in Los Angeles and also owned a home in British Columbia for use as a retreat. "We've got every room [in the apartment] painted a different color," Kala-Su said. "It'll be nice to get home. Being over here makes you appreciate things like a washing machine."

The fact the group often played for men who the next day would be blowing Communists away with machine-gun fire from helicopters did not seem to bother them. "It's very sad that they have to do the things they do," Silver said, "but we would be hypocrites if we didn't love everybody. Whether they're Americans, NVA, VC, Mexicans, or Chinese, they're still people, and we'd play for them all if we could. The world's got to get together, man, and it's got to come soon."

SIR ROBERT'S VISIT

The English guerilla-warfare expert Sir Robert Thompson visited South Vietnam in early July 1972, after the Communist Easter Offensive had been blunted. When I ran into him accidentally in Lai Khe, he told me he expected everything to be back to normal in two years at the battered provincial capital of An Loc, sixty miles north of Saigon. He had visited the city with Major General James F. Hollingsworth.

Thompson had been sent to Vietnam several times by President Nixon. On this visit he said he had been in-country for more than a week and toured most of the contested areas. He said Nixon would "be the first to get my impressions. I was sent by the president, and I will be seeing him on my return."

The author of several books on guerilla-warfare tactics, Thompson met with III Corps Commander Lieutenant General Nguyen Van Minh at the ARVN Fifth Division headquarters in Lai Khe. After an hour-long briefing, Thompson said, "Things are going very well." He added, "I've seen cities more devastated than An Loc. Most of those that were badly hit in Tet of 1968 are all back to normal now, and An Loc will be back to normal within two years. That will not be a problem."

Thompson and Hollingsworth spent a little more than an hour on the ground at An Loc, discussing the situation with ARVN commanders and Binh Long Province officials. "Great progress is being made there every day," Thompson said. "The civilians are happy and smiling. Work is going on to clean up the city ... There was a little incoming—there's always incoming—but it's not a problem. A lot of people say the siege is still going on up there, but there's no siege now. That's been over with since the enemy lost his capacity to take An Loc on May 15. The road isn't open yet, but what's that got to do with it?" I generally agreed with him because that's what my American sources were telling me at the time.

PART VIII

SCENE STORIES

PLEIKU'S LIMEY CAR SALESMAN

One story I came across that never was published involved Brian Benton, forty-three, from Norfolk, England, who was selling cars at Camp Holloway in Pleiku. Benton had served fifteen years as a Singapore policeman before returning to England in 1962 to sell foodstuffs and fertilizer. In 1968, he saw an ad in the *Daily Telegraph* for a job in Vietnam. "I was restless and bored," he told me, "and figured it was a chance to come back to the Far East." He worked out of Saigon for a while before being transferred to Pleiku and was selling twenty to thirty Chryslers a month, to be picked up in the United States, when I met him in early 1972. He fancied wearing a sky-blue bush jacket he had bought in Bangkok.

"A guy comes in here wanting a car, and we try and give him what he needs," said Benton, nicknamed "Limey." "Sometimes, they want a car they can't afford. The majority I sell to are going back to school and don't want the payments to empty their pockets. I try to help them." Benton said he took only one thirty-day vacation from 1968 to 1972 and said he enjoyed working for the Chrysler Military Service Corporation. "Long ago," he said, "cars were sold [to GIs] outside the exchange, and people were duped, so they wanted to bring it under control ... The position opened, and I wanted to get away from Saigon. We haven't been hit in a long, long time. I never think about it."

Benton said he expected to keep his shop open "till such time as there's no more people here, and I hope to remain with Chrysler somewhere in the Far East ... It's a relaxed sort of life. There's no competition. The majority know what they want. I meet all kinds of people from all sides of life. I really have learned so much about American people since I've been here, living so close to 'em."

He added, "I like to get out and talk to people. When I close my office, my job doesn't finish. I make it known I'm always available. I go to the air base, the artillery village, wherever I'm wanted."

He said of Vietnamization, "I'll be glad to see 'em go in a way. But I'll be sorry to close my shop. One of the great things you don't see now is when you go to the club, you don't see friends of yours missing. It's happened many times. Three friends were killed in '69 that I was real close to … But I never think of myself being in danger. I'm not worried. I have confidence in the American detachments here. I keep up with the news. I listen to the BBC relay every night at five."

One of Benton's customers, Private First Class Larry Stratton, of Philadelphia, bought a car from Benton and said he planned to pick it up in July. Stratton bought a Challenger RT for $3,400 and negotiated a monthly payment plan that started at $65 a month and rose to $200. "He didn't try to sell me as much as try to sell the car," Stratton said. "It has 318 horses, a small engine; it's a V-8 with three on the floor. I did stop and think about insurance. With big engines, insurance is very high."

Captain Paul Burgess, an information officer, said of Benton, "He has great relations with everyone. He's well liked, honest. If you have a problem, he can help you any way he can. I'd call him the GIs' best friend. Everybody loves him. A GI will come in and say he wants 440 on the floor with a girl on each door, and he'll talk him out of it. All the girls in the clubs come to him with their problems. He's like their father."

A LITTLE PIECE OF AMERICA

I don't remember exactly where or when it was, but it was in the dry season shortly after I joined *Stars and Stripes* in January 1972, and I remember looking to my right and seeing an American specialist fifth class radio telephone operator (RTO) humping off into some tall grass at the end of a small column of troops. He was tall and thin with boots worn brown by the dust and carrying a pack that probably weighed sixty pounds. At the end of his PRC-25's antenna was a tiny, tattered American flag flapping in the breeze. I remember thinking, *That's a little piece of America right there.* And I got choked up. The guy was long-haired and unshaven and probably wore peace symbols, but I got the feeling that he took his job seriously and that he was representing me. I was just hoping he stayed alive.

THE BORDER CAMPS

One of the first up-country trips I made as a reporter, in January 1972, took me to three of the twelve Vietnamese Ranger mountain border camps in II Corps. There had been reports of a Communist troop buildup in the area, which was believed tied to an upcoming offensive.

Ben Het, Duc Co, and Plei Djereng base camps each had two-man US adviser teams. When I visited by helicopter, each set of advisers told me all was quiet on their front. At Ben Het, in western Kontum Province and about seven miles east of the South Vietnam–Laos–Cambodia triborder, about seven hundred troops, mostly aboriginal Montagnards of the ARVN Ninety-Fifth and Seventy-Second Ranger Battalions, lived with their families in bunkers. Their mission was surveillance and interdiction, which meant looking for Communists and preventing them from getting through to the two large provincial capitals, Pleiku and Kontum.

Ben Het guarded the approach to the Dak To–Kontum area. Platoon-size patrols had been searching for the enemy in nearby forests, but their last contact had been in November, when ten VC mortar rounds had exploded outside the perimeter.

The American advisers at Ben Het were Captains Mike Perkins, of Kaysville, Utah, and Jim Worthen, twenty-four, of Phoenix, Arizona. They said they had been suggesting improvements in the camp's defenses and acting as goodwill ambassadors to nearby villages, giving out clothes, food, and candy. They said the camp had been attacked by NVA tanks in 1969, and they expected it to be attacked again.

"If they want to attack Kontum and Pleiku," Perkins said, "they must come through here first. We have info that they have twenty tanks in Cambodia. We're ready for them. We have minefields to the south and north. II Corps gives us information on troop movements. But I've been here three months, and there's been no contact, no nothing ... I'd prefer to be here, though, than sitting on my ass in Saigon."

Worthen said, "We're close to the reality of what's happening in Vietnam right now. In Saigon, you go to the officers' club, a movie, etc., and you're out of touch with the combat Joes."

Perkins said he did a 1966 tour with Special Forces and said, "I've seen more than I ever want to see. I've seen too many good boys die here for no sense at all. I don't want to kill any Vietnamese anymore; I just want to keep a few Americans alive." Perkins said he was enjoying his current tour despite the lack of action. "We sit here and tell lies to each other," he said. "Now we're trying to learn Montagnard [language]. We try to talk to the soldiers and find out what they're really thinking. It gets kinda lonely ... But we're showing the flag here, so we've got to be on our best behavior."

He added, "They don't resent us. We get along well with the Vietnamese, and the Montagnards think Americans walk on water. When you learn their language, they think you're number one."

"They're people just like Americans are people," Worthen said. "They have their families living in bunkers. There's five hundred to seven hundred dependents here."

At Duc Co, thirty miles southwest of Pleiku City, the American advisers were Sergeant First Class Irvin Dorwar, of Allentown, Pennsylvania, and Lieutenant Ronald Hendrickson, of Arlington, Texas. They said patrols of the Seventy-First ARVN Ranger Battalion were searching the surrounding forest but had not had any significant contact in months. Dorwar had high praise for the Montagnards. "These Ranger battalions," he said, "are some of the most elite troops in Vietnam. Most of these men grew up here. They have a better life here [in the camp] than they have ever known. They've got to be good soldiers, or they wouldn't put up with operations year after year. If the camp is attacked, they're fighting with their families at their backs. And you watch—the women and children will load ammo like crazy if they have to."

The mission of Duc Co, Dorwar said, was to prevent the Communists from using Highway 19 as a high-speed tank approach into Pleiku City and to defend the Thanh An District capital, or county seat, a few miles east of the camp. Dorwar said, "The whole II Corps area is historically an area where they hit the hardest. I think we're gonna get hit pretty hard. Intelligence reports say there's three hundred men [NVA] with two tanks northwest of us. They're all around us."

Hendrickson said, "There's not any of these base camps that Charlie couldn't take if he wanted to. But if he did, he'd have all the air and artillery power in 'Nam on him in a minute. There's speculation that the supposed threat is here. The camp here in '69 was attacked by armor, and they expect it to be attacked again. The intelligence says he will. You never know. He may; he may not."

Dorwar, on his third tour, said, "I think the commander here is a real good soldier. An adviser is not a commander; he's an adviser. When he fails to remember this, he's making a mistake. But we can help these people … I figure they'll either bypass us or pin us down and try for Pleiku."

Hendrickson also volunteered for Vietnam and said, "I'd rather be here than in Saigon pushing papers … out working with the people; it's more rewarding. If you're a professional in the military, you go where the combat is. We're advising their combat operations. These people are fighting for a way of life here. I've had people come up to me and say, 'You're the first adviser I've ever known that could speak Vietnamese.' It's just a matter of whether you care about people."

Dorwar said, "At a desk, you don't see the end results of your effort. I've got twenty-three years in the army, and every day I learn something new."

Plei Djereng, less than fifteen miles east of the Cambodian border, guarded what was the best infantry approach to Pleiku City. The American advisers there, Captain Jared Hawkins, of Defuniak Springs, Florida, and First Lieutenant Robert Ciccolella, of Vohannon, Virginia. They said no VC contact in the past two weeks had been reported by the ARVN Eightieth Ranger Battalion stationed there. On January 2, they said, an ARVN patrol ran into a Communist base camp and killed nineteen enemy. Another patrol killed five Communists on January 6. The advisers said Communist troops shot and killed an ARVN battalion commander with a 57 mm recoilless rifle round on December 19, 1971. "Obviously," Hawkins said, "they were a long time setting that one up. The VC are out there; we know that. They killed fourteen Montagnard villagers that day and then snuck off into the woods. The ARVNs couldn't find them."

Hawkins said most of the camp advisers had good relationships with the ARVNs, most spoke Vietnamese, and the ARVNs didn't need much help. "Some of these guys have been in this war a long time," Hawkins said. "Some of the Montagnards here were part of the old Civilian Irregular Defense Forces [trained by US Special Forces from 1961 to 1970]. They can tell if you know something from experience or from reading it out of a Sgt. Rock comic book."

He added, "I feel safer here than I've felt anywhere in Vietnam. We could be overrun, sure, but they would have to pay a terrible price. We could be sapped, but hell, they hit the American embassy [in Saigon in 1968]. No one knows if they're going to strike here, the district capital, Pleiku, or one of the other camps. But wherever they hit us, we'll be ready fo them. We can still call in just about anything that flies [on the enemy] in a matter of minutes."

He added, "It gets a little lonely, but I'd much rather be out here. I feel we're accomplishing something, and that's a good feeling. We're not really teaching them anything, just holding down the place until we [American troops] are all out. Their troops are well clothed by Vietnamese standards. They don't get rained on at night; they have good security. So I'd say morale is pretty high."

Ciccolella said, "I'd rather be with an American unit out fighting in the field, but this is the closest to it I can get. We're infantry officers, and this is a job for infantry officers."

"We're probably the best infantry approach to Pleiku," Hawkins said. "Duc Co's probably the best tank approach. And Ben Het is at the entrance to Dak To and Kontum. Our people believe these will be the cornerstones if a massive infiltration takes place."

GUARD DUTY IN THE BUSH

The hardest thing about pulling guard duty in the bush east of Saigon was not the ninety minutes I sat with claymore mine clackers at my feet, an M16 rifle cradled in my arms, and a radio telephone in my ear, staring into the inky blackness of the jungle. The toughest thing was finding my way back to my own rucksack and sleeping gear without waking up half the platoon. It was mid-March 1972, a couple of weeks before the Easter Offensive began, and pulling guard duty with an infantry unit seemed to be a piece of cake.

There was a radio at the center of the encampment and GIs at guard posts all around the perimeter. The man in the middle just kept checking the other men, asking for situation reports.

"Five-two-three, this is six-seven-x-ray. Sitrep please."

"Six-seven-x-ray, this is five-two-three. Condition green."

The condition was almost always green. That meant there was no movement in front of the observer. American troops had not had much contact lately when I visited them and slept overnight on one of their patrols. Charlie Company, Second Battalion, Eighth Cavalry, a unit of the Third Brigade, First Cavalry Division, had not had a man wounded in nine months. Nobody in the unit could recall the last time Communist guerillas had attacked a US infantry night defense position. So there seemed to be no real danger on patrol or on guard duty. It was just a nightly chore that everybody shared in the jungle to protect against the one odd chance in a thousand that the Communists might try something sneaky. Usually, the men said funny things to each other to pass the time and stay alert, such as in this exchange I heard:

"Five-two-one, five-two-one, five-two-one."

"Yeah, whadya want?"

"Short."

"Oh, yeah, how short, man?"

"Forty-one days and a wake-up—if the drops come down as scheduled."

"Don't talk to me, boy. I got nineteen and a wake-up—and I got my drop."

"Oh, okay, five-two-one. Uh, five-two-three, five-two-three. Come in, please. This is five-two-two."

"Yeah?"

"Short."

Pretty soon, it was time to wake up the next guard. That began the hard part—after my relief found me.

"Uh, excuse me, man. I'm new here. I'm looking for a tree that should be right about here. Like these four dudes were swinging [in hammocks] right across from me, you know, and the CO was to the right, and the radioman was on the left."

"Oh, yeah, just follow my finger, Mac. You're right over there."

"Thanks a lot. Uh, where's your finger? Oh, here. Thanks again."

My rifle got tangled up in a small bush, a thorn ripped a small gash on my wrist, and I got thrown off course. I cursed softly and woke up another trooper.

"Who there, man?"

"Uh, just me, a new guy trying to find my tree."

"Oh, Smith. Yeah, man. You over there."

"Oh, excuse me, man." I tripped, a man's weapon hit the ground with a loud thwack, and another soldier was roused.

"Who's messin' wit my gun, man?"

"Er, excuse me, brother. Like, I was just trying to get back to my gear, and everybody keeps pointing me in the wrong direction, and, like, I can't tell where the hell I am. Can you help me?"

I could feel tears welling up in my eyes.

"Sure, man, take it easy. You right over there, next to me. That's your stuff by that tree, ain't it?"

I felt in the darkness, found one of my canteens and took a huge swig. "Yeah, man, thanks a lot. Sorry I woke you up."

"That's okay. No sweat. Night."

It took me twenty-five minutes to get back to my position that night. The next day, somebody said, "Morning, newbie. Any problems on guard?"

"No, none at all. Went real smooth."

CAM RANH GETS HIT

Cam Ranh Bay Air Base on the central coast was about the safest place you could be in Vietnam in April 1972. That's why the three GIs who were relaxing outside their barracks on a Saturday night had no reason to expect trouble.

But four soldiers were killed and twenty wounded in a Communist hit-and-run attack on April 9, 1972. The timing was not a coincidence. The last American army infantry unit at the sprawling base, the Second Battalion, 327th Infantry Company, with 920 men, had stood down three days earlier. So the base then depended on ARVNs for perimeter security.

The US command in Saigon released nothing but casualty figures on the incident, but I felt a kinship with the soldiers at my old duty station. I had spent five quiet months as a clerk at Cam Ranh in 1971. I had a telephone directory, and that night I just kept dialing numbers until somebody answered. I finally reached a guard on duty.

"About twenty of us had a party for a few of the guys who just made E-5 [sergeant]," he said. "Most of the guys had gone to bed. Only me and two other guys were out there drinking beer at the picnic tables. When the initial wave hit—small arms, frags—we dove for cover and were pretty lucky. We didn't get hit. But the guys inside sleeping were. It was a bad scene, man. Totally unexpected. The guys came running out of the barracks toward the bunkers, thinking it was a rocket attack, and the dudes just mowed them down."

I wrote a story, but they didn't run it. The attack made me wonder what I would have done if it had come when I was there. I don't think I even knew where the rifles were kept. I was only issued one for guard duty and never had to fire a round.

THE STICKITT INN

Whenever I wanted to find out what was really happening in a battle zone, I went to the helicopter people first. The hell with the information officers. Most of them were completely worthless and were just worried about putting a positive spin on things.

The most fearless of the chopper people were the AH-1 Cobra gunship drivers. They supported ARVN troops in combat, hit enemy bunkers, and covered troop insertions with minigun and rocket fire during daredevil vertical dives that sometimes brought them almost to tree level. At Camp Holloway in Pleiku, the Cobra and Huey drivers gathered at night at the Stickitt Inn, a cave-like, air-conditioned barracks building with refrigerators, polished bar, card table, overhead lighting, and some cots where they could crash between missions.

I'll never forget the scene at that bar, the camaraderie among the men in the Custer-style cavalry hats with crossed sabers on them. It was a brotherhood that I could be around but not really be a part of. In later years, I remembered those nights like the bar scene in *Star Wars* with aliens from various planets: men of all shapes, sizes, ethnicities, rank, hair lengths, and political views—all thrown together in the crucible of war.

"ARC LIGHT THE MOTHERFUCKERS"

Another evening as I was drinking at the Stickitt Inn, the movie *Celebration at Big Sur* was being shown. It was a film about love and brotherhood generated by a California music festival. The clips showed peaceful but seemingly high hippies dancing and grooving to psychedelic music. A drunken warrant officer looked up from his shot at the pool table and said, "We should arc light [drop a B-52 strike on] the motherfuckers." And he went back to his game. I knew he was drunk, but his comment made me reflect on the disconnect between the officers and the enlisted men, and the officers and the counterculture back in the States.

TAN CANH

Colonel Phillip Kaplan, forty-three, of St. Louis, had a good reputation among the Saigon press corps. The senior adviser to the ARVN Twenty-Second Division usually was "good copy." But on April 21, 1972, I'd arrived at a bad time at the division's forward command post outside Dak To, north of Kontum in the Central Highlands.

"Afternoon, sir," I said, with full military bearing but without a salute.

"Hello, Smith … What do you want?"

"Wanna know what's going on."

"Do you want two minutes or twenty?"

"Twenty, sir, if I can get it."

"Okay … Be right with you."

In the command bunker, a half-dozen American advisers gathered around a few PRC-25 radios and a battered little coffeepot in one corner. The room was alive with the crackle of field phones and the clatter of typewriters. ARVN sergeants in starched gray-green fatigues used black or red grease pencils on cellophane-covered maps to indicate the position of enemy and friendly forces.

"Colonel," an ARVN colonel with a phone in his hands barked, "the Forty-Second Regiment needs gunships [Cobra rocket-firing helicopters]."

"They're on their way, sir," a radioman said

"My men don't see them," the colonel said.

"They'll be there as soon as they refuel and rearm," said the radioman.

And so it went. The whoosh of Cobra rockets was audible in the nearby hills. Huge clouds of smoke rose from the tree-covered mountains on all sides of the base in the middle of a verdant valley. An American staff sergeant loaded down with fragmentation and smoke grenades jumped off a hovering Huey helicopter and sprinted in to report to Kaplan.

"We just got eight of them up on that ridge there, sir."

"Any friendly losses?"

"Just one man, very slightly wounded."

"Good work, Sergeant."

"You know," Kaplan said to me, "sometimes, I get the feeling we're in a tube of toothpaste here, and the enemy is squeezing us from all sides. You never know where he's going to squeeze or how hard."

"You see that ridge," Kaplan said, pointing to the west. "They're up there. And those hills over there [east]? We know some of them have filtered through and are up there. It's coming up here; I know it. Their main effort is yet to come. I don't think the enemy has shot his wad up here by any means."

Everything seemed calm and smooth-running in the tactical operations center. Amid helmets, vests, and assorted rifles and handguns, an American captain listened on his radio to reports from the field and sipped coffee. Vietnamese officers and enlisted men worked at three rows of makeshift wooden tables. They shouted back and forth to the Americans, sometimes in English, sometimes through interpreters.

"We're busy here," Kaplan said. "We've got a lot of people to coordinate—two ground regiments, the border camps, our air assets. We work together pretty well here."

An estimated thirty thousand North Vietnamese troops were believed to be in the region where the borders of Vietnam, Laos, and Cambodia met. Three days after I visited Tan Canh, an estimated two thousand Communist troops overran the base, routing the South Vietnamese and setting the stage for their determined but ultimately unsuccessful attempt to capture Kontum, thirty miles south. The ARVN division commander and most of his staff at Tan Canh were killed or fled.

* * *

I was up early on April 24 and walking from Camp Holloway to II Corps headquarters in Pleiku when I saw Colonel Kaplan speeding by in a jeep.

When I got to the helicopter pad, the skipper of a chopper there had gotten the word that Tan Canh had been overrun. I wanted to get a ride up to the battle scene. By coincidence, Captain Geddes MacLaren happened to be making a goodies run to the firebases, dropping food, mail, and magazines off with American advisers. I hitched a ride with him to Plei Mrong. But our chopper was bounced to pick up a wounded ARVN company commander, and I was stuck there most of the day while all hell was breaking loose up north.

As it turned out, I eventually wrote a story on the fierce fighting at Tan Canh, but it was never published—perhaps because it was a major defeat for the ARVN. According to John Paul Vann, the senior American adviser in II Corps, the Communists attacked at 6:30 a.m. on April 24 using about fifteen tanks. He said US and Vietnamese Air Force strikes destroyed at least nine of them, including two that smashed through the front gates of the command post and into the middle of the base.

There were eleven Americans at Tan Canh. Three—Colonel Kaplan, Lieutenant Colonel Terry McClain, and Captain David Stewart—were evacuated to Pleiku. Six were believed fighting for their lives near Phuong Long airfield four miles west of Dak To after being evacuated there; the other two were missing and presumed still in the base. Vann said there were "pockets of friendlies" trapped in the base after it was overrun.

I interviewed Kaplan hours after his arrival at Pleiku. He said the camp had been probed by sappers on the previous two nights, "but we wanted more evidence of tanks. None had been found before today." Kaplan said as the attack began, the bunker he and his men were in was hit. "It felt like a death trap," he said. "We took one direct hit, and sandbags started caving in. I figured if we were going to die, it would be better to go out shooting than by suffocating, so I ordered everybody upstairs. We saw the tanks come in and fired at them. The closest was about twenty feet away. But we were not very good M72 gunners, and we missed them."

Nine Americans withdrew to the west about four hundred meters and waited. Vann, flying his own OH-58 helicopter, swooped in and tried to rescue a few but took fire and made an emergency landing. Another chopper landed, picked up the men, and tried to take off but was hit and turned over. No one was injured. Eventually, another chopper brought Kaplan, McClain, and Stewart back to Pleiku. But when Vann and the other six Americans tried to take off in another helicopter, ARVN soldiers linked arms and held on to the skids of the aircraft. So instead of evacuating the advisers to the Ben Het base camp near the triborder, Vann decided to drop them and the dangling ARVNs at Phuong Long airfield. (Information on their fate is contained in the next vignette.)

"It probably put the lives of the Americans in jeopardy," Vann said, "but it's understandable that [the ARVNs] would do that under the circumstances, with bombs bursting, mortar fire coming in. And the will for self-preservation is strong." Vann said he lost communication with the advisers at about eleven in the morning when they were in a firefight near the airstrip. The Communists encircled it and seized control of it just before noon, he said.

An estimated three thousand refugees fled the Dak To area, heading south on Highway 14, but the district chief, whom Vann identified as a Colonel Bao, refused Vann's offer of evacuation and vowed that "his place was with his troops and that he would fight to the death."

Vann added, "The scenario has been fairly clear for the last four months. The enemy's strategy was first to interdict the roads—from Pleiku to Kontum, Kontum to Dak To, and Qui Nhon to Pleiku. Second, to launch a coordinated series of attacks on the border camps, Tan Canh and Phuong Long. Third, he plans to drive on Kontum with the 320th Division. His plans were modified a bit when he was blocked for a time at the ridgeline."

Vann said he did not call in airstrikes on Tan Canh after flying over it in the morning of April 25 because "I knew friendlies were still in there." He said he did have tac. airstrikes destroy the artillery at Tan Canh and at the airfield to prevent it from falling into enemy hands. Vann said the Communists used one reinforced regiment in the attacks and at least three regiments "at other pressure points such as the ridges east and north of Tan Canh, the firebases on Rocket Ridge, and the highway between Dak To and Kontum."

Vann said the departure of the ARVN Third Airborne Brigade to reinforce government troops around Saigon had "probably worsened what was already a serious situation" by leaving him short of maneuver battalions in the Highlands. "The enemy will need some time to reorganize, but it's obvious with the imminent loss of the ridgeline and about twice as many enemy battalions as friendly in our area, the pressure against Kontum will get really intense in the next week. I am more confident of the defense of Kontum, though, since Colonel Ly Tong Ba moved his headquarters of the Twenty-Third Division there last week."

Vann was not optimistic on the prospects of holding Kontum. "I think it's up in the air," he said. "It's possible to hold, but it depends on how much damage the enemy has suffered; two, are there two more tank battalions, and will they commit them against Kontum? And three, the capability of the South Vietnamese forces. It depends on which way the cookie crumbles whether Kontum falls."

HIDE-AND-SEEK

"We're just glad to be back and glad to be alive," Major Julius G. Warmath told me on May 7, 1972, at the Sixty-Seventh Evacuation Hospital in Pleiku after being rescued following thirteen days in the jungle. The adviser and four others had been presumed killed when their helicopter crashed.

Warmath, forty-five, was among ten Americans aboard a UH-1H Huey shot down by the North Vietnamese on April 24 near Dak To Airfield. The chopper crashed on an island in the Dak Poko River, killing five of the men. "I never did give up hope," said Warmath, of Humboldt, Tennessee, as he rested on an operating table, his legs and midsection encased in a cast. "It was very frustrating, though. I'd just popped my next-to-the-last smoke grenade when they picked us up. We were just sitting there watching aircraft fly right overhead. But they couldn't see us."

Two of the rescued men were advisers to the ARVN Twenty-Second Division at Tan Canh, which was overrun that day: Warmath and Captain John B. Keller, twenty-six, of Lexington, Kentucky. The others rescued were Staff Sergeant Walter A. Ward, thirty-one, of Lawton, Oklahoma, whose unit was not specified; Specialist Fifth Class Rickey V. Vogel, twenty-one, the helicopter's crew chief, of Kansas City, Missouri; and Specialist Fourth Class, Charles M. Lea, twenty-one, the door gunner, of Deer Park, Tennessee.

"We had just taken off," said Warmath, "when they hit us with small-arms and .50-caliber fire. We knew we were going down. All I remember is the impact—right on a big rock—and Lea dragging me on the ground away from the aircraft. After he dragged me a couple of meters, the whole thing went up in a big, big explosion."

The pilot and copilot, Lieutenant James Hunsicker and Warrant Officer Wade Ellen, died in the crash. Three others also were killed: the medic, Specialist Fourth Class Franklin Zollicoffer; First Lieutenant Johnny M. Jones of the Fifty-Second Aviation Battalion at Pleiku; and Warmath's fellow Tan Canh adviser Major George W. Carter.

The five men who survived the crash stayed together for nine days in a grassy ditch near the aircraft. They existed on C rations, plants, berries, river water, and two catfish they managed to scoop out of a stream. Then Keller and Lea, who suffered only minor bruises, went to find help. They said they commandeered a sampan, floated downstream, and eventually found a field radio. "We're not going to say how we got it," Keller said.

They tried every frequency until they finally heard friendly voices. A light observation helicopter from B Troop, Seventh Squad, Seventeenth Air Cavalry, swooped in and whisked the two men to Kontum, from where they coordinated the rescue of the other three. The five survivors had been armed with an M60 machine gun, a .45-caliber pistol, an M79 grenade launcher, an M16, another rifle, and two grenades but never used them. There were some close calls.

"We walked up to a bunker," one of the men said, "looking for some food and checking out a blanket there—and a VC came up the trail. I think he saw us because he got down quick. We ran as fast as we could the other way."

Another time, Keller said, the men took cover on the side of a trail as two NVA soldiers on bicycles pedaled by. The five made a big SOS out of the white nylon lining from two flak vests, but it was not spotted from the air. "The aircraft were flying high because of the enemy antiaircraft sites all around; nobody got down low enough to see us," a survivor said.

Warmath, who sustained an apparent broken back, said he had been the post commander at a jungle operations training center in Panama and had a lot of survival training. But he spent most of the days propped up against a tree, unable to move. He gave Lea credit for supplying rations and keeping morale up.

"I ate some things during the thirteen days that I never thought I'd eat," Warmath said. "Like those greens. A wounded ARVN soldier joined us on the fifth day and showed us what plants we could eat—they tasted pretty good boiled. The soldier left us on the twelfth day. I guess he had given up hope. He only had a small shrapnel wound, so I guess he wanted to take his chances on foot." The survivors said they were glad they had stuck together.

WAR IN THE MORNING

The contrasts within Vietnam were incredible. I covered the war in Kontum in the morning, and in the afternoon, between screwdrivers, I was playing volleyball in the officers' swimming pool at the MACV compound in Pleiku. When I worked in the Saigon area, I could put on a helmet and flak vest, jump into my air-conditioned Rambler station wagon and drive thirty or forty miles north on Highway 13 to cover the road-clearing operations south of the battered provincial capital of An Loc. In the evening, I'd breeze back to Saigon at fifty miles an hour, dodging bicycles, Hondas, oxcarts, buses, and military convoys; take a shower; change into jeans and a sport shirt; write my story; teletype it to Tokyo; pick up my Vietnamese girlfriend, Loan; and drive downtown to have dinner in an elegant French restaurant and take in a first-run American movie.

In Pleiku, where I spent a lot of my time in the field, I could always get a ride up to Kontum with an adviser, courier, or supply mission. The army wasn't supposed to be running a shuttle service for correspondents, but since I was in the army and wore fatigues at times (although I didn't wear rank insignia), they rarely turned me down. Some of the left-leaning, long-haired correspondents for civilian newspapers and magazines envied me because I often got rides with aircraft commanders who turned them down if they didn't like their looks.

"Get Out of Kontum"

All the correspondents knew that Kontum City was about to come under attack. The trick was how to stay there to the last minute and report the action—and then get out. That's what I was trying to do. But I also didn't want to get killed. "I'm not going to tell you again, young man; I want you out of here," an American colonel told me on May 1, 1972. It was the third time I had been told to leave Kontum City. "Get your gear, and get on that chopper," he said.

But as I shuffled to the chopper pad with flak vest, helmet, camera, and suitcase, the last helicopter out already had lifted off, and it wasn't until two days later that I actually did leave. During that forty-eight hours, I drank in the sights, sounds, and smells of a city in crisis.

Refugees streamed through the MACV Team 41 Advisory Compound and were evacuated on choppers to Pleiku City to the south in almost continuous sorties. In the compound, Montagnard Special Forces troops played volleyball and listened to American cassette tapes and radios between guard-duty shifts on the perimeter. Their American advisers, most of them former or current Green Berets, drank pineapple juice and vodka, ate C rations, and joked about old times.

Along the road, refugees made desperate attempts to flee in civilian trucks. The same trucks returned later in the day, their grim-faced drivers moaning about "Beaucoup VC ... No can do Pleiku."

Choppers from B Troop, Seventh Squad, Seventeenth Air Cavalry, flew daily missions. Cobra gunships bellied in with a whoosh, quickly were rearmed and refueled, and leaped back into the fray, supporting counterattacking ARVN ground troops. Americans relaxed leaning on the sides of Hueys, drinking cold water from Coke cans, and listening

251

to transmissions from the field. In the shade of another chopper, ARVN infantrymen played cards for stakes of a hundred piasters a hand, sucked water from canteens, and chewed on fruit.

Inside the city, the black-market stalls were deserted. Some cafés stayed open, but business was slow. An American adviser wheeled a truck into town to evacuate the family of a Montagnard soldier. The whole village wanted to go too. Many toted meager possessions. "No," the sergeant explained. "Only the immediate family of the soldier can be evacuated." Some small, crying boys were helped down from the truck.

"Tell them I'd like to take them all out," the sergeant said. "But I can't. Tell them! Oh, Jesus, I wish I could take them all out. Come on; let's get out of here. I feel sick."

Sleep for two nights was interrupted by the rumble of B-52 strikes, the thunder of artillery and the pop-whistle of illumination flares. But there was no contact with the enemy at the MACV compound. "This is the calm before the storm," an adviser said. "You'd better believe the enemy is coming in strength. You'd better get the hell out of here."

On May 3, I choppered back to Pleiku. That afternoon, I swam in the pool at Camp Holloway, and Kontum City seemed like a million miles away.

A DESERTED CITY

Kontum, a city of grass huts and red tile-roofed French schoolhouses in the Central Highlands of South Vietnam, was almost deserted in early May 1972. Flying over it on May 9 in a chopper, I spotted only military vehicles and soldiers on Honda motorcycles moving over the bumpy, paved streets. Refugees jammed the US compound and were being flown daily in twin-rotor Chinooks to Pleiku, the next large city due south.

Kontum waited tensely for an expected Communist assault from the north and west. Government troops were dug in at positions around the city. Colonel Ly Tong Ba, commander of the ARVN Twenty-Third Division, headquartered in Kontum, told me, "First, we had to organize our defensive posture completely. Now, we will move out and try to strike the enemy. We want to counterattack, get the enemy to come into our artillery fan and strike him before he comes to Kontum."

Ba said he had moved several battalions of troops north of the city, and they were patrolling the jungle looking for contact. To the north, Ben Het Base Camp, near the point where the borders of South Vietnam, Laos, and Cambodia met, put up stubborn resistance and beat off several attempts to overrun it. Ba said eleven Communist tanks had been destroyed in or around the beleaguered Montagnard border Ranger camp.

"Sure we are tired," the commander of another ARVN base camp in Pleiku Province told me, "but we can't worry about that now. We must fight with all we've got. Our country is at stake now. We must meet the enemy's attack and beat him right here in the Highlands."

Civilians also were fleeing Pleiku City, about twenty-five miles south of Kontum, for the coastal cities of Qui Nhon and Nha Trang or Saigon. A Vietnamese woman who worked at Camp Holloway in Pleiku told me

253

that she gave an ARVN soldier 30,000 piasters (about $75) to buy her a ticket on an Air Vietnam flight to Saigon, but he had taken the money and disappeared.

"I've got to get more money," she said. "I have to get out of Pleiku. Everybody I know has left. I don't want to be here when VC come."

A Vietnamese Air Force officer said he put his parents aboard a giant US Air Force C-141 cargo plane bound for Saigon on the afternoon of May 10. "They are scared," he told me. "I don't know if the VC will come or not. But I don't want to take any chances with my parents' lives. They will be safe in Saigon. They have friends there who will take care of them."

In front of II Corps headquarters in Pleiku, fighting positions were being constructed. A battery of 105 mm howitzers was installed there. Several tanks were stationed near the perimeter. Six 122 mm rockets hit near the base on May 9, damaging an Air Vietnam plane and wounding the copilot and four passengers. VNAF fighters, on their way to Kontum, happened to see the lone Communist trooper who fired the rockets and rained bombs on him. The explosions could be seen from II Corps headquarters. A VNAF officer said, "We think we got him, but that's getting too close for comfort." (As it turned out, Pleiku never was attacked after the NVA drive was blunted at Kontum.)

PLEI MRONG

I got bolder as my date eligible for return from overseas (DEROS) neared. I expect I would have been killed or seriously wounded if I had stayed in Vietnam a few extra months. I took a lot of chances and got away with them. On the morning of May 23, 1972, when I was staying at Camp Holloway in Pleiku, I commandeered a van and drove up Highway 14 to see what was happening on a road clearing operation. I met a Lieutenant Colonel Waara, whom I remembered from a previous trip, and got a chopper ride with him out to Plei Mrong, a border Ranger camp midway between Pleiku and Kontum west of the highway and about fifteen miles northwest of Pleiku. We flew low-level all the way, right down on the deck, because Communists in the area were said to be equipped with shoulder-fired, heat-seeking SA-7 missiles.

Over the camp, we listened to transmissions from the site of a battle in progress less than ten miles northeast of us near Chu Pao, a mountain. Colonel Waara wanted the chopper crew to fly him near the battlefield to see what was going on, but the two young warrant officers wanted no part of that. "Not without gunships," one of them said. "Too many dinks around here; we're too short."

Waara got me a ride in a VNAF chopper with a Vietnamese brigadier general. We were set down in a field of tall grass; the chopper took off and orbited over us at 2,500 feet for the twenty minutes we were on the ground. The Vietnamese commander got a situation report from a wiry, little battalion commander, and we watched as a column of tanks, armored personnel carriers (APCs), bulldozers, and soldiers on foot wound their way through a village. An old woman squatted and smiled at the death machines as they rumbled past her thatched-roof hut. I used her in the lead of the story I wrote that night. It never ran. I never got the reason why. I guess maybe it told too much about our battle tactics.

When we flew back to Plei Mrong, I found the two resident US advisers. "We've just had a little incoming," Captain Paul Noyes told me in his tiny hooch. "No big deal. You just better stay in here a while." Noyes, twenty-six, and Lieutenant Elliott Cordell, twenty-five, two army forward air controllers (FACs), laughed off the twenty-five rounds of daily incoming they took while directing US and South Vietnamese planes on airstrikes against enemy positions.

"You missed a big day yesterday," Noyes said, climbing a ladder to his observation tower. "We had machine-gun fire at this tower, right after we put in tac. air. Surprised the hell out of me. I heard the bullets whizzing right by. I know we weren't bad shots. It's just that some of these bunkers are hard to knock out unless you score a direct hit."

Plei Mrong was manned by a battalion of Montagnard mercenaries who lived with their families inside the camp. Its mission was to interdict enemy troops and vehicles before they could reach Pleiku. The FACs estimated that there was a regiment of North Vietnamese troops west of them and other large elements to the north and east. "You don't sleep too soundly at night," Cordell said. "You never know when they might try to take this place."

While I was there, Noyes and Cordell called in several airstrikes by navy and air force F-4 Phantoms at a bunker complex 1,500 meters to their northwest. Noyes, sitting cross-legged in the tower, a field map on his knees, talked to a "covey," a light observation plane, overhead. Cordell looked through binoculars at the area to be struck and helped get the coordinates on the map as phoned in by the covey. The little aircraft was all set to fly home to Pleiku when the pilot radioed that he'd spied a series of deep, newly built bunkers near the location of that day's last previous airstrike.

"Beautiful," Noyes said. "Wish I was up there with you."

"Say, uh, two-zero," the covey replied, "how long did you say you've been down there on the ground?"

"I mean I wish I was up there to see what you see," Noyes said, laughing.

"Oh, roger that. Understand."

The covey reported seeing fifteen or twenty NVA soldiers scampering around near the bunkers. He said the middle bunker was large and oblong. There were fourteen other bunkers around it.

"From our experience," Noyes said, "that means it's the command post. Wonderful. Oh, boy—I hope you get something [bombs] in on that."

The FACs waited as the covey called to secure a pair of F-4s from either Da Nang or from an aircraft carrier in the South China Sea.

"I've found it works a whole lot better if you run this thing informally," Noyes said. "If you do it too much by the book, the guy upstairs gets uptight. If you're loose and the guy knows you're confident in what you're doing, he'll usually do a good job for you."

Noyes said he had used Vietnamese A-1Es on the previous day and had continued pounding enemy positions with AC-130 Spectre gunships during the night. "This morning's Ranger patrol came up with twelve NVA bodies," he said, "but I find it hard to believe that's all we got."

The covey radioed that he was supposed to return to Pleiku at 4:00 p.m. but the target was so juicy that he would stay around until the tac. air arrived, even though he was real low on fuel. He cagily flew off and circled around another area so the NVA troops wouldn't realize that he knew exactly where they were.

"If we knock those people out," Noyes said, "it'll eliminate our problem of incoming for a while. Just for a while, though. The enemy never seems to give up, no matter how much air we put on him"

At four forty-five, two F-4s roared in. The covey flew low and marked the NVA location with a white phosphorus grenade and peeled off. Each bomber swooped in and released two bombs. They all impacted about a hundred meters east of the smoke.

"Boo!" Cordell said. "Must be navy fliers."

Now the covey marked the position of the first bombs and gave the airplanes an adjustment. On the next few sorties, their bombs were right on target. "Okay, guys," Cordell said, checking the scene through his binoculars. "Now you've got it."

Despite the thunderous explosions and huge clouds of smoke less than a mile away, it was dinnertime at the camp. Shaggy-haired Montagnards, some clad only in the bathing suits they used for underwear, moved toward their mess hall and returned to their bunkers with bowls of rice and canteen cups of water to share with their families. They seemed oblivious to what was going on outside the wire.

"I think we'll need a couple of patrols to check out that area tomorrow," Noyes advised the ARVN base commander.

"I'll be sending out men first thing in the morning," the mustachioed little officer said through an interpreter.

"I guess you'd have to say this was one of our most active days in a while," Noyes said. "Things have been picking up lately. We put in nine sets of air today." Noyes and Cordell had been at Plei Mrong since early April and had listened to radio transmissions as ARVN base after base northwest of Kontum fell to the Communists. "I guess we're next," Cordell said. "If they want to flank both Pleiku and Kontum, they have to get us out of the way first. But we're right in the middle between Pleiku and Kontum, and we can call in any kind of air we want. They're not going to take this place without losing an awful lot of men."

Communist gunners had hit the camp with sixty rounds of 82 mm mortars on May 10 and had run the Vietnamese Popular Forces militia out of their outposts in nearby Plei Mrong Village. But with helicopter gunship and A-1E support, the Rangers killed twelve Communists the next day and drove the enemy back out of the village. Shortly after that, Cordell said he killed an NVA forward observer by hitting him with an M72 light antitank weapon (LAW) round. The advisers also taught the Montagnards to use the M72. Plei Mrong sat in a valley that was an ideal tank approach to Pleiku. But the Communists never penetrated that far south during the Easter Offensive.

"The Montagnards are sort of like children," Cordell said. "They'll run if something really unexpected comes along. But if they're prepared for something, they'll stay and fight. They're pretty good troops." He added, "We'll stay until the camp either holds or falls. We're not going to leave until the last minute. We've been here too long to miss the main attack if it comes."

PRESSURE'S OFF

When Matt Franjola and I arrived at Brigadier General Ly Tong Ba's one-room office in the old US Special Forces compound outside Kontum City on June 14, 1972, Ba was talking with two Vietnamese women about an upcoming show for his troops. His fatigue shirt was open, and his bare feet played with blue-and-white shower sandals under the creaky wooden table he used for a desk. He told the women he'd continue with them in a few minutes.

"Good morning, gentlemen," he said. "Please be seated." All was well in Kontum. The pressure was off. The remnants of two NVA regiments that had penetrated the provincial capital in late May had been driven off.

"We don't want to take too much of your time, sir," I said, "but we'd like to find out what's going on up here. Is the battle for Kontum over?"

"That's hard to say," he said. "We don't know what they want, and we'll be ready to fight again. I would like to find the last one [NVA soldier], and when the last one is killed, I'll say it's over. Some enemy units have been ordered to go [attack] again, but I think the unit commanders are almost refusing to obey now."

I asked him about the NVA tank threat. "They have only about a dozen left," Ba said. "Our soldiers are ready and know they can destroy them easily. And the VC don't know how to use tanks."

Did he consider the successful holding of Kontum a major victory for the ARVNs? "Definitely," Ba said. "I hope our success here will give our troops in Quang Tri and An Loc morale to defeat the VC. I don't see any big problems for us here. Today I saw my troops on the front. They were very happy, and I have found they were more confident than I expected them to be."

Ba said more than five thousand Communist soldiers of the 320ᵗʰ and Second NVA Divisions were killed within a kilometer of the perimeter around Kontum City. He said he never had hid casualty figures and that his losses ran about 500 killed and 1,500 wounded. "The only enemy left are suicide units," he said. "Why they stay and be killed, I don't know, maybe to prevent our units from following them [to their triborder base camp]. But day by day, we're moving out and destroying the enemy. I guess the VC commanders don't care about how many of their men die."

The general said he was proud of his Twenty-Third Division troops. He had eight hundred captured weapons on display at his command post. "We had two [NVA] regiments inside town and went three or four days without air support," he said, "and we cleaned them out. There's not a single VC in Kontum today." Ba said street fighting had ended on June 10. "We found one live tank—a T59—hiding in a burned-out building a few days ago," he said. "Today, I walked five or six clicks and shook hands with my commanders. I located the platoon that assaulted the T59 position and knocked it out. We gave the men a few thousand piasters each." He said he distributed more than 100,000 piasters (about $250).

"Okay, sir," I said. "We realize you're busy. Thank you very much for talking to us."

On our way out of town, an American adviser told us, "I think the weapons loss and the approaching rainy season will prevent the enemy from launching another big attack on Kontum."

Another adviser said, "I don't think Charles will be back until August. It takes some time to plan an attack like the last one."

An ARVN source in Pleiku, however, told us that the Communists had established a rice mill at Kon Horing Village seventeen miles north of Kontum and were supplying it with rice carried by forced laborers from coastal Binh Dinh Province. Other evidence that the Communists planned to remain around Kontum came in the form of heat-seeking missiles fired at US Air Force cargo planes, forcing them to fly into Kontum blacked out at night. But the ARVNs had withstood the worst the Communists had to offer, and for the time being, the pressure was off.

IN THE FIELD

On June 16, after the morning briefing from ARVN Captain Le Van Phuc in Pleiku, Matt Franjola of UPI, a freelancer whose name I forget, and I drove down Highway 14 south of Pleiku. We decided to stop at a Regional Forces outpost and get directions to the crash site where a big Convair 880 Cathay Pacific jetliner with eighty-seven aboard had crashed the previous day.

We were greeted by a Vietnamese interpreter who led us to a big, circus-like tent. There, two American lieutenant colonels told us about a recent operation near the firebase, which was about fifteen miles southeast of Pleiku. They said that on a recon mission, ARVNs had killed ten Communists and captured seven without taking casualties. The unit captured two NVA flags and documents that claimed the unit had gone into Pleiku City and returned to the bush with a list of the allied units there, their strengths, the number of artillery pieces they had, the number of airplanes that flew in and out of the air base in a day, the defense structure at II Corps headquarters, and the complete order of battle. I was amazed that the Americans had everything laid out in an orderly fashion and seemed eager to share it with us, as evidence of the expertise of their ARVN advisees.

PART IX

CLERK IN A WAR ZONE

PART IV

CLERK IN A WAR ZONE

"Did You Clear This Weapon, Hamburger?"

My army career had begun at Fort Dix, New Jersey, on September 25, 1970, and it had taken every ounce of strength I had to finish. Late in basic training, I had suffered from what I later found out was pneumonia. I hadn't wanted to wash out of the company I was in and repeat training, so I'd soldiered on. I had to qualify with the M16 at night on a range in a driving rainstorm. Sniffling and with bloodshot eyes, I squeezed off my rounds, and a few skipped into the target. When I was done, a drill sergeant in a Smokey Bear hat screamed at me, "Did you clear this weapon, hamburger?"

He pointed the rifle at my face. I said, "Yes, Drill Sergeant!" He turned the barrel skyward and squeezed off one round that was left in the chamber. He looked at me with disgust, then threw the weapon at me, knocking me over backward into the mud. "Sorry, son of a bitch; go on sick call tomorrow," he said.

While I was in a hospital bed, in the midst of losing twenty-one pounds, I learned that I also had qualified with the hand grenade—though I'd never actually touched one. I did my Advanced Infantry Training at Fort Jackson, South Carolina, where I went to clerk's school before shipping out for 'Nam. The possibility of serving in Vietnam as a clerk never had occurred to me.

Flying In

Flying into Tan Son Nhut Air Base outside Saigon at 3:30 a.m. on August 1, 1971, I watched the breathtaking arc of orange artillery-round tracers as they bore into the side of the hills near the South Vietnamese capital city. It was as if the army had put on a Coney Island fireworks display just to let our planeload of newfs know that there was a war going on. But that was the closest I came to combat in the five months I was to spend as a personnel records clerk at Cam Ranh Bay, a sprawling American seaport/air base on the central coast.

The day after I arrived at the 544th Replacement Detachment at Long Binh, I was among dozens of olive-clad incoming soldiers who were interviewed, received orders, and made arrangements to join units. The sergeant who interviewed me laughed and said the only way I could get shot at Cam Ranh was if I shot myself. "It's the safest place in Vietnam," he said, telling me that I was assigned to the 518th Adjutant General's Personnel Services Company. My job would be to sit at a desk six days a week and process the records of incoming and outgoing troops. At least I avoided being an infantryman. I felt good about that.

After flying into Cam Ranh, I tossed up my duffel bags and clambered into a seat in the back of a deuce-and-a-half truck. I had three quick impressions. The first was that the stench of urine seemed to be everywhere. The second was that it had to be more than a hundred degrees—and it wasn't even noon yet. The third was a weird sensation that just as tourists gape at Hadrian's Wall and other remnants of the Roman Empire in England, someday people would visit and inspect the primitive, light-green, wooden barracks that represented the furthest extent of the American empire in Vietnam.

I felt like the victim of a cruel joke. After pulling number 34 in the draft lottery following my graduation from Hofstra University in June 1970, I had enlisted in the army for three years to avoid being sent to Vietnam as an infantryman. My reward was getting to spend the summer of 1970 home with my friends. I got to choose my Military Occupational Specialty; I chose to be a clerk.

I felt that somehow this was punishment for past sins. Here I was, a single, twenty-two-year-old college graduate. I had been hired full-time as a *Newsday* sports reporter midway through my junior year. And now I would be serving what amounted to a year's prison time as a cog in the war machine. Since my grandfather Corneal had served in the US Navy in World War I and my father, Arthur, had been a Marine Corps master sergeant during World War II, I was raised to believe that military service was natural and expected. But I wasn't too keen about shooting anybody. I hoped I wouldn't have to make a decision about that. I basically went with the flow, got swallowed up by the Green Machine, and was ready to do my thing for God and country.

HOW I GOT THERE

The trip to Vietnam was a nightmare. After a thirty-day leave at home on Long Island, I reported to Fort Lewis, Washington, on July 25, 1971. Following four days of orientation and processing there, I was flown to 'Nam by a circuitous route that started at Seattle-Tacoma Airport; featured stops in Anchorage, Alaska, and Yokota Air Base outside Tokyo, Japan; and included three mechanical delays and two hotel stays. Because we failed by three and a half hours to land in-country in the month of July, I forfeited a month's combat pay (sixty-five dollars). I figured if the army was as inefficient as the trip I had taken, I was in for a heap of trouble.

Thankfully, Cam Ranh Bay wasn't nearly as bad as the replacement detachment had been. There were mountains on all sides, sand everywhere, sun shimmering on the bay. It was like a Caribbean resort city. There was no water worth drinking, but Coca-Cola had a gold mine there. At the replacement detachment, I had pissed through a wire-mesh cover into an oil drum and seen roaches the size of small mice scurry across the barracks floor. Cam Ranh was different. It was clean and seemed orderly.

I took consolation in the fact that I would be among the last few thousand lame ducks in a war that America continued to protest as it sputtered to its sad end. There were more than two hundred thousand troops in-country when I arrived. When I flew home 365 days later, there were less than fifty thousand, almost all in support roles. One of the first soldiers I met in Vietnam was wearing a camouflaged jumpsuit and carrying a crutch. He gave me a tray with four half sandwiches on it and left without saying a word. I figured he was stoned. The tuna and lettuce tasted great, but I wondered what the guy's story was.

Somebody told me that the words *Cam* and *Ranh* in French meant "miserable hardship frontier," which seemed appropriate. The landscape all around us was arid, but the amenities on the base made it bearable.

Racial Tension

"This is a knockout, rabbit, you dig?"

The tall, slender black soldier uncorked a roundhouse right, and his fist, enclosed by a plaster cast, caught the white soldier flush on the nose, sending him sprawling into the dusty street.

"Hey, brother," the white man said, getting up. "What's the matter? I lived with brothers all my life. I ain't never done 'em wrong. Is this the thanks I get?"

"Don't call me brother, motherfucker!" The black soldier slugged the unresisting white again and would have moved in for more if his laughing friends had not grabbed him and led him away. "The cat ain't even fightin' back, man," one said. "You killed him."

Another black approached the white soldier, who was me, and offered a towel to stop the steady stream of blood from my nose. "Take it easy, man," he said. "You're not hurt. Just wait here till that cat gets over the hill."

"I don't believe this happened," I said. "I never messed over a black cat in my life."

The night had started peacefully. It was "soul night" at the enlisted men's club in Cam Ranh Bay in August 1971, just after I arrived in Vietnam from the states. I liked soul music, so I went to the show alone. The place was packed, mostly with blacks and their Vietnamese whores. The Filipino band was terrible, but the blacks did not seem to mind. They were exchanging ritualistic handshakes (daps), putting on an arrogant display for the few whites who dared try to share the evening with them.

After the show, I walked back toward my barracks alone, my mind clouded by five beers and two rum and Cokes. As I was walking up a hill, I heard a voice behind me call, "Hey, brother." I turned around and saw a pack of blacks and kept walking. Another voice said, "That ain't no brother: that a rabbit motherfucker."

The black with the cast jogged up the hill in front of me and blocked my path. "When I call you, you rabbit motherfucker, you stop, understand?"

"Yeah, man, sure," I said, trying to step past him.

"You ain't goin' nowhere, whitey. This is a knockout, dig?" That's when I got clocked.

My nosebleed had stopped, but my hand was covered in blood. I wiggled my nose and was relieved to find it wasn't broken, I had a cool T-shirt on that I had brought from home. It said "Chevys Blow Your Mind" on the front and "Endless Summer" with a sun and a surfer on the back. It was torn and bloody.

"I don't believe this happened," I said again to the black with the Sherlock Holmes pipe and wire-rimmed glasses who offered comfort and the towel. His name was Chuck Holmes.

"It did, man, it did," he said.

"But why?"

"You meet all kinds over here, man. All kinds. You all right? Can you make it home?"

"Sure, man, sure. I know where I'm going. Thanks a lot, brother. Thanks a lot."

"Don't take it too hard, man. There's a lot of messed-up people on both sides."

"Why do there have to be sides, man? We're over here together. We're supposed to be fighting together. Why do we have to fight each other?"

"Blacks been taking shit for a long time."

"Not from me, man. I never messed over them. You know it doesn't hurt me here [on the nose] as much as it hurts here—in my heart, man."

"I dig you, man."

I continued on up the hill and made my way to the barracks. "What happened to you?" somebody said. "Damn niggers jumped me," I said. Then I sat on my bunk, disgusted over what I had said. (As it turned out, I never was involved in an incident like that for the rest of my tour.)

A Mundane, Boring Job

At the 518th, I worked in a big wooden office building/warehouse from seven thirty to five thirty with an hour and a half for lunch and Sundays off. There were daily formations at seven a.m., one p.m. and eight p.m. They took head counts. Like, where did they expect us to run off to? We were surrounded by mountains. The village was off-limits. We basically were captives. We could have been in Albuquerque, for all the contact we had with the war or the Vietnamese people. With four lines of bunkers and wire between our company area and the perimeter, I figured if an enemy soldier made it that far, I deserved to die.

I was making $180.90 a month as a private first class when I arrived and got a raise to $249.90 a month (plus $65 combat pay and $13 overseas pay) when I was promoted after a few months of good behavior to specialist fourth class.

The food was fine, but water was scarce, and because of the heat, most of us clerks drank at least four Cokes a day. The job was typing and copying the paperwork for troops to process in and out of the country. On my first day on the job, I noticed that the thermometer outside our office read 106 degrees at eleven in the morning. I couldn't imagine how grunts in the field could cope with such oppressive heat. One night early in my tour, I was writing a letter to my parents, and my sweaty forearm stuck to the notepaper.

There was a big movie screen outside our barracks. Just about every night, we watched first-run movies. Some nights, we had barbecued steaks that were stateside-good. I made friends quickly. Life was simple. The work was monotonous but easy. I occupied myself at night by reading novels, rapping, drinking, and listening to or recording music. Eventually, care packages began arriving from home every other week with purified water, cassette tapes, *Newsday* sports sections, magazines, snacks in tin containers, Handi Wipes, and other goodies. I shared the water so as not to be branded a momma's boy.

We also sometimes received care packages and letters from our hometowns via the Red Cross. My friends shared their care packages with me. One guy gave me a piece of pumpkin bread his mother had baked and mailed from St. Louis.

HOW WE LIVED

The barracks hooches were about eight feet by ten feet, two men to a room. Men had black lights, spotlights, desks, streamers, beads, posters, bookshelves, beach chairs, night tables, rugs, wall lockers, footlockers, and fans. Some troops had small refrigerators for beer and soda. As people left, they sold off their stuff. By late September, I had bought a refrigerator for thirty-five dollars. Coke was $2.40 a case. We kept hard liquor, cheap and available at the base PX, under lock and key. There didn't seem to be a lot of marijuana around, but it was available at parties, usually held on Friday or Saturday night from nine to midnight when the lifers were at their clubs getting loaded.

One morning during an inspection, a shoebox of marijuana was found in our barracks and burned, ceremoniously. The inspection had been announced in advance, which gave guys time to bury or hide their stashes.

A couple of troops were addicted to heroin, which they snorted or smoked. I never saw a needle. The boredom was oppressive. A friendly black troop from Missouri was addicted. He seemed to be mellow and tired all the time. I never took the time to ask why he began using skag. I was concentrating on making it through my own tour. Nobody judged anybody else. You did what you had to.

I started a short-timer's calendar and began crossing off the days. I picked up the familiar expressions that remain a part of my vocabulary to this day: bye now, beaucoup (a lot), *tee tee* (a little), number one (good), number ten (bad), same-same (exactly like), cut me some slack (give me a break), there it is, I notice that, don't mean nothing, back in the world, *dinky dau* (crazy).

Whenever any of us was threatened by lifers, we mumbled under our breaths, "What are they going to do to us, send us to 'Nam?" That was the joke. We were already at the worst place to which we could be banished.

Whores in the barracks were forbidden, but somehow guys managed to sneak them in. The prostitutes were called "gators" because of the big bites they took out of GIs' wallets. After attending mandatory health classes and hearing horror stories about venereal diseases, I never got involved with gators. One night, our CO happened to be riding home from the officers' club in a jeep when he spotted a couple of guys strolling arm in arm with whores in our company area. He ordered a dawn formation the next day.

"Men," he said, "there are specific rules about the presence of foreign nationals in the billets after hours. There will be no foreign nationals in our billet area after hours, and to ensure this fact, we will have a courtesy patrol of E-6s, E-7s, and E-8s [sergeants] in the barracks every night." It worked for a couple of weeks, but then the sergeants slacked off, and the men started sneaking the whores back in.

The rules about haircuts were pretty relaxed, although there were periodic crackdowns on that too. I got my second haircut in four months on October 11 at the PX. It included a shave; facial massage; back, arm, and chest massage; and antipimple cream on my face. The price: $1.25. One thing about 'Nam: everything was cheap.

PACIFYING THE TROOPS

The army tried to keep us amused by sending over Miss America and a half-dozen other stateside beauty queens to sing and dance for us. The Miss America show was held on a hastily constructed stage on the dusty, grassless baseball field. Dozens of MPs encircled the stage. Security was tight. What did they think—that us horny GIs would storm the stage and grope or rape the women? About two thousand men attended, most sitting on the side of a sandy hill wearing fatigues or civilian clothes. The girls were gorgeous. But their numbers had been prerecorded. They danced and lip-synched but seemed to be going through the motions.

We booed the MPs every time they did anything. Like when the girls came dancing up to the front of the stage, two dozen MPs formed up with their gleaming white helmets and pistol belts, tapping clubs into their palms. They looked like the riot police at the 1968 Democratic Convention. We hooted at and taunted them. I got a laugh from my buddies when Miss New Jersey did her number. "That's close enough!" I said. They all knew I was from New York. You had to be there. It was funny.

There also were American civilian women volunteers called "Donut Dollies" who played guessing games and board games with us. They refused most offers to play spin the bottle. There were Vietnamese and Filipino bands that played a couple of times a week at the enlisted men's club. They knew all the right songs and usually encored with "We Gotta Get out of This Place." There was a band that played on weekends at Tiger Lake, a sandy rest-and-relaxation site within the base. They did songs by Led Zeppelin, the Temptations, the Four Tops, Iron Butterfly, Three

Dog Night, and the Cowsills—anything to help us forget where we were. Sometimes we did.

There was a base chapel. I took advantage of a priest's giving general absolution and went to Communion for the first time in six years. I figured I might as well cover all bases. Who knew when a rocket might blow up my barracks while I slept? I made a tape describing life at the base for my family and asked my *mama-san* (hooch maid), Renee, who washed my clothes and made my bed for five dollars a month, to say a few words about how good I'd been. "Why GI do beaucoup cocaine?" she said into the microphone, exploding into laughter.

There was a base library from which it was easy to steal paperbacks. I must've read twenty-five in five months, including *The Godfather*, *The Decline and Fall of the Roman Empire*, *From Ghetto to Glory*, *Day of Infamy*, *The Andromeda Strain*, *The Sun Also Rises*, *The Power and the Glory*, *Honor Thy Father*, *1984*, *Time Machine*, *The Great Gatsby*, *The Hobbits*, *The Jocks*, *Confessions of a Dirty Ballplayer*, *The Kennedy Legacy*, and *Rock from the Beginning*. We had a lot of free time.

I read everything I could get my hands on, including the *Stars and Stripes* daily newspaper and *Overseas Weekly*, the underground servicemen's newspaper that reported troop reductions and redeployments. There was a country-wide lull in battlefield action. But that did not mean we weren't vigilant. There were periodic alerts, some coinciding with significant dates in enemy history, such as VC Revolutionary Day when my company provided eighteen guards at night instead of the usual four. But nothing happened.

Monsoon Season Begins

By mid-October it was windy and rainy most of the time. At nights watching movies, we wore field jackets and ponchos. There was mucky water in the shower shack, and for a few weeks, hundreds of frogs called the place home. The flow of people into our office for processing, in conjunction with Nixon's Vietnamization policy and troop pullout, started to wane. Six of us in my section had processed about fifty newfs a day when I arrived. By mid-October, in a four-day span we processed only twenty-five men and got off early twice. In mid-November, I was transferred to another part of the office.

In the new office during monsoon season, a half-dozen dogs would stroll in the open front door, shake off the rain, and plop down in the middle of the room. Nobody chased them out. We gave them names. One night, two dogs, Rat and Doofus, fought each other as twenty-five men surrounded them and cheered. Another dog, whom we called Dollar, interceded to help Rat, and they drove Doofus down the street yelping. Money was exchanged by those who'd bet on the fight. The dogs were celebrities. Like, we'd walk by a dog, and even if nobody was around, we'd say, "Hello there, US, how's it going?"

We had heard there was incoming at the airport on the night of August 23. I got up at three thirty in the morning to get a drink of water and saw the sky light up in the distance. But I had no sense of being in danger. Some clerks volunteered weekly for Tiger Patrol, in which they carried weapons like infantrymen and patrolled the hills around the base a couple of times a week. They got tiger patches to wear on their fatigue shirts, and they could tell the folks back home that they were warriors. Not me. If I had wanted to be a grunt, I would have allowed myself to be drafted and served two years instead of committing for three. I enjoyed nightly chess games in the comfort of my hooch. One guy got bitten by a snake while on patrol and was hospitalized for a few days. Like I needed that.

A Friend in Deed

Renee was about forty-five with betel-nut-stained teeth. My prescription sunglasses disappeared from my hooch one day. She got them back. I figured she hid them herself so she could then ingratiate herself to me. But who cared? I bought her cartons of Salem cigarettes from the PX that she sold on the black market. I gave her cans of fruit and vegetables that came in my care packages.

On slow days at the office, the clerks wrote letters and read books. I never wrote so many letters before or since. I'm not sure why, but I reached out to my extended family, relatives, and friends, including a girlfriend who sent me a Dear John letter a couple of months into my tour. She told me she had met a guy at Fordham University and that they were dating. She hoped I understood. It was a good excuse to get drunk. I found a different excuse four or five nights a week.

I knew nothing about Vietnamese history and did nothing to find out anything about it. I had no sense that America was losing a war, but there was a feeling among us that the country had decided it wasn't worth winning. We all tried to make the best of the situation. I participated in many late-night debates. I heard rage coming from paranoid potheads. I heard antiwar logic from college graduates. To me, it seemed that we were doing the right thing: we were arming and fortifying an ally while withdrawing gradually from the battlefield. To me, that made sense.

We bonded by playing softball and touch football. I got a lot of laughs with my Howard Cosell impersonations. I "broadcast" some of our unit football team's games using a Cosell-like voice, recording myself on cassette tapes and playing them back at postgame parties. I cracked everybody up by trying to stir up trouble, suggesting that one player was handicapped on the field by alcoholism, another was a glory seeker, a third was playing out his option to join another unit, and so on. We celebrated victories by strumming guitars, popping popcorn, and drinking. After some big wins, we doused each other in spray, as if we had won the Super Bowl. We laughed at inane jokes until our throats hurt. The NCOs and our lieutenant joined in the celebrations but faded away early so they would not be compromised by the team's grass smoking. After one victory, which I attended fully dressed for guard duty, the team bus dropped me at the guard shack. I got an ovation for attending on a night on which I had duty.

By early November, I had switched my stuff into a hooch near three friends—Red Irwin, of Austin, Texas; Rich Ledford, of Virginia Beach, Virginia; and Bill Haendler, of Dumbarton, Pennsylvania. We did a lot of rapping about each other's lifestyles at home. Irwin described in great detail how he cleaned and waxed his car every Saturday morning. When I asked him what he did on Saturday nights, he said, "Take it down to the dirt track and race it."

We beat Ninety-Second Finance for the base football championship, 18–6, and the commanding general of Cam Ranh, whose name, ironically, was Kissinger (Major General Harold A.), awarded trophies to us, including a big trophy for winning the title. Our CO, Major Casey, accepted it, and we gave him an ovation. People were snapping photos and hugging each other. I recorded the general's speech by standing next to him with a microphone and tape recorder. Then we celebrated in my hooch. The lifers all came, and we listened to my broadcast. I stayed up till midnight with a few guys discussing the game. It seemed *so* important.

FLAG FOOTBALL IN THE MUD

On November 24, we were bused about fifty miles north along the coast to Nha Trang for the regional best-of-three playoffs against the Sixty-Eighth Signal Corps and beat them on a safety 2–0 in mud caused by a driving rainstorm. The army gave us what had to be the best coach bus in Vietnam. It had heat, plush seats, and loudspeakers for the radio. On each side of Cam Ranh's main gate, barbed wire was coiled like giant slinky toys. The bus rumbled past a plywood village outside the base. We saw rows of shacks with tin roofs. We saw people on bicycles, children pissing in the street, and families with six inches of rainwater in their living rooms.

In some areas, the bay overflowed across the causeway. The bus slowed down when we hit puddles, but sometimes it sent up a spray on each side of us that soaked some folks. The driver, a tall, muscular redneck from Alabama, was enjoying it. He was scaring the shit out of us, though, by swerving in and out of traffic on the two-lane highway, passing people on motorbikes. There were two bunkers at every bridge we came to. On the other side of one bridge, there were a few homes made of concrete blocks and presumably occupied by the more wealthy residents of Cam Ranh.

We drove a half hour on an open road before entering another populated area. There were all kinds of little roadside shops: a hardware store with lumber and odds and ends, a dress shop, a barbershop with one chair, a motorcycle repair shop. A man was driving cattle along the side of the road. I got a flash of the inside of a plywood hut and saw ten little kids running around. We were heading toward mountains that looked dark and forbidding. We drove into the suburbs and saw thatched-roof houses that were clean and organized, surrounded by wooden fences and shaded by palm trees.

An ARVN convoy of deuce-and-a-halfs passed us going in the opposite direction. There were resolute pint-size ARVNs behind M60 machine guns on top of many trucks. That reminded us that we were in a war zone. We saw an Esso station, but the only thing it seemed to be dispensing was air for bicycle tires. Gray clouds hung low over the mountaintops. Here we were, with seventy-five-dollar cameras shipped from Japan, taking photos of kids with no shoes riding water buffaloes. We were ensconced in a heated bus, and I figured the people outside didn't see seventy-five dollars in a year. In the distance, a small boy poled a sampan through a rice paddy to a tiny island where a pup tent was set up.

The houses outside Nha Trang looked like some that I remembered seeing gypsies living in near Coney Island's amusement park. Some were gaudily painted. The poverty was depressing. As we headed into the main business district of Nha Trang, we saw buildings that looked like the seedy motels at Myrtle Beach in the '70s. We entered a traffic circle where six streets converged. We snaked our way around bicycle-riding Vietnamese girls in flowing white ao dai dresses. Some girls walked together arm in arm. Small people, small trucks, small bikes, small roads, small buildings. I saw a boy of about ten trying to blow up an inner tube he'd fished out of a mud puddle. I felt empathy but had no sense of wanting to help the Vietnamese raise their standard of living. I was an American. I deserved the royal treatment.

We arrived at the American base at Nha Trang and played the football game in the mud. I don't remember the score, but we lost. People slid through puddles. The lines on the field were obscured by the downpour. Nobody could hold on to the ball. The absurdity of it all struck me. But who cared? It helped us forget where we were.

The day after that game, we traveled back to Nha Trang and lost 7–6 for the championship in another rainstorm, having three touchdowns called back due to penalties. We felt we were robbed by the officials but came back to Cam Ranh and had our party anyway. There was beer, Bacardi, and Coke on the bus and more drinking back at the barracks. But the party broke up before ten o'clock because people had to go back to work the next day. After that, we focused on softball.

PASSING TIME, CROSSING
OFF THE DAYS

I spent a lot of nights recording friends' music. When I wrote letters home while I was drunk, I'd quote obscure lyrics from rock songs. My parents must've thought I was high all the time. At night, you could stroll through our barracks and hear Merle Haggard, Marvin Gaye, Rare Earth, Jethro Tull, The Who, the Rolling Stones, the Moody Blues, and Country Joe and the Fish in a dueling-stereos competition. Usually, people were respectful of each other's space and kept the volume reasonable. Sometimes, people got drunk and cranked their stereos up. That could result in cursing matches and fights.

A Mexican and a redneck lifer once wrestled with each other in the sand for what seemed like a half an hour as we passed around a joint and egged them on, refusing to break it up. During another fight, a pocket knife flashed and drew blood on a man's cheek. But mostly, relations were cool. Most of us were clerks and had some education and common sense.

The monotony of our lives was numbing, though. One night, for lack of anything to do. I came up with a list of the top ten people I admired: John Kennedy, Mick Jagger, Robert Kennedy, Che Guevara, Peter Fonda, Ralph Nader, George McGovern, Ted Kennedy, Mickey Mantle, and Arnold Palmer.

A pig farmer from Minnesota had an enormous reel-to-reel tape player he'd had shipped from Japan. He let me record a bunch of my favorite groups: Three Dog Night, Creedence Clearwater Revival, Tommy James and the Shondells, Melanie, the Beach Boys, Cat Stevens, and Blood, Sweat & Tears. When I played those tapes on my little cassette player,

284

they sounded better than some of my prerecorded music. On Labor Day weekend, the AFVN radio station played three straight days of oldies with narration by commentators. Everybody recorded as much as they could. One commentator said, "The Rolling Stones brought an insistent, individualistic, working-class drive to rock music ... a kind of youthful alienation in their place and time." I made fifteen tapes in seventy-two hours.

Here's what I wrote one night, obviously drunk: "I was thinking—because there is the boooom of artillery shells in the distance—that if this barracks were blowing up right now, I don't think I'd get up off this bed because I'm so enthralled with these sounds. My life is flashing before my eyes, musically. (two more Buds, please.) ... Oh, screw the guns. Screw the cat playing Sly's Greatest Hits upstairs. Screw everything. I'm listening to the Beatles."

In October 1971, the most frequently played singles on the AFVN radio station were "For What It's Worth" by Buffalo Springfield, "In-A-Gadda-Da-Vida" by Iron Butterfly, "Goin' Home" by the Stones, "Five O'Clock World" by the Vogues, "Riders on the Storm" by the Doors, "Take Me Home, Country Roads" by John Denver, "Sweet Hitchhiker" by Creedence, and "Maggie May" by Rod Stewart. If I hear "Take Me Home, Country Roads" play now, tears well in the corners of my eyes.

SNORTING HEROIN

In Cam Ranh Bay, we slept in hooches with streamers and beads for doors, about thirty-two to a two-floor barracks. At night, socializing broke down to the lifers, draftees, blacks, juicers, heads, and so on. Since I had enlisted, the draftees didn't know what to make of me. One guy, an addict with bulging eyes, was particularly abusive to me, taunting me about being "a lifer and a snitch." To get him off my back, I snorted powdered heroin through a dollar bill at a party. After hallucinating and combining the skag with alcohol, I slept like a brick for twenty hours. But I was finally one of the guys. And I never touched anything outside of grass again.

There were so many addicts afraid to pull guard duty that I used to pull it for them at thirty to fifty dollars a night. Most times, I'd shine my boots and use starched fatigues to get named sergeant of the guard, so I'd stay in a shack manning a radio in contact with the dudes on the wire. When I got home, I had enough money to walk into a Chevy dealership in Queens and buy a 1973 Chevy Monte Carlo for cash: $4,107.

I sat in on card games, usually losing my shirt. I talked to guys about the lives they left and to which they would return—Bill, a college-grad truck driver from Pennsylvania who expected to become a teacher; Rich, a nerd from Virginia Beach who had no plans; Varney, a carpenter from rural West Virginia who I hoped would enter a drug rehab program; Donnie, a naive coon hunter from Ohio who was considering staying in the army.

A few of us used to sit in the bleachers watching the nightly movie. Most of the movies were PG, and we talked through them. A guy at the end of a row would pass an empty cup and say "ice." Each guy, in turn, would say "ice" as the cup made its way to the end of the row, where somebody filled it with ice and 7-Up from a cooler and passed it back. "Ice." Real brains, we were.

Sometimes we'd all go to the club to drink and listen to rock bands. And we'd have periodic company parties. At one of them, the lifers provided a band from Manila called the Living Legends. We had barbecued steaks, baked beans, salad, and beer. The show was held inside, in an unused section of the records office. Seating was based on time in-country: short-timers up front, newfs in the back. Two men with a week to go were ushered to seats of honor close to the stage. "Short!" they yelled. The band played all the usual stuff. Three dancing girls gyrated. Lights flashed. Then a chunky Mama Cass type came out and sang some Janis Joplin tunes. By the end, there were officers onstage dancing and lifer NCOs clapping sullenly, and then we all helped each other stagger out the door and home to the barracks.

I fired nine rounds with my M16 from a prone position early in my tour at range targets twenty-five meters away. They were the only rounds I remember firing the whole year I was in 'Nam. I mailed the targets home as evidence that I could hit what I aimed at. The day of my brushup course in rifle shooting, they gave us the rest of the day off. I hitched a ride to Tiger Lake, sunbathed on a sandy beach, and floated in lukewarm water on an inner tube. The heat and humidity were unbelievable. After a short walk up a hill, your fatigue shirt stuck to your back.

We became so tight in the barracks that whenever anybody went anywhere at night, he got grilled. One night, Haendler was seen emerging from the minicourt trailer-park home of the Donut Dollies. Red and I confronted him on his return and started lisping like homosexuals. "My heavens, where have you been?" I said. "We were so worried. Don't you ever go away again without telling us, you savage."

A BREAK FROM THE
CLERICAL POOL

I got time off from clerical chores to pull duties such as driving fence posts, stringing barbed wire, picking up trash, hauling garbage to the dump, and performing guard duty and charge of quarters. On one detail, three others and I had to roll sixty-five heavy truck tires, most filled with rainwater, a hundred feet through sand to load them on a five-ton truck. Then we had to drag them off and roll them into a clover-leaf pattern on the side of a hill as part of an erosion-control plan. The same day, we drove to a dump, loaded two trucks full of tires, drove back to the hill, and dropped them off for others to arrange.

Probably the worst job I ever had in my life was burning shit at Cam Ranh Bay. We all took turns going to the outhouse, rolling the two-gallon drums a few yards to the side, and lighting them with a torch. After the crap cooked off, we had to roll the drums back into place. The smell stayed with you for days.

I also periodically was drafted to fill sandbags. One day, fifteen others and I built up protection around a bunker on the top of a steep, sandy hill. When there was a report of a typhoon headed our way, all sorts of preparations were made, especially putting sandbags and wire mesh around barracks windows. But the storm changed course and headed north. We rooted for it to hit Hanoi.

I spent the morning of my twenty-third birthday on post police, picking up Coke cans and candy wrappers on the side of a road for a mile. In the afternoon, we did the same thing along another mile-long stretch of dirt road. It was just like being a garbage man in the world. Two of us stood on the two running boards of the deuce-and-a-half. We'd jump off, snatch some garbage, throw it into the back of the truck, and jump back up. After we were done, we drove two miles to a deserted, off-limits beach, picked up some trash cans, and emptied them into the back of the truck. Then we had to sit in the stuff. A roach crawled up my arm and disappeared beneath the huge mass of sticky cans, cartons, and gunk. Man, did I take a long shower that night.

Ten days later, while I was stringing barbed wire, we had a thundershower, got soaked, and took refuge in an abandoned school bus. They took us back to the mess hall for hot soup and cardboard fish for lunch. We went back out in the afternoon and got soaked again. My buddy Rick was cursing and swearing. I congratulated myself for being cool and not grumbling. I was mature enough to cope. I'd finished college, gotten my foot in the business world at *Newsday*, and was secure that I would have a job when I returned—unlike Rick, who'd joined the army out of high school.

One guy paid me thirty dollars to pull guard duty so he could play touch football. Another had been on guard in June when some VC sappers blew up a bunker and wounded a few GIs. Since then, he paid people to pull all his guard-duty shifts.

The neatest troops with the shiniest boots got to stay in the guard shack all night, so I always showed up looking good. Half the time, I never left the shack. When I had guard duty, I pulled out my starched fatigues that I saved for the occasion. I never had to fire my rifle on guard duty, never came under attack. Most of the time, I guarded places like the NCO club while the less fortunate or less prepared were stationed at ammo dumps or in bunkers on the perimeter.

The only scare I had was on the night of October 2 when the truck driver of the two-ton vehicle that delivered the guards to their posts was stoned. Twice he drove us into sand dunes. We all had to get out and push the big truck out. Eventually I finally was dropped off at my post, Support Command Headquarters (SUPCOM). SUPCOM was on top of the highest mountain, overlooking the bay. I spent the night humming oldies tunes to myself and gazing at the moonlight reflecting off the bay. It looked like Long Island Sound. No sweat.

HUNJ

The Filipino rock band inside the NCO club was wailing into a distorted medley of Creedence Clearwater Revival songs as I slid my M16 off my shoulder. In the shadows, a seemingly furtive figure approached, stopped, and stared. A moment passed. It seemed like an hour. My finger tightened on the trigger. This was during my stint as a clerk.

"Hey, man, what's up?" the man said, coming closer. "It's me—Hunj."

A relief. It was only the little Vietnamese guy who worked the night cleanup detail. I slung my rifle and continued pacing around the building. Can't be too careful. VC could be anywhere.

"You had me scared there for a minute, Hunj," I said.

"How come?"

"The way you stopped when you saw me."

"I didn't know who you were. I was afraid."

"So was I, man."

Actually, I'd lucked out that night. My reward for putting an extra coat of polish on my boots was an easy post—the NCO club. While most of the other guards pulled three hours on, three hours off at far-flung posts around the perimeter of the huge base, I only had to "guard" the club from six to eleven at night. And I still got the next day off.

Walking guard, my steel pot gave me a headache. My pistol belt was a notch too tight. Or my stomach was an inch too large. I had two magazines of ammo: thirty-six rounds. I wondered what would have happened if the VC really hit. Would I have fired? Could I have killed somebody? I'll never know.

In the distance, Cobra gunships spit rockets into a hillside, lighting up the sky. The war was going on out there. But I felt pretty safe on the sprawling, well-protected base.

"Where you from, Hunj?" I asked, sitting for a spell on a folding chair one of the cooks had left outside the kitchen.

"Up north. I come down 1954. Now live cross bay."

I noticed that Hunj's right eye was a misshapen, caved-in mess. "How'd you get that?" I asked.

"I fight," he said, "year and a half in the army. Something blow up. A piece goes in my eye. Doctor say he can put in a plastic one, but I no want. Then maybe no can see at all. Rather be this way."

Hunj was about five foot two and looked about eighteen with his close-cropped hair. "Twenty-six year old," he corrected. "Have two *babysans*. One die. He only a few days old. Nobody knows what happen. He just die." The other child, he said, was in his wife's stomach, due in about four months.

"I no like war," he said. "I no like army either. They no pay nothing. I make more now."

"I know what you mean, man," I said.

Hunj turned serious. "Before Americans come," he said, "we can go anywhere we want. Now we can go nowhere. We're afraid to leave village. Now worse than before. Why?"

"A lot of people made a lot of mistakes, Hunj."

"You like be here?"

"No, man. I don't want to be here."

"Why you come?"

"They had my name on a piece of paper. I had to. Or go to jail."

"I would not fight again. I no like killing."

"Me neither, man. Well, time to do my guard thing again."

I continued pacing around the building. The club was for the ranks of E-5 through E-9, buck sergeant through first sergeant. Lifers. Some were pigs; some weren't. Go-go dancers were gyrating wildly, distracting the men from the fact the music was horrible. A lifer staggered through the doorway and saw me. "Give 'em hell, kid," he said. I flashed the peace sign and kept pacing.

I started humming a song by Melanie with the lyrics "There's a chance peace will come in your life."

Hunj, stepping out of the shadows, said, "I pray for peace too. I am a Catholic. So is my wife."

"So am I."

"You know," he said, "I wonder what happen when all GI go home. I wonder if we have peace, like before, or more war. I wonder what GIs do here."

"So do I, man, so do I."

SAIGON BOUND

On November 15, 1971, I saw an ad in *Stars and Stripes* for a reporter's job, so I telephoned the daily newspaper's Saigon office and inquired about it. After hearing my background, office manager Dick Berry said he'd hire me if my unit could be persuaded to let me go. As an enlisted man, I had leverage to request a transfer to a job in which I had "a civilian-acquired skill." So I immediately put in an application for a transfer. Berry sent a message to my CO, saying he'd hire me if I were released. I waited for the paperwork mill to grind. It had to make its way through successive steps up the chain of command: Special Troops Headquarters in Cam Ranh, USARV, USARPAC, and so on. Berry withdrew the ad, told me I was the only one who had applied for the job, and said he would hold the slot for me.

In the meantime, I pitched and played second base on our unit softball team. The weather turned windy, and often during games, sand would swirl across the infield, stopping the action as we covered our eyes with our mitts. The wind blew snow-like drifts two feet high around the barracks. Once it was so windy we had to cancel a practice. We wore field jackets outside at the movies. On November 21, I saw that my CO had stamped "recommended for approval" on my paperwork, so I expected to leave in two weeks. Most of the NCOs and officers knew me from my affiliation with the football team and liked my sense of humor. But as it turned out, it took five more weeks because the paperwork got lost and had to be refiled. Typical. On November 23, I was told by a clerk at Special Troops that I shouldn't expect to leave until about January 1. In a way, that was good, because I got to spend more time with my friends while still feeling upbeat about my impending transfer.

Many of my barracks mates were getting drops off their tours and shipping out early. There were a lot of happy faces around. Everybody felt the rough stuff as far as US involvement in the war was over. We spent entire days verbally dumping on each other about being queer, being a rebel, a Yankee, or whatever. But nobody got ticked off. It was just a way of getting by.

I wrote only eleven pages' worth of letters home in December. By December 15, I was notified that my paperwork had made it as far as USARV headquarters in Saigon. One day, I killed time by playing tennis and miniature golf with Red and Bill, who was preparing for a two-week leave. Compared to most of the soldiers in Vietnam, we were living like kings. I saw some of the infantrymen's barracks, and they didn't even have partitions, just two dozen beds, twelve on each side of a big open area. No privacy. That would have driven me insane. One of the grunts told me he had scored 151 out of 160 on the army's general intelligence test. He'd had twenty-nine hours toward a law degree at the University of Pittsburgh when he'd been drafted. And they had made him an infantryman. When I heard that, it validated my decision to enlist for the extra year.

At nine in the morning on December 27, a fellow clerk told me, "We gotcha, buddy." He'd just gotten my transfer approval papers back from USARV. He cut my request for orders, and a Vietnamese man at a computer banged out a mat for me. I took it to repro, and a friend put it through the ringer, and I had fifty copies of my reassignment orders. You needed copies at several steps along the way to get through all the red tape of a transfer. I gave a friend my desk radio, threw away my office calendar, gathered up my nameplate, and hightailed it out of the office.

Over the next few days, I got my clearance papers from the orderly room, went to finance and got my records, cleared the education center and the library, and packed some of my odds and ends in cardboard boxes, taping the tops. I got my specialist fourth class chevrons sewn on my dress uniform, dusted off my low quarters, put some Brasso on my belt buckle, and so on. I picked up my medical records at the dispensary, drew my savings (about $1,000) out of the bank in the form of a note that could be cashed only by me, cleared the motor pool, supply room, and so on. I said my good-byes to the guys, exchanging addresses with a half-dozen men. They had a small party for me the night before I left. I supplied crackers and cheese from my last care package. Somebody brought a case of Bud. We passed around a joint.

The next day, I got paid, loaded my baggage onto a deuce-and-a-half, and was driven to the airport. Hallelujah. No more guard duty. No more fence-post driving. No more garbage detail. No more monotonous records to process. I was finally getting the hell out of Cam Ranh Bay. I was going to the big city. I was going to find out a little about what the war was all about.

ARRIVING IN SAIGON

Almost two months after I began the paperwork to get myself transferred from my personnel records clerk job at Cam Ranh Bay to *Stars and Stripes* in Saigon, I shipped out on New Year's Eve, December 31, 1971. I flew in a C-130 cargo plane outfitted with beach-chair-like webbed seats. There were about seventy of us crammed into the plane. The only two windows were portholes on each side of a sliding door on the side, so I couldn't see any of the countryside. Mostly, I read H. G. Wells's *War of the Worlds* and mused about freedom from the boredom of the base camp.

When I arrived at Tan Son Nhut Air Base, two *Stars and Stripes* staffers met me and helped me load my suitcase, duffel bag, and six cardboard boxes full of junk into their Scout station wagon. They settled me in a room at the paper's compound downtown. It looked like an old hotel with high ceilings, concrete walls, and tiled floors. Since it sat on a main thoroughfare, there was an incessant putt-putt and vroom of Hondas, Suzukis, and other two- and three-wheeled vehicles on the street outside. It made sleeping before curfew tough.

After I got settled and showered, six of us drove in two vehicles to a French restaurant called Ramuntcho's and had a heck of a New Year's Eve dinner. The drive was hairy because all these idiots on scooters were darting in and out of the four-wheeled traffic. I thought we were going to kill a couple of them. At the restaurant, it was first-class all the way: hot towels, white tablecloths, sparkling glasses, shimmering silverware, a great steak with french fries and green beans, a few Vietnamese beers. It was hard to believe I was in a war zone.

On New Year's Day, a bunch of us drove forty miles east to Vung Tau, a sandy-beach rest-and-relaxation site on the coast. We stayed a couple of hours, jumping over the waves, bodysurfing, and throwing a football around—it was just like Rockaway Beach in Queens. Then we went to the snack bar, where they were giving out free food, I guess because it was New Year's Day: shrimp, french fries, hamburgers, Cokes, pickles. Quite nice. Then we cavorted in the waves again before settling down to watch the Giants lose to the Eagles, 41–28, on television.

The drive back to Saigon in our air-conditioned Rambler station wagon took two and a half hours. The melody of Richie Havens's song "Freedom" was all I could think of all day. "Freedom … freedom … freedom … freedom … Sometimes I feel like a motherless child … Sometimes I feel like I'm almost gone … a long, long way from my home."

The next day, I got processed for my press card and was taken to a tailor and measured for some jungle suits, the generic, lightweight, solid-colored leisure suits that the *Stripes* reporters wore. That night we began by having a drink at the bar in our air-conditioned television room and then drove downtown to a restaurant called La Dolce Vita. I had a shrimp cocktail and a sausage pizza. The other guys had steak, veal, spaghetti, and crab. We paid a guy taking Polaroids 400 piasters (about a dollar) to take a shot of us at the table. After that we went barhopping.

For some reason, we taught a drunk bar chick how to say "Happy Hanukkah," and she kept saying it, and we kept banging glasses together. We arrived back at the ranch a little after one in the morning, and I slept like a rock until I was awakened by the noise of the eggbeater vehicles and buses grinding up and down the street outside my window. I guessed I wouldn't have to worry about getting an alarm clock.

I was given a desk and a maid and made to feel at home, I got a rations allowance of $77.10 a month and had the option to pay fifty cents a meal at the US servicemen's mess hall just down the street. We also could buy provisions from the American commissary, and one of the first nights I was in Saigon, we barbecued steaks and made french fries. There was a lull in the war, and we were enjoying ourselves. Everything was informal. Nobody on the staff wore any rank insignia. We wore little eagles on our collars. The whole thing seemed run like a civilian newspaper.

Our office was right down the stairs from the living quarters. Everything was air-conditioned. I had a fairly new typewriter sitting atop a gray desk. I couldn't have asked for a better situation. I was looking forward to getting out and writing some features. After attending the daily afternoon briefing given by the South Vietnamese and US commands for a few days, I figured a lot of the work was going to be dull—writing about casualty figures, unit stand-downs, drug raids, B-52 strikes, and so on.

OUT IN THE FIELD

After spending my first twelve days in Saigon learning the basics, I went out in the field. UPI broke a story quoting Brigadier General George E. Wear, the commanding officer at Camp Holloway in Pleiku, as saying that the Communists were building up for a massive offensive in the Central Highlands to coincide with the Vietnamese New Year (Tet) and the arrival of President Richard M. Nixon in China. Our Tokyo office suggested that we get a man to Pleiku immediately, and I volunteered.

I flew on a C-130 from Saigon to Cam Ranh Bay, where I had been stationed the previous five months. I picked up a story on the guys who x-rayed and otherwise checked airplane and helicopter parts for cracks and corrosion—my first bylined story in *Stars and Stripes*. The next night, I met with a colonel and wrote another story on the security precautions he'd taken to prevent sabotage at the big air base.

I had another flight from Cam Ranh to Pleiku and found the post information office, where writers were buzzing around from *Time*, UPI, AP, *Newsweek*, Agence Presse, and the Vietnamese press corps. It was cool to be among them. I flew with four ARVNs in a chopper to a series of base camps west of Pleiku and Kontum, just inside the Cambodian border, and did a story on the mission of the camps, quoting the American advisers there. What I did was establish contacts for future reference, figuring that when things got hot, I'd have some sources to work with, and I'd have places to sleep where people knew me. In the time I spent in Pleiku, I was eating three meals a day in the officers' mess hall with the civilian correspondents. My impression was that the wire-service and magazine guys were real pros. I kept my mouth shut, did a lot of listening, and tried to soak up as much information as I could.

After arriving back to Saigon at about seven in the evening, I joined the *Stripes* staff at a party at Reuters. There were too many beautiful people around to suit me, so my friend Ken and I left and went to the Melody Bar for some slow dancing in the dark and a floor show. Not with each other. We both picked up bar chicks. A couple of days later, I needed a penicillin shot.

SAIGON SCENE

I spent a few more days doing puff pieces off the daily briefings and butterflying around to bars and discotheques with Ken at night. On January 18, we went to the Melody, where you could play cards with the bar girls (if you bought them teas at 500 piasters a drink) and listen to old records for ten piasters a play. I met a woman there that night, and she gave me a warm reception. I got my ration orders that said I would be getting $154.20 on February 1 to cover January and February. I quickly calculated that I couldn't afford to be out on the town every night, or I'd spend all my allowance in a single week.

The quality of our food amazed me. We had privileges at the army snack bar across the street from our office and could buy toast, pastries, and coffee in the morning. For lunch, we usually went to the Casa Grande at Tan Son Nhut for a ham-and-cheese or tuna sandwich or a hamburger pizza. The place was clean and air-conditioned. The pizza was the best I'd had outside the Roma Cafe in Albertson, New York, where I lived in the world.

For dinner, the staffers sometimes went to the local US mess hall, where we paid seventy cents. Otherwise, we went to the NCO club for sandwiches or a steak or sometimes downtown to an intimate, elegant restaurant. The waiters and bar girls treated us like kings. *Stars and Stripes* guys had the reputation of being big spenders. I did nothing to destroy that reputation. Within three weeks, I was known in three bars and greeted on arrival by a woman in each bar as if I was her long-lost lover. I figured what the hell, you only live once.

"Six thousand p, maybe you take me home, yes, GI?" a woman would ask me.

"No, I don't think so."

"Maybe five thousand—you give half me, half to *mama-san* [the madame]."

"No, not tonight." *Not in the market for the syph, thank you. But I'll play kissy-face in the dark a little.*

"You buy me one more tea, yes?"

"Yeah."

The traffic was unbelievable. There were hundreds of Hondas and pedal bikes, bicycles, Renault taxis, and motorbikes with sidecars, vehicles in all shapes and sizes. People darted in and out of traffic, battling for every inch of space. I never drove more than thirty-five miles an hour in the first month I was in Saigon. I'd signal for a right turn, and invariably, just as I was turning, a jerk on a Honda would come rocketing past me, between me and the curb, only to go straight. I'd be doing thirty, and a cowboy would cut in front of me with six inches to spare with a deadpan expression on his face.

But we took the bad with the good. We filled up our cars with gas for free at the army filling station. The four writers on the staff had two un-air-conditioned Scouts and a Rambler among us. The three lifers on the staff, who did the administrative work, telexed our stories, and so on, had the other three Ramblers—Staff Sergeant Carlos Ramirez, the sergeant major (whose name I forgot), and the Captain, James George. I read some old clips from 1968 that said that during Tet that year, 660 Americans were killed in street fighting in Saigon in an eight-day period. I couldn't imagine that happening in 1972. It seemed as if we were living in the Paris of the Orient.

I was trying to write cute features and not step on anybody's toes. It seemed as if every time I telephoned somebody for information, like how many shells had landed at Cam Ranh the other day, I got the runaround. It amazed me how much stuff was leaked to the wire services. I quickly realized that it was not likely that I would break any significant battle action stories. We were considered the American servicemen's house paper and were expected not to print anything that would reflect discredit on the troops. I was in a mode where I was just counting down the days until I was shipped home.

CONCLUSION

When I got home from Vietnam, I was stationed as a clerk for ten months at the Army Chaplains School at Fort Hamilton in Brooklyn. I got to go home on weekends. Great duty, after being in a war zone. I was in Brooklyn from August 1972 to June 25, 1973, when I got an early out and was discharged. Then I had what I call three "lost" years until I met my wife, Lynn, in 1976. I was working as a news reporter at *Newsday* and making good money, but I was pretty wild. I once passed a garbage truck by driving parallel to it through a gas station and cutting it off. I carried grass and Jack Daniels under the seat of my car, had a DUI on October 18, 1973, and had a traumatic episode on April 30, 1975, as I watched the final evacuation from Saigon of Americans and South Vietnamese who had worked for us.

As CBS showed footage of that helicopter on the top of a building with Vietnamese climbing a ladder toward it and then showed helicopters on an aircraft carrier being pushed into the South China Sea to make room for others to land, I coughed up blood. I ran from the couch at our family home to the bathroom and locked the door. I slumped to the floor, and my nose started to bleed too. I grabbed a towel to stanch the flow and cried uncontrollably. My parents banged on the door, and I told them I was okay. But the trauma I felt was worse than anything that had happened during my tour.

I think all at once it hit me—what a waste the war was. Fifty-eight thousand Americans lost their lives, and for what? To aid an ally that couldn't save itself when push came to shove. After watching the South Vietnamese beat back attacks during the Easter Offensive, I just couldn't believe what I was seeing three years later. It was one of the worst moments of my life.

My position on the Vietnam War changed over the years. In 1966-67 as a college freshman, I actually debated from the pro-war side against a twenty-four-year-old Vietnam veteran who opposed the war after returning from it. In 1971, before I was sent to Vietnam, I considered the protesters against the war to be loyal Americans. But in early May 1972, when I heard the news that President Nixon had mined Haiphong Harbor as a response to the Communist Easter Offensive, I raised my rifle over my head and cheered. I was traveling on a daytime patrol with one of the last remaining American infantry units left in the country. They were ecstatic over the news that Nixon had taken an offensive step against their enemy.

There were sixty thousand US troops left in-country at the time, and Nixon vowed not to let them or their South Vietnamese allies be jeopardized. "There is only one way to stop the killing," Nixon was quoted in the May 10, 1972, *Stars and Stripes*. "That is to keep the means to make war out of the hands of the international outlaws of North Vietnam." US notification said, "The entrances to the ports of North Vietnam are being mined, commencing 0900 Saigon time May 9, and the mines are set to activate automatically beginning 1800 hours Saigon time May 11."

The longer I was in Vietnam, the longer I supported the war. But at the end of April 1975, as I watched Saigon fall, I viewed it as a tragedy. I wound up putting my feelings on hold until 1991, when I went to a support group and found out what survivor's guilt is. Eventually I worshipped with the Quakers and joined Veterans for Peace.

The only conclusion I can draw from my tour in Vietnam is that I and others went off and did our jobs to the best of our abilities in a war that we had no business being in. I did nothing there that I'm ashamed of, and I met people that I'll never forget, people who did their jobs the best they could. I admit that I was caught up in the adrenaline rush of that conflict and was pretty damn lucky to have survived it. A lot of others weren't so fortunate.

NOTES

Part I: Combat Heroes

1   "Freaky Killer" from notes and "Door Gunner: Cool Is the Word," *Stars and Stripes,* January 26, 1972.
2   "The Hillbilly Chicken Man" from notes and "War Still Hairy Business to Rotor-Winged Fighters," *Stars and Stripes,* January 21, 1972.
3   "Looking for the Dudes" from notes and "Dudes Waiting for Tet, Helo Pilot Reports," *Stars and Stripes,* February 13, 1972.
4   "Silver Dollar" from notes and "U.S. Rangers Keep Commies Hopping," *Stars and Stripes,* March 31, 1972, and "3 Sgts. Head Home and Jungle Safer for Reds," *Stars and Stripes,* June 26, 1972.
5   "Football Hero Turned Ranger" from notes and "Gridder Moore Finds More Rewarding Goal," *Stars and Stripes,* April 1, 1972.
6   "Two Heroes: Geddes MacLaren and Jim Stein" from notes and "We Thought We Had 'em but Reds Almost Had Him," *Stars and Stripes,* May 11, 1972, and May 26, 1972, "Ups and Downs of Flying," *Stars and Stripes,* May 26, 1972.
7   "Both Sides Showed a Lot of Guts" from notes and "FAC Tells How ARVN Fought Inch by Inch to Hold Base," *Stars and Stripes,* April 21, 1972.
8   "Captain Glen S. Ivey" from notes and "Fire Base Hit as War Sneaks Up on Pleiku," *Stars and Stripes,* May 12, 1972.
9   "Drawing a Line in the Dirt: John Paul Vann" and next two vignettes from notes taken in April, May, and June 1972.
10   "Captain Robert A. Robertson" from notes taken in June 1972.
11   "Surviving a Missile Hit" from notes and "Flier Knocked Down—But Not Out," *Stars and Stripes,* June 25, 1972.
12   "King of Tac. Air" from notes and "Adviser Praised in Phu My Defense," *Stars and Stripes,* July 17, 1972.
13   "Twenty-Three Days on the Ground" from notes and "Rescue Flier Hiding 23 Days in N. Viet," *Stars and Stripes,* June 5, 1972.

305

14   "Surviving in No-Man's-Land" from notes and "Five Days in Hill Village Weren't Dull," *Stars and Stripes*, July 1, 1972.

15   "A Reporter Killed on the Job" from notes of conversation with Huntley and Chad Huntley, "Reporter's Ordeal Behind Red Lines," *Stars and Stripes*, July 1972.

Part II: Do-Gooders

1   "Trying to Leave with Goodwill" from notes and "Capt. Races Clock in Fight to Aid Needy Tribesmen," *Stars and Stripes*, January 17, 1972.

2   "Stoking Vietnamese Nationalism" from notes and "S. Viet Youth Turning on to Nationalism," *Stars and Stripes*, February 6, 1972.

3   "Civic Action" from notes and "Civic Action Aim: Boost the Arm's Image," *Stars and Stripes*, February 22, 1972.

4   "Vietnamization Was Working" from notes and "AF's VNAF Pupils Taught to Teach," *Stars and Stripes*, February 20, 1972.

5   "God Squad Member" from notes and "AF Capt. Ready for His Biggest Mission," *Stars and Stripes*, February 13, 1972.

6   "Afro Workshop" from notes and "Blacks Launch Afro Cultural Workshop," *Stars and Stripes*, February 23, 1972.

7   "NFL USO Tour" from notes and "Skins [sic] Alderman Anonymous after 12 Years," *Stars and Stripes*, February 20, 1972.

Part III: American Units

1   "Finding Needles" from notes and "Find the Needle—But Don't Move the Hay," *Stars and Stripes*, January 14, 1972.

2   "Testing His Mettle" from notes and "He Asked for Active Duty and Really Got It," *Stars and Stripes*, January 31, 1972.

3   "The Men of 'Blue Max'" from notes and "'Blue Max' Up and at Them in a Hurry," *Stars and Stripes*, January 27, 1972.

4   "Cav. Hats" from notes and "One Look at the Hats Tells You It's F Troop," *Stars and Stripes*, February 2, 1972.

5   "Packing" from notes and "U.S. Is Taking Its Gear Home," *Stars and Stripes*, February 17, 1972.

6   "Defending Cam Ranh" from notes.

7   "New Look Fire Base" from notes and "A New Look in Fire Bases: Cold Beer, PX, Pool, Maids," *Stars and Stripes*, February 26, 1972.

8   "Having It Easy in Pleiku" from notes and "GIs Have It Easy at Pleiku—And That's the Problem," *Stars and Stripes*, March 3, 1972.

9   "Yanks in Kontum" from notes and "Yanks at Kontum: Relaxed but Ready," *Stars and Stripes*, March 6, 1972.

10   "Saigon MPs" from notes and "Policing Saigon—'Just Routine,' like Any City," *Stars and Stripes*, February 10, 1972.

11   "The Red Barons" from notes and "Red Barons Fly VIPs High and Safe," *Stars and Stripes*, February 21, 1972.

12   "Basic Training" from notes and "Viet Tour? It's Just Basic Training ...," *Stars and Stripes*, March 21, 1972.

13   "Fire Base Melanie" from notes and "GIs at FB Melanie: Warriors Without a War," *Stars and Stripes*, March 20, 1972.

14   "Convoy Man" from notes and "His 650-Mile-a-Week Job Is Really a Low Down Pain," *Stars and Stripes*, March 24, 1972.

15   "Doc Holliday" from notes and "Planes to Land Fast and Take Off Quick," *Stars and Stripes*, March 7, 1972.

16   "Tanks for the Memories" from notes and "Armored Squad Through; Tanks For the Memories," *Stars and Stripes*, March 14, 1972.

17   "Peacock Hill" from notes and "VNAF Learns How to Handle Its Planes," *Stars and Stripes*, March 7, 1972.

18   "Medics" from notes and "Combat or Not, Being a Medic in Viet Is a Busy Business," *Stars and Stripes*, March 22, 1972.

19   "Fire Base Bunker Hill" from notes and "Bunker Hill—1ˢᵗ and Maybe Last," *Stars and Stripes*, March 27, 1972.

20   "XM3" from notes and "Guerillas Dogged by XM3," *Stars and Stripes*, March 23, 1972.

21   "Standing Down" from notes and "Viet Vets Given U.S. Base," *Stars and Stripes*, April 4, 1972.

22   "Deadly Fire" from notes and "Copters Facing Deadly Fire," *Stars and Stripes*, April 21.

23   "Patrolling the Pleiku Bush" from notes and "Yanks Patrol Pleiku Bush—And Ask Themselves Why," *Stars and Stripes*, May 23, 1972.

24   "The Men of MACV-SOG" from notes and "Advisers: Ready to Stay, Die," *Stars and Stripes*, May 7, 1972.

25   "The Eighty-Second Weighs In with TOWs" from notes.

26   "Delta War" from notes and "Pilot's Report: A Hot War in the Delta," *Stars and Stripes*, June 4, 1972.

27   "Smart Bombs" from notes and "Say Smart Bombs Reduce Casualties," *Stars and Stripes*, June 30, 1972.

28   "Up Highway 13" from notes and "Advisers—Duty, Devotion," *Stars and Stripes*, July 7, 1972.

29   "Battle Tactics" from notes and "Battle Tactics Changed," *Stars and Stripes*, July 29, 1972.

30 "East of Quang Tri" from notes and "Ready to Kill or Save," *Stars and Stripes,* July 23, 1972.

31 "Jolly Green Angels" from notes and "Jolly Green Giants Are Angels to Fliers," *Stars and Stripes,* July 30, 1972.

32 "Nighthawk" from notes and "Nighthawk Flights Keep Red Rocketeers on Toes," *Stars and Stripes,* July 23, 1972.

Part IV: South Vietnamese and South Korean Units

1 "'Kit Carsons'" from notes.

2 "Abandoning Fire Base Charlie" from notes and "Ridge Vital to Kontum Defense," *Stars and Stripes,* April 20, 1972.

3 "Captain Le Van Phuc, Man in the Middle" from notes and author's memory.

4 "Delta's Sporadic War" from notes and "It Looks Peaceful—But They're Out There," *Stars and Stripes,* June 3, 1972.

5 "Close to the Action" from notes and author's memory.

6 "Optimism Reigns" from notes and "Optimism Reigns in Tiny Phu Bon Province," *Stars and Stripes,* June 27, 1972.

7 "The Browns" from notes and "'Browns'—Trouble for Reds," *Stars and Stripes,* July 4, 1972.

8 "'We Are Here Every Day' (VNAF)" from notes and "VNAF Chopper Pilots: We Are Here Every Day," *Stars and Stripes,* July 3, 1972.

9 "The ROKs" from notes.

Part V: Vietnamese People

1 "Rice Wine" from notes and "To Flee or Not to Flee Imperiled Kontum," *Stars and Stripes,* April 30, 1972.

2 "We Think They're Dead" from notes and "Refugees: Down the Road to Nowhere," *Stars and Stripes,* April 28, 1972.

3 "I Can't Go Home" from notes and "Montagnard Boys Go Where Yanks Go," *Stars and Stripes,* May 10, 1972.

4 "Newspaper Pioneer" from notes and "New Viet Paper Appears Doomed," *Stars and Stripes,* June 5, 1972.

5 "War Brides" from notes and Newsday, "Taking Their Vows (In Triplicate)," Jim Smith, May 7, 1972

Part VI: Close Calls, Indiscretions, and Unconfirmed Reports

From notes and author's memory.

Part VII: Invited Guests

1 "The Bob Hope Christmas Show" from notes and author's memory.
2 "Froehlke Gets the Big Picture" from notes and "Froehlke Gets the 'Big Picture,'" *Stars and Stripes*, January 15, 1972.
3 "A USO Band That Was Far Out" from notes.
4 "Sir Robert's Visit" from notes and "Guerilla Expert Optimistic on An Loc," *Stars and Stripes*, July 4, 1972.

Part VIII: Scene Stories

1 "Pleiku's Limey Car Salesman" from notes.
2 "A Little Piece of America" from author's memory.
3 "The Border Camps" from notes and "Border Camps Ready for Anything," *Stars and Stripes*, January 20, 1972.
4 "Guard Duty in the Bush" from notes and "Guard Duty Not Like It Used to Be," *Stars and Stripes*, March 19, 1972.
5 "Cam Ranh Gets Hit" from notes and "Reds Attack Barracks in Cam Ranh," *Stars and Stripes*, April 11, 1972.
6 "The Stickitt Inn" from author's memory.
7 "'Arc Light the Motherfuckers'" from author's memory.
8 "Tan Canh" from notes.
9 "Hide-and-Seek" from notes, *Stars and Stripes*, May 9, 1972, and "Johnny Mack Jones," casualty report on http://1-22infantry.org/kia2/jonesmpers.htm.
10 "War in the Morning" from author's memory.
11 "'Get Out of Kontum'" from notes and "Kontum: They Say Get Out," *Stars and Stripes*, May 5, 1972.
12 "A Deserted City" from notes and "They 'Have to Get Out' of Imperiled Kontum," *Stars and Stripes*, May 13, 1972.
13 "Plei Mrong" from notes.
14 "Pressure's Off" from notes and "Pressure Is Off Kontum—For Now," *Stars and Stripes*, June 16, 1972.
15 "In the Field" from notes.

Part IX: Clerk in a War Zone

From notes and author's memory

APPENDIX

Excerpts from My Letters

The following are excerpts from letters I wrote home that my mother saved.

August 6, 1971:

This is perhaps the biggest test of character I will ever undergo.

August 17, 1971:

The only latrines we have are oil drums with wire mesh covering. Just to urinate requires tremendous effort to avoid vomiting because of the stench. There are daily formations at 0700, 1300 and 2000. People have to pull various crappy details. I saw roaches the size of a small mouse crawling across my barracks room floor … What a screw job being sent here. But I guess I'm one of the last few thousand men to get the shaft. That's at least some consolation …I have had no water in 48 hours because our well is going dry and it is carefully rationed …There is only lukewarm Kool-Aid and Coke. Barracks fall apart and are abandoned. The paint is cracked and peeling.

August 24, 1971

There was incoming at the airport last night. I couldn't sleep and got up at 0330 to get a drink of water. I saw the sky light up … you know, like bombs bursting in air. The gooks must be coming … What the hell is this? You'd think there was a war on or something.

September 4, 1971

If I died tomorrow, how would you describe my good and bad points? What would you remember most about me?

September 7, 1971

All those letters every day
May be alright in their way.
But I'd like to see your face
When I come home in their place.
—Rolling Stones, "Comin' Home"

September 9, 1971

Your worst enemies over here are the soul brothers, not the VC. But believe me, there's more danger in East Harlem than there is where I am … I sleep just as soundly here as I have anywhere else in my life.

October 10, 1971

I'm writing these letters for a double purpose. First, to have a record of what I was thinking about at this point in my life and second, to tell you how I am and answer your questions.

October 15, 1971

Every time I hear this tape, I just get a lump in my throat, you know. I wonder if I'll put it in a cabinet and play it when I'm 40 and still dig it. Right now, it's very real to me ... Something just stirs inside me when I hear this tape.

Sometimes I can't help but crying.
People when I think about the dying
... While the powers of the world are struggling,
The children of the world are starving
While the prayers of peace are rising
The sons of war are dying.
People we gotta stop—my God, yeah, people we gotta stop
We gotta stop
Sisters and brothers can you hear me.
We gotta stop killing one another.
—Jesse Colin Young

I don't know, I'm just in one of those moods again tonight. Geez, I got a helluva long time to go over here ... I notice I've got nine months and two weeks left ... I hope I can still write coherent, lengthy letters at that time. I hope I break out of this purple haze ... I just realized ... In two weeks I'll be 23. It's scary, man.

October 22, 1971

I feel like I've always been here, you know? I mean, it won't ever be the same when I come home.

November 11, 1971

I'm mature enough to cope with my surroundings. I'm happy I finished college and I've got my foot into the [newspaper] business and all that because if I came into the army right out of high school I'd probably be grumbling a lot more.

When I left my home and my family
I was no more than a boy
In the company of strangers
—"The Boxer," Simon & Garfunkel

November 15, 1971

Well, today was an eventful day. I saw an ad for reporters in the *Stars and Stripes*. I called Saigon, and the cat said he would hire me if my unit here could be persuaded to let me go. So I put in for a transfer.

November 26, 1971

It's just one big lame duck thing over here. Everybody knows the rough stuff is over.

December 11, 1971

I've lived my life over mentally a hundred times since I've been here.

January 15, 1972

The first 10 days [after being transferred to Saigon] I spent in the office, learning the basics, learning our style and covering the dull briefings in Saigon. Then, the fun started.

January 16, 1972

Saigon is quiet but tense. Saboteurs are blowing up stuff all around us. Just a matter of time before we take some rockets, I guess ... I flew with four

ARVNs in a chopper to do a series of articles on base camps just inside the Cambodian border. Riding in a chopper was cool. What I did up at Pleiku was establish some contacts so that during Tet [in mid-February], when the place gets hit, I can go back there and get what I need ... I ate three meals a day in the officer's club up there ... I think I am going to like being a war correspondent.

January 26, 1972

I've been getting out around the country a little. I really enjoy the job ... I work when the spirit moves me. I've been banging out some good stuff ... Tokyo's been very happy with the features I've been sending

February 4, 1972

I just can't hack a system where a man's rank (if it's higher than yours) determines whose opinion is right. You know, like just because Capt. George wants something done a certain way, you do it that way. I know more about the business than any of these duds and yet I have to bend to their judgment ... No big hassle, though. I'll just write little PR pieces for a few more months and stay away from anything controversial. This *Stars and Stripes* employee from the Tokyo office who came to Saigon to pick the next bureau chief said I'd be "slinging hash in the Mekong Delta" if I sent the recent story I did on the deplorable living conditions at a Bien Hoa training center. No problem. I'll write it their way for now.

February 19, 1972

If you're wondering why I haven't written for a while it's because I've been busting my tail out in the field for the past eight days. I've been in Pleiku, Nha Trang and Pleiku again. And all over, nothing's happening. There's not much of a war up here. So I'm buzzing around doing feature stories like crazy. Tokyo has nine of my stories that haven't run yet, so I'm just going to cool it for a while ... I've met a lot of good people wherever I've gone and wherever I go, I seem to get good chow, a good place to sleep and somebody to give me a ride to the airport or to the next unit I'm doing a story on … If I'd been stuck at Cam Ranh Bay my whole tour, I'd never have known what was here.

February 27, 1972

My grist mill really has been grinding. I went to Pleiku, Nha Trang, back to Pleiku, Kontum and back to Pleiku … I'll just tell you a little more about my trip, which has to be one of the most memorable experiences of my life. I got some more chopper time, flying to base camps in the northwest part of Kontum province where the borders of South Vietnam, Laos and Cambodia meet. I went to one camp on Friday that was rocketed on Tuesday, Thursday and Saturday. I traveled back to Pleiku in a pickup truck with a Korean engineer over the same road that a Vietnamese truck convoy had been ambushed on by the VC in the morning.

Saturday I met Pat Smith, an American civilian who has run a hospital for Montagnard tribesmen in Kontum for 13 years. I banged out 1,000 words on her and I'll bring it back to Saigon tomorrow instead of dictating it over the phone because it's something that can run any time. Altogether, I guess I got a dozen stories in 16 days. (This story did not run in *Stars and Stripes*, and my notes on it were lost.)

I went to a Vietnamese orphanage where these army cats were turning over money and food to some French-trained nuns. They fed us some musk melon and various other fruits. Got some good pix. Everywhere I went, I was treated well. I'm really developing the confidence as a writer and interviewer that comes only with experience. A few times this trip. I learned that to get a story, you've got to give that extra effort. A couple of times, just as a story was slipping away, I'd ask the right question, get some cat to take me to see someone else and boom—there it was.

I'm good and I know it. I can write as well as all these cats from the wire services that are running around. When I interview a cat, whether he's a PFC or a colonel, I take the SOB in the palm of my hand and monopolize the dialogue and manipulate the cat until I get what I want. I know my sportswriting will benefit simply by the extra confidence I've derived from handling myself as a brash, cocky and good reporter when I deal with these servicemen.

March 6, 1972

I have today requested that I not be given a drop (early release from one-year tour in Vietnam) and that I spend my whole tour in 'Nam. I've done this because of this chick I met last week. I'm really flipped out. This chick is something. She told me last night that when I leave Vietnam, no sweat, she can't go to America. But if I break up with her while I'm still here, she'll kill herself, or words to that effect. She said a lot of GIs want to talk to her at work and take her picture but she tells them no, she has a boyfriend. I mean, I'm totally spaced. We've gone to dinner, the movies and the park the last three days. She's coming over to the office again after work today. She's Catholic and I gave her that white beaded rosary as a present. If you want to know whether I believe in magic, I do. I feel like a high school kid again.

When I came to this godforsaken country last year, I never thought I'd do what I did today. I requested that I not be given a drop to return home three months early. We received a message from Tokyo saying our strength here would be five people (total) by May 1. We have 10 right now. But Rich Haines leaves today and one cat ain't working out and the sergeant major leaves next week. But the CO leaves May 1. Sergeant First Class Frank Castro (acting bureau chief) said it's up to us—whoever wants a drop could take it ... But I said I wanted to stay, so Frank chopped Mark Treadup, who's leaving in June and sort of wanted to stay a little later.

So the final crew is me, Castro, Ken Schultz, Allen Schaeffer and Staff Sergeant Carlos Ramirez from Long Island. Great five. Real tight. I made the decision first because of Loan and second because I'll never have a job as good as this as long as I'm in the service ... I really am having the time of my life over here ... My articles are running, I've got a great boss, no lifer hassle, a car I can use as often as I want, sleeping quarters right upstairs and an air-conditioned office with my stereo set up right on my desk and a drawer full of tapes. If I was back in the States, who knows what I'd be doing? I'm so happy I could scream … I haven't been counting the days since I left Cam Ranh. I'll tell you what really happened there some time.

The following is an excerpt from the letter I sent to *Stars and Stripes* brass regarding my request to stay in Vietnam:

I, James R. Smith, 057-42-2759, SP4, US Army, do on this sixth day of March, 1972, state that I want to serve a full year in Vietnam and am not interested in a drop of any form for any reason. I would appreciate any attempts to declare me "mission essential" so I could complete a full year in Vietnam.

March 12, 1972

Well, nobody forced me into it, although my editor thought it would be a good idea, and here I am out in the jungle 30 miles southeast of Saigon. That's a damn poor lead sentence but so are my surroundings.

I'm traveling with Charlie Co., 2nd Bn. 8th Cavalry on patrol in the so-called "rocket belt." The infantrymen are one of the last U.S. combat forces in action. They sweep through the jungle, making sure no Communists set up housekeeping [to fire rockets at Saigon]. I covered a half mile through some of the most dense jungle imaginable today, carrying an M16 and 50 pounds of equipment. I'm bushed, hurting all over, especially in my shoulder sockets. And I've got the runs and I haven't had a decent meal in a week.

I'm sure the stories I turn out of this will be good ones but I'm sure I'm never going to go out in the field with a grunt unit again. Right now my thoughts are on my girlfriend Loan in Saigon. I can't wait to see her again. I've been out in the field five days. Today is Sunday, though you'd never know it, and I'll be back in Saigon in three more days, hopefully. I'll get out with the next supply bird coming in Tuesday. These kids are stuck in the field for five more days after I leave. I really feel sorry for them after seeing the way they live.

The other night I had the runs right in my pants and you can't change in the field, so I'm stuck with my stinking self. It's quite unpleasant and yet it's not really that bad because I've been driving myself and if I had never been out with the grunts, I'd always have wondered what it was like. Now, I know.

I just want to get out of here now. I don't know how anyone could keep his sanity if he had to do a full tour in the jungle. I know I couldn't last past Tuesday. I like being a REMF. The first two letters stand for rear echelon. But I have tremendous respect for these cats out here beating the bush.

March 13, 1972

Another day just like yesterday in the jungle. Some of these kids eat it up. But to paraphrase an old song, "Monday just won't go. Tuesday comes too slow. 'Cause I got Friday on my mind." And I'm going to have fun in the city, be with my girl (she's so pretty) and all that.

Beating the bush is for the kids. We set up about 1 p.m. on a tree-covered hill and the CO led an eight-man patrol for about two hours back and forth across a winding stream. No dinks, no nothing. Just two very old bunkers, he said. Well, I'm holding up pretty well. Only two more days till I get back to the fire base and then get extracted. I'm getting to dig it a little, I guess. This morning I had some hot cocoa and crackers and jelly. That's the most I've eaten in three days. If I get anything out of this trip, maybe it'll be a waistline a few inches smaller.

Well, I just had supper. First hot food I could eat in four days. I had half a C-ration can of hamburger meat and beans, four crackers with grape jelly and some water out of my canteen. Surprisingly, I feel just as full now as I did the other day when I took Loan out to eat in Saigon for 4,000 piasters (about $10) in a French restaurant. I've got tomorrow's breakfast set aside—crackers and cheese and all the ingredients for hot cocoa. Oh, yeah, I forgot I also had a can of fruit cocktail for supper tonight and it was good.

Yesterday we were really humping and I kept thinking about all the hairy spots I've gotten into in my life and I said this was one of the hairiest. But I said I always pull through somehow and I would this time. So today, instead of having to hump 800 meters, we only had to do 250. I spent most of the day on my back while the guys went on patrol without packs.

The lieutenant asked me to pull guard again last night and I did—7:30 to 9 p.m. with a radio and a set of clackers for Claymore man-detonated mines in front of me. It was really something as I sat there staring into the eerie darkness. I mentally ran through a rosary and prayed that nothing would happen. It was really far out. I think I'll remember these few days the rest of my life.

I talked with a kid today who was born in Cuba and escaped in 1961 with 15 of his family and friends on a fishing boat. He said he joined the army so he could get training to help retake his country from Castro someday. Makes a great story. I've got a half-dozen of them from this trip. I wish I could get out tomorrow but log day isn't till Wednesday so I have to wait.

No sweat, though, I'm feeling all right and down with the real people, as the Lt. says—the ones that matter in Vietnam.

March 14, 1972

The captain has just had a cat get out some goofy grape [smoke] to let the colonel circling above in a chopper know exactly where we are. Col. Blagg is looking the area over for a possible "log" site—an open area—where we can be re-provisioned by chopper tomorrow. I've only got one more night out here, thankfully, and then tomorrow'll take a resupply bird to the fire base and then hitch another bird back to Bien Hoa. From there, I'll get one of the guys from our office to drive up and get me. I had my cocoa this morning and it really hit the spot because it was cold as hell this morning and I woke up shivering.

Some cats are playing cards. Others are just laying in hammocks, waiting to see what will happen. It's remarkable how organized everything is. If I was a dink, I think I'd pack it up. We're camped near a river again today and should be moving out shortly.

April 19, 1972

Being a war correspondent is cool but it's cooler when you're in Saigon. I'm in Pleiku—have been for the past three days—and nothing much is happening at "the front" some 50 miles northwest in Kontum province. I'm not very inclined to fly to some godforsaken Vietnamese outpost to get a story. I'd just as soon sit here and get the daily war notes from an ARVN spokesman.

Why should I risk my life for a story? If I was working for Newsday, I could see it. But my loyalty is not very strong to Stars and Stripes. I admit I haven't been doing as much as I could but why should I? I've got 101 days left until I finish a full year in 'Nam and that will be no small accomplishment. I want to stay alive and go back to being a jock reporter and screw this stupid war.

I just don't think it's a measure of a man or his talent that he writes a first-person story about being wounded in action. It's just not that important for me. I'll be content with being a base camp reporter. I don't have anything to prove to anybody about how brave or fearless I am. Stars and Stripes is just an opportunity I'm using to keep my hand hot in writing and enable me to be in the Army without really "playing" Army. It's been a cool trip. How many people can say they live in a hotel with an air-conditioned office downstairs and an air-conditioned car at their disposal and draw $77 a month ration money and $75 a month combat pay? Not many. But I'm playing it for all it's worth and I'm not anxious to stick my life on the line for a few stirring inches of copy. I'd get a much better kick out of writing a good piece after covering a Ranger playoff game.

True, I went out "in the bush" last month. But I knew it wouldn't be dangerous. I waited until things settled down before I suggested that I go out with some American ground troops. I'm not crazy. I hate this damn war and I hate myself for glamorizing the people who revel in fighting it. I've had to do this to keep my job and it was a "sell out" to some extent. The only justification I can make is that I'm taking advantage of the army, which has taken advantage of me by sending me over here. Rationalized that way, I can salve my conscience.

April 20, 1972

I saw my people on a movie screen tonight. They were wearing uniforms but they were hardly military. They were "freaks" at the Big Sur Festival in California and seeing how free they were and what a great time they were having made me homesick. Homesick for freedom.

I'm getting tired of the army. Sure, I've had it good while I was in. But it's still the army, you know, and there are messed up heads all around me. People who think killing is cool. And I realize I've sold out by glorifying this type of moral degenerate in some of my articles. I hope you can dig that I've undergone some changes in my 19 months in service.

I can tell you that when I leave the straight world of the Army, I'm gonna be a full-fledged member of what the news media likes to refer to as "the counterculture." I'm going to dress sloppy and natural. My hair's going to be real long. My only concession to the establishment will be a complete devotion to my job at Newsday.

April 21, 1972

Well, I'm in Kontum. Sounds like Khartoum, you know? You think of huge mountains and a cast of thousands with pointed spears and gleaming helmets. And Kontum has a lot of mountains. But the battle is waged with Cobras and automatic weapons these days, not swords and shields.

April 22, 1972

I got plastered last night on five double rum-and-cokes with a shot of cognac chasing them down. I met an old friend from my first trip here—Bud Cavanaugh, about 65, who works as an engineer at the army compound here. I went over to meet his wife (common law) and the children she cares for in a little house in town. Seems like they have a nice life together, even though it will be over when he goes back to the world later this year.

Last night at the tactical briefing, Colonel Bachinski, who looks an awful lot like the guy who played Toody on Car-54, said the next 48 hours would be critical here because "the enemy seems to like weekends." He said he felt the recent actions north at Dak Pek, where 170 Reds died in two pre-dawn attacks on the remote outpost earlier this week, were diversionary. He indicated that the fighting near Saigon at An Loc also was a diversion and that he expected the primary thrust of the enemy to come in the Highlands northwest of Kontum and that it would come in the next 48 hours. So this is where I want to be in the event it does break out.

June 16, 1972

Pleiku—You know, it's really funny. I enlisted in the army for three years so I wouldn't have to fight in the jungle. But as a reporter, I've probably put myself in more danger than I ever would have faced as an infantryman. My friend Col. Waara said that to me yesterday and I had to agree with him.

June 17, 1972

The sounds of Bangkok are still ringing in my ears, though I've been back "in the stuff" for six days. It was great. I happened to link up with a Ranger super-killer I'd interviewed twice in my travels to Bien Hoa and we traveled everywhere with our chicks in Bangkok.

Jimmy's got 107 kills and won the Silver Star when his three-man team blew 26 dinks away in an ambush last fall. I bought a watch, two pairs of bellbottoms, two tie-dyed freak shirts and a couple of old records—"Introducing the Rolling Stones," "Got Live if You Want" and the "Yardbirds' Greatest Hits." We hired a driver—$25 for seven days—and he was on call from 8 a.m. to midnight every day. Like whenever we wanted to go somewhere, we went. His name was Mr. Tia.

The hotel was the place that all the Special Forces people stay at and Jimmy and me had some interesting raps with some weird heads. The charge at the place was $28 for seven nights.

I was shocked to learn that John Paul Vann, the senior adviser in II Corps, was killed in a chopper crash last week. His personal aide, Sgt. Black, called me in Saigon and asked me to come over to MACV headquarters. He said Vann often treated me as though he believed I was a naive kid. But he said Mr. Vann told him he had a lot of respect for me. I always seemed to be bumping into him in Kontum [and Pleiku]. It really made me feel bad that Vann got it. He was the sixth man I knew well in Vietnam that's been killed.

The following day, I typed a personal letter to Col. Koch asking him to reconsider and allow me to extend my tour over here. I told him like I was committed to seeing this thing through and stuff like that. I am, I want to come home, and I will in about 42 days. But I want to come back. If I can.

Dad, you might be interested to know that U.S. Special Forces troops are being dropped behind enemy lines with special assassination teams and guerilla units. I saw one Green Beret (they're not supposed to be over here, you know) teaching some ARVNs how to mortar an enemy position on a hillside yesterday.

If my extension request is turned down, I plan to see as much of the country as I can in the next 42 days. I'm not going to hang back in Saigon away from the action … I've really lucked out to the max. I happened to write a few stories that some generals up here didn't care for on my last trip. So [my boss] hid me away in the Delta for five days and then I went on R & R [June 4–11].

Meanwhile, Kontum was erupting in flames. I was told that 5,636 Communists were killed within a mile of the city between May 14 and June 7. Friendly losses were put at 500 killed and about 1,500 wounded. Fighting erupted inside Kontum on May 25, the very day I left for the Delta on Frank Castro's orders. Matt Franjola was almost hit by automatic weapons fire three times, he said, and he kept flying into Kontum even while there was house-to-house fighting there.

Well, it's been a long, tiring day. I've been working 18-hour days lately. There's so much to do. I'm sitting on a chartered C-46 plane flying from Cheo Reo to Pleiku. In it are newsmen, representatives of five embassies and British Cathay Pacific Airlines officials. We're just coming back from the site where a big 880 Convair with 82 persons aboard exploded in mid-air and crashed two days ago.

It's like miles from nowhere, you know. Anyway, I saw—and smelled—54 bodies today. What a terrible tragedy an airplane crash is. The investigators aren't sure of the cause but they're not ruling out the possibility of a bomb having been placed on board.

I'm happy with myself because besides the crash story I got another piece today on Phu Bon province and its dreams for the future; I'll quote U.S. and Vietnamese officials.

It's cool in here and dusk is pretty in the Highlands. I see Devil's Mt. up ahead, so we must be near Pleiku City, into which I've flown about 20 times. I'm happy also cause I got a byline in today's paper on a war notes story out of Capt. Phuc's briefing. Usually [the editor] goes with the AP or UPI war notes, so it's cool. It also helps to have my name in the paper while I'm working an area, cause then people realize that I'm a real, live reporter who gets stories in the paper and not just some dumb Spec. 4 in the Army ...

The aircraft is over good, old Camp Holloway now. I'm going to the NCO club for some chow. I haven't eaten anything since breakfast except a bottle of French biere in Cheo Reo. We've just touched down.

June 17, 1972

I'm sitting with Matt outside the 180th Assault Helicopter Battalion. operations office waiting for a Chinook to Cheo Reo, near where a British Cathay Pacific Airliner went down with 82 aboard Thursday. Matt and I drove 30 miles south of Pleiku yesterday, through primitive villages and over dirt roads in VC territory trying to get to the crash site but failed. The airliner went down in dense jungle 10 kilometers north of Phu Thien, a small town we reached in early afternoon.

Matt and I flew up to Kontum again on a hook Wednesday and took pictures of each other on a Russian-built tank just north of the abandoned US compound. Just before I snapped a shot of Matt, Communists shot four 122mm rockets into the MACV compound, 200 meters away, and we hit the dirt. One rocket impacted 20 feet in front of a dozen US First Cavalry Division soldiers standing near some TOW tank-piercing missiles mounted on jeeps.

VNAF aircraft knocked out eight more Red tanks yesterday north of Kontum City. Meanwhile, ARVN tanks and armored personnel carriers are meeting stiff resistance as they try to drive past Chu Pao Mountain south of Kontum. I flew into a little village two miles from the heavy fighting with the Vietnamese general in charge of the operations and got some great pictures of US M41 tanks rolling past bewildered primitive Montagnard villagers.

June 30, 1972

I don't believe this week has gone so fast. It's been really great because [Bureau chief] Frank Castro has been on R & R in Hawaii for six days and the CO is leaving the country at midnight tomorrow, so he ain't hassling us.

Sunday I drove with Loan to Vung Tao, a resort town 50 miles southeast of Saigon on the coast. We had my radio on the dash and were listening alternately to American and Vietnamese music. That night, we had dinner in town (Saigon) at Ramuntcho's as usual, then went to her pad to watch TV. Tuesday night, we went to see "Romeo and Juliet," which brought a tear to this reporter's eyes. Last night she cooked some of her famous Vietnamese chow for me. Work has been real good. I've been working in the Saigon area since my last trip to Pleiku. I've driven 30 miles north of Saigon to Lai Khe three times in the last week and I'm heading back up there today. We got a call from our sources there yesterday that something would break today. I think the allies are just about to rout the last few hundred dinks out of their entrenched positions on the west side of the highway about six miles south of An Loc.

GLOSSARY

Units

A Battery, First Battalion, Twenty-First Artillery. Artillery Hill, Pleiku, unit of thirty-eight men who worked in six-man crews handling three howitzers, associated with the First Cavalry Division.

B Troop, Seventh Squad, Seventeenth Air Cavalry. Flew daily AH-1 Cobra missions from Camp Holloway in Pleiku in support of ARVN troops.

Charlie Company, Second Battalion, Eighth Cavalry. Unit I pulled guard duty with east of Saigon.

Civil Operations and Revolutionary Development Support (CORDS). A pacification program of the United States and South Vietnamese that included military and civilians whose objective was to gain support for the central government from the rural population.

D and E Companies, First Infantry Battalion, Twelfth Cavalry. Infantry units based at Pleiku's Artillery Hill that largely were kept out of contact before the Easter Offensive and then were transferred to Fire Base Bunker Hill east of Saigon.

Da Nang Support Command. I Corps headquarters for US advisers' efforts.

Delta Company, Seventeenth Cavalry. Another infantry unit that patrolled the area around Camp Holloway.

Eighteenth Special Operations Squadron. A joint army–air force unit with Hueys, an AC-119 airplane, and choppers from Delta Troop, Seventh Cavalry, and F Troop, Eighth Cavalry, at Marble Mountain Army Air Base that targeted enemy rocketeers.

Eleventh Armored Cavalry, "Blackhorse Regiment." Worked mostly in Tay Ninh Province and then Binh Duong Province north of Saigon until it stood down in March 1972; had more than a hundred Sheridan tanks and armored personnel carriers.

F Battery, Seventy-Ninth Aerial Rocket Artillery Company. The last army aerial artillery unit in Vietnam during the Easter Offensive; consisted of thirty Blue Max AH-1 Cobras based at Plantation Army Base near Long Binh, working to blunt the NVA drive toward Saigon at An Loc. It was among the first US units to engage and destroy the NVA's Russian-built tanks.

F Troop, Fourth Air Cavalry. Served at Lai Khe and Long Binh in III Corps before relocating to Da Nang during the Easter Offensive; was one of the last US Army units to leave Vietnam in February 1973. It staged out of Tan My just south of Hue in late July 1972, performing mainly rescue missions.

F Troop, Ninth Cavalry. Scout helicopter unit that flew Loaches to provide reconnaissance for Third Brigade, First Cavalry Division, infantry around its Bien Hoa base.

F Troop, Eighth Air Cavalry, "The Blue Ghosts." A helicopter assault unit that supported ARVN troops in I Corps around Da Nang during the Easter Offensive.

Fifty-Second Aviation Battalion. The last helicopter assault unit in II Corps; located at Camp Holloway in Pleiku until late April 1972.

First Cavalry Division, Third Brigade. One of the last two American combat units to be withdrawn from Vietnam in June 1972, it was responsible for the defense of Saigon, Vietnam's capital city.

501st Engineer Company. Remained attached to the Third Brigade after its parent, Eighth Engineer Battalion, stood down in 1971; it built Fire Base Bunker Hill.

518th Adjutant General Personnel Services Company. My clerical unit at Cam Ranh Bay from August 1 to December 31, 1972.

520th Transportation Battalion. An army aircraft maintenance support unit based at Phu Loi that stood down on April 1, 1972.

Fourteenth Medevac Company. Helicopter rescue unit that operated out of Camp Holloway.

457th Tactical Squadron. Air force unit based at Cam Ranh Bay; used C-7 planes to fly resupply missions to ARVN bases and US advisers.

483rd Civil Engineer Squadron. Air force unit based at Cam Ranh Bay that supervised a Korean contractor's removal of thousands of square feet of runway made of aluminum planking for use at other US bases.

483rd Field Maintenance Squadron. Air force maintenance unit based at Cam Ranh Bay.

557th Engineer Company. Army unit that helped build Fire Base Bunker Hill seven miles northeast of Bien Hoa in March 1972, from which First Cavalry Division troops ran patrols in the "rocket belt" to protect Saigon.

H Company, Seventy-Fifth Infantry, Third Brigade, First Cavalry Division. Last Ranger outfit in Vietnam; based at Bien Hoa and consisted of seven six-man teams that ran ambushes and recon patrols in a forty-mile radius of Saigon.

Military Assistance Command, Vietnam–Studies and Observations Group (MACV-SOG). Small, highly trained infantry unit comprised of members of various services and civilians; ran covert operations and ambushes with Montagnard troops in II Corps during the Easter Offensive.

Military Assistance Command, Vietnam (MACV). Joint-service headquarters of US military in Vietnam from 1962 to 1973; based at Tan Son Nhut Air Base near Saigon.

Ninety-Second Combat Engineer Battalion. Its C Company helped with the hammer-and-nail construction at Fire Base Bunker Hill and also helped build Fire Base Gibraltar, twenty-five miles east of Saigon.

921st Air Control and Warning Center. Air force unit based at Peacock Hill in Pleiku at which Americans trained VNAF airmen to guide aircraft in and out of the facility.

Ninetieth Replacement Detachment. Processing unit at Long Binh where incoming and outgoing troops awaited reassignment.

196th Light Infantry Brigade. Last US ground combat unit in Vietnam; based at Da Nang in I Corps and deactivated on June 30, 1972.

Peacock Hill. An American radar site in Pleiku.

716th Military Police Battalion. The seven-hundred-man American unit responsible for enforcing rules governing behavior of US troops in Saigon and its suburbs.

Second Battalion, Eighth Cavalry, Third Brigade, First Cavalry Division. Based at Fire Base Amy, twenty miles east of Saigon; was one of seven combat battalions left in Vietnam in March 1972.

Second Battalion, 327th Infantry. The last American infantry unit at Cam Ranh Bay Air Base; stood down on April 6, 1972. The next day, an enemy rocket attack and ground assault killed four GIs and wounded twenty at the base.

Sixteenth Air Cavalry. Its C Troop was the sole air cavalry unit in IV Corps in the Mekong Delta region during the Easter Offensive. It was based at Can Tho Army Airfield.

361st Aerial Weapons Company. Pulled maintenance for Camp Holloway choppers.

Third Aviation Assault Company, Fifty-Second Aviation Battalion. Unit with twenty Hueys that flew out of Camp Holloway.

Thirty-Seventh Aerospace Rescue and Recovery Squadron. Unit at Da Nang Air Base that included Jolly Green Giant helicopters and crews that exposed themselves to enemy fire in late July 1972, accompanied by A-1 Sandys, OV-10 Broncos, and F-4 Phantoms, to rescue downed American airmen.

201st Aviation Company. Camp McDermott Nha Trang–based home of "the Red Barons," which provided VIP helicopter and fixed-wing flights for American advisers, mostly in II Corps.

Twenty-Sixth Chemical Detachment. Bien Hoa unit that used Hueys equipped with XM3 body-sniffing devices and was accompanied by Cobra gunships to detect Communists in the jungle southeast of the base.

US Air Force Advisory Team (AFAT). Air force unit at Nha Trang with thirty-six men who helped VNAF operate a training center.

Weapons

B-40. A bazooka-like, handheld, antitank grenade launcher.

C-4. Plastic explosive with a texture similar to modeling clay.

82 mm mortar. Indirect fire weapon that launched an explosive projectile from a tube in high-arcing trajectories.

.50-caliber machine gun. A belt-fed, antiaircraft gun that could be used from a ground mount or on a vehicle for use against low-flying US aircraft.

57 mm recoilless rifle. Bazooka-like weapon that fired artillery-type shells; could be carried by an infantryman.

M16. Basic US combat rifle that used a twenty-round clip and could be fired on automatic or single-shot. The United States had provided the ARVNs with 640,000 before the Easter Offensive.

M60. Belt-fed American machine gun that weighed twenty-three pounds and was fired using a tripod.

M72 light antitank weapon. Tubular antitank weapon that could be shoulder-fired or installed on a vehicle or helicopter.

M79. Shotgun-like grenade launcher that fired 40 mm grenades.

105 mm howitzer. Mobile army artillery piece introduced in the Vietnam War for helicopter and light infantry operations; could be airlifted into and out of firebases to support ground troops.

122 mm rocket. A surface-to-surface artillery rocket delivered by a multiple rocket launcher used by the NVA to terrorize civilians and against dug-in ARVN troops.

PT-76. Amphibious light reconnaissance Russian tank that had three-man crew; was useful crossing streams in I Corps in the NVA drive against Quang Tri.

SA-7. Shoulder-fired, heat-seeking missile launched from a tube that NVA troops used to knock down low-flying US aircraft.

.37-caliber antiaircraft gun. Russian-made weapon on wheels for use against low-flying planes or helicopters.

TOW missiles. Tube-launched, optically tracked, wire-guided missiles. They could be shoulder-fired by an individual or affixed to jeeps or helicopters.

Aircraft

A-1 Skyraider. Carrier-based, single-seat attack airplane nicknamed "Sandy" that was a close-air-support workhorse for the VNAF; had a long loiter time and large ordnance load.

AC-119 Stinger. Twin-engine airplane gunship often operated in tandem with Spectre, nicknamed "Truck Killer." It had four miniguns with 31,000 rounds of ammunition, multiple-barrel Gatling guns, and 4,500 rounds of 20 mm ammunition.

AC-130H Spectre. Converted C-130 flown by US Air Force that had a crew of fourteen and brought devastating firepower against enemy troops via an assortment of weapons including 105 mm howitzer rounds; also had sophisticated sensors to provide night-fighting capability.

AH-1 Cobra. Twin-blade, single-engine attack helicopter nicknamed "Snake" that had two-man crew and was equipped with rocket pods, miniguns, grenade launchers, and TOWs.

A-37 Dragonfly. Light attack plane used for close air support. About 250 were delivered to VNAF before the Easter Offensive; they were equipped with high-explosive bombs, rockets, and miniguns.

C-7 Caribou. Small cargo plane used to move troops and material into and out of small, unimproved airstrips; could accommodate up to thirty-two passengers.

C-123. Twin-engine, fixed-wing troop transport plane that could carry sixty-two combat-ready troops.

C-130. Big, lumbering four-engine plane used to carry material and up to ninety-two troops.

C-141. Enormous cargo-carrying airplane that could transport up to 150 troops or 80 patient litters and medical personnel.

F-4 Phantom. Most extensively used fighter-bomber in Vietnam; had laser-guided bombs that could be steered toward targets; could be based on land or aircraft carriers; armed with missiles and bombs; supported ground troops in contact.

F-105 Thunderchief. Conventional strike bomber eventually replaced by the F-4; was used to bomb North Vietnamese military targets and bridges; single-engine, two-seat fighter-bomber used in April 1972 when President Richard M. Nixon ordered resumption of bombing of North Vietnam.

HC-130. Extended-range version of the C-130 used for search-and-rescue operations; could refuel in the air and drop rescue forces.

HH-53 Super Jolly Green Giant. Large helicopter used for special operations and search-and-rescue missions. It was equipped with Gatling guns and countermeasures to deal with heat-seeking missiles. It had a crew of five, including two rescue men.

OH-6 Cayuse. Nicknamed "Loach," this light observation helicopter flew low-level scout missions to pinpoint enemy troop locations and often worked with an AH-1 Cobra on hunter-killer teams.

OH-58 Kiowa. Single-engine, single-rotor helicopter used for observation or direct fire support or armed reconnaissance missions. It also was employed for artillery spotting or bomb damage assessment.

O-1 Bird Dog. Small-engine, two-seat airplane used to adjust artillery and observe enemy troop concentrations.

OV-10 Bronco. A rugged, maneuverable, twin-turboprop airplane whose mission was to find and hit battlefield targets close to friendly troops. It also was used for helicopter escort.

UH-1H. Produced by Bell and nicknamed "Huey," seven thousand of these multipurpose helicopters served in Vietnam for troop insertions, medical evacuations, cargo transport, and aerial attacks.

U-21. A medium-size aircraft, built to hold eight or ten passengers and crew. It was used mainly by the army, to a lesser extent by the air force, for transporting VIPs.

Bases

Ben Het. Camp in northwestern Kontum Province seven miles east of the Laos-Cambodia-Vietnam triborder manned by two ARVN Ranger battalions and two US advisers.

Bien Hoa. Sprawling base fifteen miles northeast of Saigon; home of the Third Brigade, First Cavalry Division.

Cam Ranh Bay. Massive base on central coast opened in 1965 whose last infantry unit stood down in 1972.

Camp Holloway. Home of the Fifty-Second Aviation Battalion, a helicopter assault unit, in Pleiku.

Da Nang. A major air base eighty-five miles south of the Demilitarized Zone in I Corps for army, air force, navy, and marines during the entire course of the Vietnam War; was a base for secondary bombing missions during the Easter Offensive.

Duc Co. Camp thirty miles southwest of Pleiku City manned by an ARVN Ranger battalion and two US advisers.

Fire Base Amy. Forty miles east of Saigon; was home to a thirty-eight-man artillery battalion that was moved in 1972 to Pleiku to provide cover for Camp Holloway during the Easter Offensive.

Fire Base Bunker Hill. The name of the first (1965) and last (late March 1972) firebases built in Vietnam. It sat on a hill overlooking the Dong Nai River in the "rocket belt" east of Saigon and was home to the First Battalion, Twelfth Cavalry, in 1972. It was built by the 501st Engineer Company.

Fire Base Charlie. Vietnamese base guarding the approach to Kontum City that was overrun on April 14, 1972, by human wave assaults by the NVA, which lost a thousand killed.

Fire Base 42. Outpost eight miles north of Pleiku at which a friend was killed.

Fire Base Melanie. Home of the Second Battalion, Eighth Cavalry, one of seven combat battalions left in Vietnam in March 1972; twenty miles east of Saigon.

Lai Khe. Staging area thirty miles north of Saigon for Bien Hoa–based VNAF chopper crews that supported ARVNs encircled at An Loc during the Easter Offensive.

Long Binh. Home of MACV headquarters and the largest American base in Vietnam; had about four thousand Americans stationed there in August 1972. It was about twelve miles northeast of Saigon and also home of a stockade in which US military criminals were jailed. It was turned over to the South Vietnamese in November 1972.

Long Thanh. Airfield and staging area for US helicopter missions around An Loc.

LZ Crystal. Home of the Forty-First ARVN Regiment and US advisers just south of Phu My on the central coast.

Marble Mountain Army Air Base. On a strip of beach between the Marble Mountains and China Beach, southeast of Da Nang, it was controlled by the US Army until August 1972, when it was turned over to the Vietnamese. It was home to D Troop, Seventeenth Cavalry.

Phan Rang Air Base. Former American facility on the central coast used by VNAF A-37s and helicopters to support ARVN ground troops.

Phu Loi. US Army base fifteen miles north of Saigon turned over to the Vietnamese on April 1, 1972.

Plei Djereng. Camp fifteen miles east of the Cambodia border that guarded the best infantry approach to Pleiku City and was manned by an ARVN Ranger battalion and two US advisers.

Plei Mrong. Site of ARVN camp about fifteen miles northwest of Pleiku manned by a battalion of Montagnards and two US advisers.

Pleiku. Capital city of province of same name and site of II Corps headquarters and Fifty-Second Aviation Battalion. The city was not threatened during the Easter Offensive.

Polei Kleng. Camp fifteen miles west of Kontum manned by ARVN Rangers and US advisers.

Qui Nhon. Central coastal city in Binh Dinh Province that was home to the Republic of Korea (ROK) forces in Vietnam. There were thirty-seven thousand ROKs left in July 1972. They were responsible for patrolling a section of the central coast.

Tan Canh. Headquarters of ARVN Twenty-Second Division northwest of Kontum City that was overrun by NVA troops in late April 1972, setting the stage for their unsuccessful assault on Kontum City.

Tan Son Nhut Air Base. Major airport near Saigon into which most arriving US troops flew and out of which most departing troops exited.

Team 41 Advisory Compound, Kontum. Key US facility in the besieged provincial capital from which advisers directed airstrikes during the Easter Offensive.

An Loc. City sixty miles northwest of Saigon that was target in early April 1972 of 30,000 North Vietnamese troops with a hundred tanks during the Easter Offensive. The attack was repulsed by 6,800 ARVN troops supported by artillery, armor, and US airpower, a victory largely unreported by the US media. By early July, the NVA had withdrawn to base areas in Cambodia.

Can Tho. Major city (population: 170,000) in the Mekong Delta (population: 6.9 million); the breadbasket of South Vietnam, which largely was untouched during the Easter Offensive.

Cheo Reo. Central Highlands interior city and provincial capital of Phu Bon with a population of about fifteen thousand about fifty miles south of Pleiku City. Of Phu Bon Province's seventy thousand people, 84 percent were Montagnard.

Hue. Walled city in the northern part of South Vietnam (I Corps) that was threatened but not captured during the Easter Offensive.

Loc Ninh. Provincial capital eighty miles north of Saigon that was captured and held by the North Vietnamese during the Easter Offensive.

Kontum. Provincial capital city of thirty thousand in province of same name in the Central Highlands. ARVNs repulsed an NVA attack there in May 1972 with the aid of massive B-52 strikes and drove the Communists away by early June.

Mang Buk. II Corps city forty miles north of Kontum that sat astride one of the main Communist infiltration routes during the Easter Offensive.

My Tho. A Mekong Delta provincial capital city about forty miles from Saigon that was relatively calm during the Easter Offensive.

Nha Trang. Relatively quiet central coastal city about two hundred miles northeast of Saigon where GIs took in-country R&R.

Pleiku. Provincial capital city of province of same name about thirty miles south of Kontum in the Central Highlands. It was home to the Fifty-Second Aviation Battalion helicopter unit.

Quang Tri. Northern provincial capital that fell in early April 1972 to a Communist assault but was retaken by the South Vietnamese in late June.

Vung Tau. Extremely quiet beach resort east of Saigon used by GIs for in-country R&R.

Xuan Loc. City near rubber plantations that was a staging area for US helicopter assault teams forty miles northeast of Saigon.